The Theme of Nazi Concentration Camps
in French Literature

New Babylon

Studies in the behavioral sciences

12

MOUTON · THE HAGUE · PARIS

The Theme
of Nazi Concentration Camps
in French Literature

by

CYNTHIA HAFT

MOUTON · THE HAGUE · PARIS

Library of Congress Catalog Card Number : 72-79993.

© 1973, Mouton & Co, Herderstraat 5, The Hague, The Netherlands
Printed in France

Acknowledgments

Many years ago, I became acquainted with Charlotte Delbo. When I was ready to begin my investigations in the pursuit of a dissertation topic, she suggested that I explore the literature of the deportation. It is thus that this book owes its existence to her. The illuminations and such mastery of the subject matter as I was able to gain have been the result of her tutelage. During these past years, her encouragement and guidance have helped me throughout on many levels, both intellectuel and personal, including the invaluable editing of the first draft.

I am also greatly indebted to Drs. Adèle Bloch, Sidney Braun, Henry Hornik, Rosette Lamont and Yvette Louria for their suggestions and patient assistance.

I wish to thank the staff of the Amicale d'Auschwitz in Paris, the staff of Yivo Institute and the Library of the Jewish Memorial in Paris for their help.

For their advice in the compilation of the Appendix, I am grateful to Drs. Gisela Isser-Mosher, Miezeclaw Maneli and Wallace Lipton.

This treatise though, would not have been possible without the aid of Olga Wormser-Migot who not only furnished indispensable information but also put into perspective the task before me, communicated her own feeling of *élan de travail* towards the subject and made me realize it was possible.

To all the deportees who talked to me, particulary Cécile, Lulu, Carmen, Marie-Elisa and Mado, all survivors of Auschwitz-Birkenau, I owe a debt of gratitude because they helped me to understand.

Contents

Publisher's Note: In keeping with contemporary standards of scientific publishing, the reference material has been incorporated into the text itself.

Introduction

Fifty years from now, there will be no living witnesses to the atrocities committed against humanity by the Nazis. Those who returned from concentration camps realized their own mortality : they realized that they had partaken of an event which surpassed human imagination. They therefore wanted to communicate in some lasting way to those yet unborn, to those who had not shared their experience, what they had seen, endured and survived, so that this phenomenon, unique, unreal and beyond human imagination might never be forgotten and might never be repeated. They wrote because they felt an obligation to those they left behind, of whom only ashes remained, and because they felt an obligation to themselves. They wanted to tell. They were urged to write by the fact that they felt themselves to be a part of history, the history of all men, and also because they feared that, as time passed, they might very well doubt the verisimilitude of their own experiences.

These writings took on many forms : poems, novels, plays, narratives and hagiographic literature. There are also history books, biographies and autobiographies, * eye witness reports (témoignages), songs and movie scripts, and there are new forms of literature which emerge for which we do not yet have any classifications. The forms invariably fit the content.

Confronted by the mass of varied works, some more elaborate, some more brutal, the reader and the critic discover that certain among them succeeded in transmitting the experience to them. We will attempt to discover, by analyzing the characteristics of the varied

---

* There are also medical reports which we choose to eliminate from discussion here.

works under consideration, if it is possible to find criteria which permit us to place certain of these works on the level of literature, rather than of concentration-camp literature.

After the liberation of the camps, an immense number of the survivors wanted to communicate, to transmit their personal experiences. A mass of works, encouraged by the terrified curiosity of the world, appeared. No one was looking for literature. Rather, it was a quest for the knowledge of what had been undergone, lived : history, the proof of crimes committed against humanity. Among these *témoignages* of the first days, few are remembered. With the passage of time, more was demanded of these works : they had either to surpass the individual experience and become historical, metaphysical or philosophical explanations or they had to constitute a literary work of art.

This question becomes important because it is our contention that only by its entrance into literature can the phenomenon of concentration camps penetrate the individual and collective consciousness of men. Only when this phenomenon has become a literary theme, a poetic theme, will its intense ramifications be felt. The power of language is to contain and transmute all passions, all human experiences of men. For the man of letters and the humanist, no experience can remain outside the scope of language. We propose that among the many who wanted to talk about that moment of their life and those who were inspired to talk about the experiences of others, there are some who relate in ways that surpass the mere eye witness reports of the phenomena. We will speak of all the genres, but we will dwell upon those whose extraordinary literary value distinguishes them from the mass.

We are aware that a certain discrimination will have to be exercised. We realize that the task of discussing the works is the simpler one, that the complications come to the fore at the time when we propose to decide what constitutes a valuable contribution to literature. We proceed therefore with caution knowing that many may disagree with our opinions and choices. We can only say that each opinion is equally valid and that our study is not attempting to be definitive in that respect.

There are those, of course, who consider the phenomenon of concentration camps sacred, not to be approached by those who were not themselves a part of the inferno. There are also those who believe that this phenomenon, because of its vastness and intensity, surpasses the scope of literature. In the first case, we can only answer that we hope this treatise will serve as a reply to their resentment, and will show that we share their goals, that we too want this event, so unique, never to be forgotten, that we too feel obliged to join with them in their efforts to remind others and to bear witness, without in any way violating the sanctity of the subject matter. In the second case, we answer that by its own definition, language and literature must be able to absorb within themselves and render to the reader the passions of all men.

Of the several hundred people who have made contributions to the French literature about concentration camps, some were already established authors ; others began by writing about concentration camps, and went on to other themes. These are men and women who are authors in their own right, who would have been authors without the theme of concentration camps to inspire them. Their work, while sometimes superior when speaking of deportation, is artistic and demonstrates that they are literary masters. There are others (bakers, priests, doctors and midwives) who had never written before and would never write again. Their only contribution to the literary scene is their book or poem which they hoped would tell all, which they hoped would serve to help us remember what happened in the 1930's and 1940's. Unfortunately, the fact of having been in a concentration camp, or the fact of having seen or heard what happened to others in these camps is not always sufficient to bestow literary talent upon an author. Therefore, no matter how praiseworthy the intentions, the results are not always literary. The mass of writings serves to elucidate a phenomenon which none will ever totally comprehend. They will be discussed to glean important information about what the deportee was like, how his torturer appeared to him, what methods he used to survive — mentally and physically — by what an entirely new and different moral code he lived, what he thought about as he dug ditches, what he dreamt about at night and finally what happened to him when he tried to re-adapt himself to society. We will discover how, in a completely new context, men created a new language, a moral code, new heroes and a different system of values : how in fact they lived in a heretofore unknown world. We will see too that the concentration camp world is a separate world, new to the history of mankind, with all the attributes of a closed society. We will follow the experiences : the trip to the camp, the camp life, the return, the reflections, dreams and daily routines as they are presented to us by literature, to see how the experiences are transmitted and transformed by literature. We have chosen to use the element of time as the key to the unfolding of this study since time was so all important to the deportee and because we feel that by following a time pattern, we can better bring to the fore the metamorphosis undergone by the prisoner.

We will see too that the theme of Nazi concentration camps has penetrated the works of authors who were not deported and we will realize that it is certainly possible and indeed an immense contribution to literature and to history that these men have chosen to touch upon this sacred phenomenon in their works. By incorporating these historical moments into their creation, they have permitted them to enter the realm of literature and thus that of the subconscious and the conscious. We are much indebted to those who have been able to write about concentration camps without themselves having endured the experience. It is thus that we can be reassured that this phenomenon will not be forgotten, will not die with its survivors' deaths. For those who were not deported, this is a vicarious experience, that is, they are integrating into their works an experience which is incomprehensible and unimaginable for those who lived it. For these others, their sensitivity is their guideline to interpretation.

It is important to note that there are two ways in which the phenomenon of the deportation can be considered. For some, it is one in a long series of incidents which form a historical canvas, that of the long martyrdom of the Jewish people — a martyrdom that they have the privilege to endure because of their birthright and which they endure without any element of choice. These writers talk to us of concentration camps and they talk to us of many other plagues visited upon the heads of the Jewish people. Their preoccupation is with the Jewish question and the phenomenon of the deportation as an intrinsic part of this long series of incidents in the history of the Jewish people, the history of a martyred people.

For others, the phenomenon of deportation is unique in that it surpasses the martyrdom of a single people. The context is broader and different. These writers therefore dwell rather upon the vastness and uniqueness of the phenomenon. For them, it is not a part of a long history of suffering. It is an event apart from all others, incomparable and infinitely more horrible than any which preceded it. And it is terrifying to conceive that it could be repeated. It is a part of the history of all mankind. For them, the element of choice is very strongly reflected. They show that many chose the road their lives followed because of their political or humanitarian ideals. These writings broaden the scope of the question. The aim of the writers in both groups is the same : to force his story into the readers' conscious, to have it gnaw at his subconscious, in some cases by a superb poetry and tenderness.

We will see that each author views the immense phenomenon from his place in the universe ; each brings to it his own background. All fight to keep their own personalities throughout the camp struggle because this is the principal method of survival, and they retain this personality almost intact after the long fight. It is this personality that seeps through and penetrates the work. The details rarely change in those who recount their stories honestly — because frauds come to the fore even here, but we will see that, at some levels, reactions are uniform while at others, the reactions vary. The validity of Nietzsche's commentary will be proven here : men react differently to the prick of a pin, but to burning charcoal in the palm of the hand, all have the same reaction. To minor pains, men manifest different reactions ; to overwhelming suffering, the reaction is a universal cry. We must also take into consideration that within the Nazi network there are degrees of horror. It is impossible and unfair to compare the writings of Holleischen with the writings about Auschwitz. Even in this world of the macabre, there are degrees of the unimaginable. There will be no archetypes of the deportee. On the contrary, the most contradictory images will emerge. All will be valid. The microcosm of the concentration camps had many things in common and many divergent points : this must be taken into consideration since it is reflected in the literature.

Because of a desire to render their works as faithful to detail as possible, many authors lost the perspective of their role as writers. The role of the writer is to recreate through language the passions that he wishes to convey to his reader. But a recreation is not rendered most effective by the precision of the details included in the rendering. Not all things are measurable, and in the human mind, not all things can be represented. To tell us how high the blocks were, how many miles were walked in the fields, how much water there was to drink is not pertinent to literature. And these facts taken out of context, recited without recreating the life in camp, will not evoke in the reader's mind what a camp was. The artist's role is not to tell the number of miles that a prisoner walked each morning in order to reach the swamp where he worked. It is rather to impress upon the reader's mind how the prisoner's legs felt, to impress upon the reader that distance is relative and that the longest walk he can take is along a path where at every step his foot digs into a fresh cadaver. These feelings are conveyed not by a strict attention to details in ounces and miles. They are rather given by a poetic recreation of what the prisoner felt and the pain that his mind and body suffered. Details will not communicate the reality of the experience. The passions, the conditions will be transmitted to the reader by the effective and lyric author who never mentions the miles. The reader cannot reconstruct in his mind what Auschwitz was, but, by realizing the totality of the phenomenon, he recreates the subjective truth of the experience.

The System of Nazi Concentration Camps

Concentration camps were a dynamic aspect of the Third Reich. They were, out of necessity, constantly changing and growing to accommodate the changing political climate of the Third Reich. It is important to differentiate from the beginning between the Final Solution of the Jewish Question and the System of Concentration Camps. The two are not synonymous. The first had its roots in the Nuremberg Laws and theoretically in *Mein Kampf,* but was explicitly formulated only in 1941-1942. The latter began much earlier, in the 1930's, supposedly as a political measure taken against socialists, syndicalists and liberals.

From 1933 to 1939, the system of concentration camps was a national one and pertained to citizens of the German nation. The period from 1939 to 1945 can be divided into two phases : 1939 to 1942 and 1942 to 1945. The latter division differs from the former in that during the latter period, the Third Reich was in need of workers in its factories to replace those Germans who had left to fight. The final decomposition of the system began in January, 1945. The SS had become fearful when they realized that Germany was losing the war. The liberation of the camps and the end of the system was reached in April, 1945 (Wormser-Migot, *Le Système concentrationnaire nazi,* p. 26). *

The goal of the system of concentration camps was originally one of reform : to make a good German from a dangerous Marxist. A prisoner either obeyed or was broken. Theoretically, when the internationalization of the camps took place, the prisoners from other nations were to be integrated into the system, each playing a role

---

* For full details of the references, see the Bibliography, pp. 213-225.

previously destined for him (Wormser-Migot, p. 22). The theory was never put into practice. The roles were determined by nationality, but based upon the prejudices of the formulators of the system. There was often a stereotyping of the deportees, by the German Kapos (see Appendix), which went according to their nationality.

In 1941 (January 2), the Chief of the Security System of the Third Reich established four categories of camps. The first category was for aged prisoners. The camps destined for them were supposedly Dachau, Sachsenhausen and Auschwitz One. Those who were guilty of very little and who were able to work at gardening and similar chores were to be placed in Dachau. The third group of prisoners, those who were hardened criminals but capable of being reformed, were to be placed in Auschwitz Two (Birkenau), Buchenwald, Flossenburg and Neuengamme. The fourth group, those who were considered very difficult to reform, whom the Third Reich did not consider possible to re-educate, were to be placed in Mauthausen. This, however, was purely theoretical. The prisoner, in actuality, was never judged and the camp discipline had nothing to do with the four categories.

The first camp created was Dachau, considered the model camp. Buchenwald was created in 1937 and Ravensbrück was created in 1939 as a camp for women only, which in fact it was. It was in 1942 that the formula which would dominate the camp discipline was finally proclaimed : the extinction of prisoners by work. The idea of the participation of the prisoners in the war effort had however been prepared since 1941 by Himmler's decrees. The names which are perhaps the most important in the history of concentration camps are SS Oswald Pohl, Himmler, Kaltenbrunner, Speer and Hoess. It is important to realize that by 1942, manpower was needed, and the need for manpower superseded the desire for the Final Solution. Therefore, by 1942, those who were incarcerated, including Jews, were not necessarily gassed upon arrival into the camps. It can thus be concluded that beginning in 1942, deportees were used for the economic necessities of the Third Reich. The Final Solution was, in a sense, being prolonged. The SS (see Appendix) was invented and created by Himmler. It was to be a ruling elite which would eliminate all opposition to the Third Reich. The concentration camps, run at the highest level by the SS, had the same goals. Socialists, communists and liberals were considered as active opposition to the Third Reich. The Jews and eventually the other non-Aryans in the conquered territories were considered static opposition. They opposed the goals of the Third Reich by their mere existence, without being engaged in any activities directed against the Reich, but merely because they could not be totally assimilated. It is estimated that from nine to ten million people were killed or died in German concentration camps, six million of whom were Jews (Colette Audrey, in Delbo, *Aucun de nous ne reviendra,* 1965, p. 129). Four million of these were deliberately exterminated ; the others died in the camps from varied causes. 220 000 Frenchmen were deported to German camps. Only eighty thousand of these were Jews. About 36,000 in all returned. * The concentration camps were invented to make sure that these people, enemies of the Third Reich in one way or another, would be rendered innocuous.

The deportees could also serve as guinea pigs for medical experimentation. Why not ? The subjects would have to consent ; the camp was thus the perfect locale for working undisturbed. The camps mushroomed. They grew to proportions for which they had never been planned mainly because of the constant need to replenish the slave labor, and because the gas chambers did not function rapidly enough. Each camp was equipped with its own crematoriums.

Although the camps were supposedly better or worse by degrees already mentioned here, this was quite theoretical. There were, however, other real differences, quite marked, actually, in the camps,

* Statistics furnished by the Ministry of War in Paris.

and of which the deportees themselves were aware. A deportee being transferred from Auschwitz to Ravensbrück, upon arrival at Ravensbrück and upon seeing the aged inmates, still alive, announced to her travelling companions, somewhat relieved : 'Ici, c'est la pension de famille' (unpublished remark made by Delbo). What then caused the differences in the camps ? It is important for us to note these dissimilarities because they are certainly reflected in the literature written about the camps.

The camps which the prisoners and the SS were building together, the newest, were the worst because of the element of uncertainty. This element having been eliminated, the 'misery at least consolidated itself' (Kogon, p. 37). There was, however, a general curve which can be followed in the camps : from 1939-1940, the situation verged on disaster. The food was rationed very strictly and famine threatened. This recurred in 1944-1945 and was worsened by the fact that the camps were extremely overcrowded. The so-called normal level of camp life (except in Auschwitz) was reached during the war years, 1940-1944 (Kogon, p. 39).

The camps comprised several different categories of prisoners, usually designated by the color of their triangles (see Appendix). There were basically four groups : political prisoners, criminals, ethnic minorities and social criminals *(Berufsverbrecher)*. The minorities were primarily the Jews and the gypsies. Almost all the gypsies perished in camps ; at first they were truly just told to relocate, but after a certain time they began to bother the German maniacal sense of order and they were sent to camps. The Jews, even if they fit into certain of the other categories simultaneously, were always incarcerated as Jews. They were in special barracks and they were generally treated worse than the other deportees. However, the SS felt that it would serve their purpose to mix the different nationalities and categories as much as possible in the barracks and in the camps in general. Alas, they were right. Charlotte Delbo, writing in *Le Convoi du 24 janvier,* a story of 230 non-Jewish women deported from France for mixed reasons, explains why, out of her group, the number of survivors — 49 — is higher than a random sampling would give :

... en outre ces Juives ainsi rassemblées à la veille du départ ne formaient pas de groupes homogènes, solidaires. Mêlées dans leurs blocks à des Juives d'autres pays, dont elles ne comprenaient pas la langue, qu'elles ne connaissaient pas, elles ne rencontraient ni amitié, ni entr'aide. Si notre convoi a eu un si grand nombre de survivantes... c'est que nous nous connaissions déjà, que nous formions, à l'intérieur d'un grand groupe compact de petits groupes étroitement liés... que nous nous aidions de toutes les manières, souvent bien humbles : se donner le bras pour marcher... (p. 17.)

The preceding passage illustrates exactly what the SS tried in every way to avoid : the building of morale among the prisoners. The psychology of the SS worked hard to destroy the mutual help system. The principle was clearly 'divide and conquer'. Groups were played off against each other. And deportees were used to control other deportees, following the idea explained in *Mein Kampf* : 'Les prisonnières souffriront par les prisonnières *{sic}*' (Rosane, p. 115). It is for these reasons, among others, that a small group was able to control an enormous camp and that revolts were very scarce ; * this indicates the effectiveness of the SS system.

In order to understand what happened in concentration camps, it is necessary to understand — or make an attempt to understand — what comprised the corps of elite called the SS. In general, they were men and women who had volunteered for the job. They had families and played normal roles in everyday life. They were men who preferred anything to giving up these normal lives in order to fight on the front. However, while they outwardly appeared to be functioning normally in family situations, it also appears that they

---

* The revolt of Treblinka has been recounted. Also that of the *Sonderkommando* in Auschwitz and one in Sobibor. Recent documentation shows there may have been 2 or 3 other revolts in camps. There is little else, and few personal stories of escapes, other than those which took place while the prisoner was in transport.

engaged in heavy promiscuity and drinking. Most of them did not think too much about what they were doing. The SS mode of living let them enjoy whatever pleasures they wished to indulge themselves in, and this appealed to them as did the high ideals of SS elite conduct which they heard about so much during their training : clean family life, fellowship among the SS brotherhood, the Third Reich above all, patriotism, the chance to rid the world of its ills, the greater glory of Germany. They compensated for the strict obedience which was demanded of them by taking it out on the prisoners. They were basically not idealistic though, and they were certainly not so by 1944 or 1945. Most of them were characterized by a sense of failure and of inferiority. They therefore hated any men of accomplishment or prestige. The camp gave them the opportunity to play games, where the penalty was death, with some of Europe's most talented and accomplished citizens. One of the principal motives that guided the SS was a desire for power. The SS was put in a position in which he was independent in a way, but in which he had to be able to know what should be done. He therefore was playing a role where obedience and subordination were curiously mixed with the need to make important decisions (Kogon, pp. 258-261). Neither history nor literature has succeeded in understanding the motivation of the SS. We offer the following suggestions as partial explanations : robbery, gluttony, luxury, hedonism. It is important however to retain what little we know of their psychology so that we can later see it in interaction with that of the deportee.

The SS were given very rigorous training, usually at Dachau itself, in the methods of debasement and cruelty. Since the penalty for non-conformity was incarceration in the camp, those who chose to join and train for the SS became masters of their trade. They were given deportees to practice upon and then later, if they proved trustworthy by SS standards, they were given positions of responsibility in other camps. The camps, then, to some degree, also served as training grounds and the need for the trainees to prove themselves is a partial

explanation for some of the excesses of brutality. The prisoners existed only to serve their masters, they had no other *raison d'être*.
There was no reason not to use them as implements in training
their future guardians.

A part of the psychology of the SS as practiced in the camps
must be underlined. This was the practice of using privileged deportees to occupy key positions. The positions of Kapo, Blockhova (see
Appendix) and all other positions relating to the immediate supervision of the deportees were occupied by deportees. They were chosen
either because of the friends they had or because of the packages
they received ; these two assets meant that they could pay back the
favor. The Kapos were rarely Jews. They were almost always 'green
triangles' (see Appendix), but in certain camps, such as Buchenwald,
the 'red triangles' managed to infiltrate these ranks after a while.
It is generally considered that once these positions were held by the
political deportees, conditions for the deportees improved at least
slightly. This system of utilizing deportees as guardians for deportees was extremely effective because the guardians realized that this
could be a life and death game and viewed it as such. They used
their positions as an insurance that they would survive. However,
failure to properly discipline the deportees that were under their
authority would result in the loss of their position and could ultima-
tely result in their own death. Since the guardians considered that
their survival was at stake, they were flagrantly inhumane. They
wanted to prove that they were capable of the task they had accepted.
These jobs were coveted by some of the deportees ; others refused
them entirely because they felt that any position of authority would
involve beating their fellow deportees. It was rare that Frenchmen
held these positions. This presented a communication problem. The
German who spoke only his native tongue and was in charge of the
French deportees, who did not necessarily understand German, inspired a great deal of fear. It is difficult to follow an order that one
does not understand. But punishment would be meted out all **the**

same. The Kapos were generally German and Polish. It was the Kapos and Blockälteste who were in closest contact with the prisoners. These were then supervised by the SS. There are instances of decent Block-hovas, but they are in the minority. The efficiency of the Nazi system is proven by the fact that it was able to reduce victims to the level where they would commit acts of brutality against their fellow victims in order to better nourish themselves, such as beating their fellow deportees in order to avoid losing their jobs and in some cases, killing their fellow deportees because it was what they decided to do. They were not always following orders ; they were, at times, acting upon their own judgment. The Germans were highly successful in their attempt to corrupt the deportees.

The interior organization of the camp was the following : at the head of the camp was the Kommandant and his staff. His rank varied with the size of the camp. The Administrative Office was responsible for the running of the camp. It contained the *Arbeitsta-tistik* which was responsible for work distribution among the depor-tees and therefore a key department for the deportees' survival. It was under the direct supervision of the Kommandant. There were Lagerführer (see Appendix for further explanations of the German terminology) who were in charge of the deportees. There was one on duty at all times. The Gestapo was directly responsible for the supervision of the camp and was represented in the camp by a poli-tical department called the *Politische Abteilung*. This department interrogated deportees and inspired an enormous amount of terror. The organization of the remainder of the camp was undertaken by the Blockälteste and the Kolonneführer. Besides carrying a gun, the SS were armed with police dogs and bloodhounds which, in addi-tion to inspiring fear, were used to detect possible escapees and to punish misdemeanors such as breaking rank during a march to get a drink of water. This system led to an emphasis on bribery, un-equal and very arbitrary justice, misuse of authority, and most obviously, unimaginable cruelties.

The basic weapon of the Nazis was fear. It took on many forms. Because of the way political suspects were arrested — usually their homes were invaded by the police and they were informed that they were under arrest — and interrogated at police headquarters but never tried, and because they would never know what was to happen next, fear reached optimum proportions. Instrumental in this was the weapon of secrecy : fear mounts disproportionately when it confronts the unknown rather than just the painful future. Because secrecy was an intrinsic part of the Nazi system, fear was easily maintained. It was perhaps not so much even the fear of death, but rather the fear of how one would die. In the case of Jewish prisoners, they were merely rounded up wherever they could be found and loaded into cattle cars in which they were transported to destinations unknown to them. In camps such as Auschwitz-Birkenau and Maidanek-Lublin, selections of the Jews were made upon their arrival in camp. The physically able might get a chance to work. Others were gassed immediately. Occasionally when the camps were too crowded, and the gas chambers were not, there were no selections. All passengers went from the trains to the gas chambers. The details of the arrival in camp vary but they usually consist of certain paper work, forms to fill out, and then a series of formalities which will be discussed later ; the chief aim of these procedures was the debasement and humiliation of the prisoners. It is difficult for a prisoner who is stark naked in front of his child to think of his pride. The thought of revolt is out of the question. The stress at the entrance to camp, in the first few hours, was to make the prisoner realize that he was no more than a number, a triangle, a sub-human. He was expected to show total obedience. The object was to crush any idea of personality or any concept of self that might help the prisoner to survive. It was hoped that the deportee would no longer consider himself a human being because his superiors certainly did not consider him as such. He was henceforth perhaps a useful commodity. At the point when the supply of this commodity exceeded the demand, his usefulness would be terminated and extermination would generally follow. Chance and luck were also to play a crucial role in the deportees' lives. These factors are mentioned here as objectively as possible. We will examine, in the later chapters, how this psychology of the SS affected the deportees and how it was transmitted and transformed by literature and time. It is necessary to make these brief, introductory remarks because there is little or no literature written from the SS point of view; there are rather only historically oriented documents.

Shortly after his arrival in camp, the prisoner was dressed in a tattered uniform, after having stood outside for many hours and only after having been disinfected. Of course, this became more painful in harder climates and in winter, especially since clothes were insufficient and never fitted properly. All his belongings were removed; he was instructed to put them into his suitcase for safekeeping, and turn them over to the officials. All his hair, from head to toe, was generally shorn. The same applied to women. The conditions varied in each camp. In some, the deportee was immediately designated a place to sleep each night. In others, he was told which barrack he would be in and there was a fight each night for covers and a place to sleep. The barracks were made of bricks or wood. In some of the camps, there was, at first, a period of quarantine during which the newcomers were kept apart from the others because of the fear that they might be carrying disease. For example, in Buchenwald, 'le petit camp' was set aside for this purpose.

The day in camp began between 3 a.m. and 6 a.m. depending on the season of the year and the camp. Generally, breakfast consisted of a cup of hot water tinted green. The systems varied but occasionally bread was issued in the morning and occasionally it was issued at night. Whenever it was issued, it was only once a day. Its supply could be withdrawn as a penalty or for no reason at all. Breakfast was followed by roll-call, during which the entire camp had to be counted in one way or another. Since this usually involved thousands and thousands of inmates, roll-call could last from several hours to all day, if something went wrong, or if the SS were in a particularly sadistic mood. Inmates of Ravensbrück remember a Christmas when they spent the entire day at attention for a day-long roll-call (unpublished anecdote recounted by Charlotte Delbo). Standing in the snow, in sub-freezing temperatures, in a pair of striped pyjamas or other tattered garments, sometimes in shoes and socks, without having eaten all day or night, was an experience that ended the lives of many prisoners. After roll-call, the next order of business was work. Deportees worked at varied things, many at useless things, such as transporting rocks from one pile to another and the next day back to the first pile, to further reduce their self-image. At times, work served a useful purpose, either in the building of the camp, or in the personal accommodation of the SS. Conditions varied but generally the deportees worked fourteen hours with about half an hour for lunch — a bowl of soup. In some camps, there was no lunch. In any case, this meal was no more than a bowl of soup that was usually composed of rutabagas and water. In the evening, roll-call took place again. In some camps, roll-calls were complicated by the fact that the morning ones necessitated the transportation of the dead deportees from the barracks to the roll-call to be counted, and in the evening by the fact that the deportees who had died during the day had to be transported back to the camp center by their comrades so that they too could be counted. Since the comrades usually had enough trouble supporting themselves on their own two feet, the extra weight was an added torture. After the evening roll-call, some drink or food was issued. It generally consisted of a cup of soup and, if no bread was issued before, the bread ration of the day, approximately four American slices of bread, and either a quarter of an ounce of margarine, one slice of sausage or one teaspoonful of jam. The sausage was not made of meat and the jam was not made of sugar. No further commentary seems necessary about the state in which the deportee found himself after he had

lived on this diet for even a few weeks. Many did not survive because
of the hunger and thirst.

The trick was to get into a Kommando (see Appendix) that worked
indoors, and was better fed. It is impossible to state categorically
how this could take place : there were no rules. Occasionally, it was
according to skills, most often according to whom one knew and
what one had available as bribery.

The French were not well treated, as a whole, in the camps, and
their nationality was looked down upon. They, therefore, did not
have much chance to get into the 'good' Kommandos. There were
Kommandos to which a deportee was assigned as a punishment
like the one that cleaned latrines, when these existed. There were
other Kommandos for which the deportees volunteered : the *Sonderkommando* in extermination camps is a famous example. It consisted
of deportees who stacked bodies in the ovens for three months, at
which time that deportee himself would be killed and replaced by
another volunteer. Many deportees agreed to do this work ; three
months of grace, during which they would be well-fed and suffer
comparatively less, seemed like a lifetime grace. Judgment cannot
be passed. Certain people were sent to work outside the camp ;
others stayed within it. It is difficult to judge which was easier ;
this too varied in each camp. There was a general fear of being
separated from the large camp and being sent to work in a Kommando or outside of the boundaries of the central camp. This was
the case in Buchenwald, where there was an overwhelming fear
of being sent to Dora from which nobody saw anybody return.
The deportees also were kept busy making things for the SS and
their families, building, repairing and cultivating their gardens. There
were night shifts and day shifts. Details are not necessary here nor
is it our place to furnish them. Our objective here is merely to give
a fundamental knowledge of what happened in the camps according
to historical recordings, so that we can consider the literary transfor-
mations of the material later.

Various punishments were devised for the deportees, or groups of deportees, who committed minor offenses — often considered major by the SS. These varied from not singing the proper marching song, taking one's hat off too soon or too late at roll call, oversleeping, not washing and not being able to control one's physical needs because of diarrhea or kidney trouble. Punishments varied from death to forced calisthenics, to beatings. These were often administered to the naked prisoner in full company of the entire camp. Of course, there were hangings, also public, which the whole camp was forced to watch, motionless, eyes glued to the victim, and transferals to special punishment Blocks ; 25 was famous for this at Birkenau. All this was part of daily life. Camps which had gas chambers sent their incarcerees there to die as punishment for more serious offenses. In other camps, serious offenses could be punished by shipment to a worse camp ; this was called a Black transport (see Appendix).

Most of the camps had infirmaries. However, these were sometimes the worst places of the camps. There was no anesthesia to perform operations. There were few doctors. If there were doctors from among the ranks of the deportees, they tried. But if they were SS doctors, the fate of the inmates was usually worse. From the infirmary, in camps where there were gas chambers, selections were made. Fear was constant and survival depended on physical fitness and the compliance of the aides. Often however the medical personnel was composed of people who had successfully bribed to get these sought-after positions and had little medical knowledge.

In camps having gas chambers, fear was much greater because of the constant danger of selections. Deportees not in good enough shape to work, or those already in the infirmary, were often selected to be gassed. The Germans had tremendous fears of being hit by epidemics. Typhus was rampant because sanitary conditions were non-existent. This led, all too often, to selections. The camps, having no sanitary facilities and no toilets, were havens for all types of bugs carrying infectious disease. The SS carried on furious campaigns against this vermin by de-lousing procedures which did nothing whatever to combat the vermin and only succeeded in further torturing the prisoner who waited hours, sometimes in the cold of winter in Silesia, naked, to get his clothes back. In many camps, death was the penalty if lice were found upon the person. Death took many forms : hangings, whippings, injections of poisons, gas, firing squads, destruction by dogs. Death certificates, seldom issued to the family, completely distorted the truth, since the routine was to state that all the deportees who died on that day were reported to have died of pneumonia and on the next day of intestinal trouble. There were four or five official causes of death. There were in fact a very minimal number of deportees who attempted to escape and very few who succeeded. Reprisals were often meted out not only to the deportee when he was brought back, but also to those who may have plotted with him — those with whom he lived or worked. Escape efforts meant endangering the lives of fellow prisoners. The risk was not only to oneself, but to the others.

Deportees were classified in many ways. Those who were *NN* (see Appendix) were not permitted to receive mail or packages. This was the case of many political prisoners. Those who could not receive mail suffered more because packages received, although generally pilfered by the Kapos, permitted them to exchange the remains for favors or to eat the contents and fortify themselves and their friends. Because of the conditions of these human beings, at starvation level, many men were led to perform inhuman acts against fellow inmates, to steal a package or to share it.

The liberation of the prisoners from the camps took many forms. It basically depended on the geographical location of the camps. Those camps which were nearer to the Soviet Union were evacuated first and the prisoners were marched to other camps. These marches were often death marches because the prisoners, hardly able to breathe, were forced to walk immense distances, for many days, under SS guard, with almost no food, until they reached other, already overcrowded camps. The camps were evacuated because the SS feared the discovery of the camps and of the state of the prisoners by the advancing armies. Other camps were liberated by the Soviet or Allied armies. Others were deserted by the SS personnel and the prisoners were left to their own devices until the arrival of the Allied or Soviet forces. The prisoners were eventually repatriated and many were forced to spend considerable time in sanatoriums and under doctors' care. Many died after the camps were liberated because they no longer had the strength to hold out and because medical help could not reach them quickly enough.

This brief historical panorama will, it is hoped, serve as a basis for putting into proper perspective the literary works which these camps inspired. There were thousands of Kommandos, probably over 3,000. We cannot mention them all here. Since the climate and geographic locations of the camps affected the life of the prisoners, it is important to have a general idea of at least the location of the principal camps. Since, though, our considerations are literary and not documentary, we presume that the preceding short summary will suffice (see also Appendix).

2

The Trip

Sol de Compiègne
Terre grasse et cependant stérile
Terre de silex et de craie
Dans ta chair
Nous marquons d'empreinte
de nos semelles

. . .

Plus dur que le silex
Plus docile que la craie sous
le couteau

Robert DESNOS,
Sol de Compiègne.

The trip to the concentration camp contains all the elements of the concentration camp existence. It can be viewed as a metonomy. It is a part of the whole which exemplifies the whole. From the beginning of the trip the prisoners were passive, transported like cattle. We will see that certain writers, when speaking of the trip maintain the same artistic freedom that they maintain later, when speaking of the camp life. The skillful writer affirms his freedom as a writer by the use of the time sequence, as he integrates the different moments of his life into a structured pattern of free association.

For most Nazi victims, it was a one-way trip. It was the first hurdle. A ten year old, when asked to describe this phenomenon stated with perfect simplicity : 'Ils allèrent à l'autre bout de la terre et ils ne sont pas revenus.' * The impact of the trip varied with the conditions under which it was taken. In general, the physical

---

* Engraved into the floor of the Memorial to the deportation, Paris.

3

conditions were characterized by overcrowding and ensuing suffocation. Thirst was so overwhelming that hunger no longer mattered. And the same methods that were used by all the prisoners to maintain themselves — methods that they would not be able to use in camp — psychological combat, mental combat, are still possible on the penultimate level. We are made aware that they have not reached the ultimate :

... les souvenirs précieux viennent à leur aide ; les heures exaltantes de la Résistance, les souvenirs familiaux, les aventures banales ou grisantes nourrissent une sorte de rêve éveillé. (Pineau, p. 14.)

The impact of the trip also varied in relation to the place from which the deportee was coming. As he sets foot into one of the cattle cars, the erstwhile prisoner becomes a deportee. The transformation of human to sub-human begins. As Pineau states : 'Nous commençons à devenir des animaux' (p. 13).

Herein lies the difference which is to make this incarceration distinct from all others, for many had been imprisoned before the Nazis, many still are. It was this transformation, this transportation away from home, this *dépaysement* which was one of the essential elements of the Nazi system and therefore one of the essential *points de départ* for those who wrote when they returned.

Robert Desnos, who died in deportation, started his trip from Compiègne. Because he did not survive the deportation to take the trip home, his incantation to Compiègne can contain only one level of reality. It is not written retrospectively. Desnos does not view Compiègne with a lapse of four years or more, nor does he view it in the light of his experiences in Buchenwald and Flossenburg. The words Desnos uses to describe Compiègne could well be used to describe the camps through which he passed : 'Terre grasse et cependant stérile / Terre de silex et de craie.' His preoccupation is the same at Compiègne as that of others in death camps elsewhere in Nazi territory : 'Nous marquons l'empreinte de nos semelles.' This preoccupation, this idea of leaving a trace of oneself, of the experience itself, is the same preoccupation that haunts all camp inmates. It haunts the writers until they return and can execute what they feel to be a part of their destiny :

> *Nous laisserons notre poussière*
> *Dans la poussière de Compiègne*
> *Et nous emporterons nos amours*
> *Nos amours qu'il nous en souvienne*
> Chœur : *Qu'il nous en souvienne.* (R. Denos, p. 187.)

This is the beginning of the trip for Desnos. He describes his thoughts at the time just before his transport to the other end of the world. We will later see the end of the trip for him : the end, but not the return.

There are several ways in which this trip can be presented to us. In general, the authors write several years after the trip was taken. The perspectives vary. Those who desire a strictly realistic portrayal are most faithful to details and isolate the incident in time, that is to say, they describe the incident as if they had just lived it a few moments ago. They do not add to it the perspectives of the life in the concentration camps which they came to know later, nor do they speak at the same time of the return trip. They follow an objective time sequence. For them, the trip was yesterday. They cannot tell about its relationship to tomorrow because they have not lived tomorrow yet. In some cases, there are religious overtones. Many priests were deported. Those who are religious pray, talk of God, of Christ. And they are indignant of the humiliations endured by their religious leaders :

Je revois encore ce digne prêtre orthodoxe, avec sa grande barbe, tenant en une brassée sa soutane relevée. (Bonifas, p. 42.)

But the elements of time rarely vary :

On nous fait monter dans des wagons à bestiaux par groupes de soixante. 'Hommes 40, Chevaux en long 8' : nous avons à peine la place de nous asseoir, imbriqués comme des sardines en boîte. Un peu de paille, l'inévitable tinette, et nos portes verrouillées. Sous la paille, nous trouvons un outil dissimulé, déposé là sans doute par quelque cheminot. (p. 43.)

The overcrowding, the first element which is described, will be found again in camp life. There is little poetic transformation in what we have just quoted. The *'inévitable tinette'* introduces us to the Nazi disregard for human needs among sub-human prisoners. The same elements which make the suffering in the trip unbearable will be re-encountered in camp life. They are recounted, in the selection we have just quoted, with a goal, we suspect, of realism and transmission rather than transformation.

The entrance of the prisoners into the cattle cars was often viewed by a public who looked on with mixed reactions. Here at Compiègne, our author is rather sympathetic towards the Compiégnois and finds them courageous :

Devant tous ces regards, à la fois malheureux et fiers, qui nous scrutent avec tant d'ardeur, on a envie de crier : Merci ! Merci ! peuple de Compiègne, pour la force qui est en toi et que tes regards contiennent. Merci, peuple de France que nous aimons entre tous et pour lequel nous tiendrons. (pp. 42-43.)

Let us see a contrast. The first contact with the oppressors is also the first time that the prisoners are in contact with the outside world in their roles as deportees. Elie Wiesel was not deported from France. He was deported as a Jewish child from a little town in which he lived in Hungary. He is haunted from the beginning of the Night, as he calls his trip to the other end of the world, by a face in the crowd, that of a person who refused Tsipora, his sister, a glass of water. Because this man did not get up and find water for the child who was thirsty, because he remained passive in this situation, he is guilty. Non-activity, passivity, for Wiesel (*La ville de la chance*), is equated with negative activity ; therefore the man is guilty of collaboration.

Vous étiez en dehors du cercle magique. Votre devoir était clair : il fallait choisir. Nous battre ou nous aider. Dans le premier cas je vous aurais haï, dans l'autre je vous aurais aimé. Vous êtes resté à la fenêtre : je vous méprise. (p. 185.)

There is a third reaction, perhaps the most common, the indifference of the passer-by :

En entrant dans la ville, nous avons vu quelques passants. Les uns promenaient leurs chiens, les autres se hâtaient. Peut-être allaient-ils à la première messe. Ils regardaient à peine les camions dans lesquels nous étions debout. Nous chantions et nous criions pour les faire au moins tressaillir. 'Nous sommes des Françaises. Des prisonnières politiques. Nous sommes déportées en Allemagne.' Ils s'arrêtaient un instant au bord du trottoir, levaient les yeux, vite les baissaient, continuaient leur chemin. (Delbo, *Le Convoi du 24 janvier,* p. 9.)

The confrontations that will take place later between the workers walking to their Kommandos and the townspeople who see them will be characterized by the same three types of reactions. And the deportees will have the same feelings towards these reactions.

Each writer presents the phenomenon of deportation from his unique place in the universe. A most significant example will be Elie Wiesel whose perspective is quite distinctive ; haunted by a mad woman with the power to predict, whom none will believe or heed, he presents this mad woman on the train to Auschwitz. She predicted and the others did not accept. She hallucinated, or dreamt, perhaps saw. She cried out from the depths of the cattle car : 'Regardez ce feu. Des flammes, des flammes partout' (*La Nuit,* p. 49). Of course, the veracity of her vision is verified by the first view of the crematorium. The rest of the train, Wiesel tells us, thought she was just a mad woman and refused to believe her and ardently wished that she would keep quiet.

Those who were not deported but who write about deportation begin to sketch their characters' reactions to camp life at the point in which the character enters this phantasmagoric world. Tanguy is a young boy (Del Castillo, *Tanguy,* 1957). He is completely innocent. He is being deported because his mother was a Spanish political prisoner. He is nine years old at the time that the trip begins. (We must point out that the book is a novel, and that the historical premise is not correct : children of non-Jewish prisoners were not deported from France.) The same reactions that characterize the young Tanguy during his trip characterize his life in camp. He cannot believe what is happening to him. He blames the organization, the bureaucracy of the world, and says that it has made a mistake. He still believes that he will make them understand it was all a mistake and that he will then be freed. Therefore, Del Castillo shows, he is entering this other world slowly. He is not fully there by the time his trip begins. For a child of nine, his thinking is mature. He wonders how such things can happen. The same tinge of indifference which emerges in his character is seen here too : when the first child in his convoy dies, his reactions are the same as when he sees the dead being carried back from the swamps — calm acceptance.

Vercors' Clémentine (in *Sur ce rivage*) is a person who is characterized throughout her life by her need to serve others, to be with others. Vercors shows us that the trip and the later camp experience will not change her in this respect. He shows that the personality traits which he wishes her to maintain are indeed maintained throughout the trip and, more important, during her life in camp and later, after her release. Vercors realizes that they must come to the fore during the trip. Aware of the horror of the trip and of what is going on around her, Clémentine is well able to calm the others, to begin in her role as helpful friend. And since she is basically not unhappy in camp, she is not unhappy during the trip. For Vercors the camp experience begins in the train and therefore the structuring of his heroine must begin there too.

'Nous nous sommes installées comme pour un long voyage, les amies côte à côte', writes Mrs. Delbo (*Le Convoi du 24 janvier,* p. 10). The key word here is 'comme'. This is of course, a long trip, the longest anyone will ever take. Then why the word 'comme' ? To show us that this trip is not a 'long voyage' as one takes to go on vacation, as one takes to change locale : it is a trip, a long one, but one that bears no resemblance to anything that has ever taken place in the history of man. It is unique unto itself. A long trip is real ; a trip to the other end of the world, beyond human borders, is in the realm of the surreal.

As soon as the trip begins, all illusions are broken :

J'ai heureusement pu conserver à côté de moi Bonamour, furieux devant son illusion détruite d'un confortable voyage dans un somptueux wagon de troisième classe. (Pineau, p. 8.)

It is interesting to note that the comparison is with a third class car, not a first. The desire is to find oneself with the few people, the few friends one has there, to take the journey together. This remains a prime consideration later in camp, too.

One fact, which dominates much of the literature about the deportation, must be mentioned here :

Nous avons essayé de disloquer des planches. Dans mon wagon, rien à faire. Dans celui où était Madeleine Dechavassine, elles y sont parvenues et l'ouverture aurait été assez grande pour sortir. Les raisonnables ont démontré que quelques-unes s'évaderaient peut-être mais que les autres seraient fusillées. Si elles avaient lu l'avenir... (Delbo, *Le Convoi du 24 janvier,* p. 10.)

This story is recounted countless numbers of times. Holes were made in the boards. Some prisoners, at least, could have tried to escape. But the Nazi psychology is already visible from the beginning. They told their prisoners that if some escaped, or tried to, the others would be shot. This is exactly the same technique that was used in camp. And the psychology was effective from the beginning, as seen by the former quotation. Here, we have the first inkling of the idea of subjective time. 'Si elles avaient lu l'avenir...' The author, in the middle of her description of the trip, takes us into the realm of subjective time and lets us see the future. She hints at it by telling us that the worst is yet to come. As we read more, we understand the way in which the word *'raisonnables'* might be taken and then, by the end of the story, we conclude that *'raisonnables'* is meant most sarcastically.

The element of time and the transmission of the surrealistic world, that indeed begins with the trip, and is contained in the trip, is most effectively done by Jorge Semprun in *Le Grand voyage,* who realizes the immense dimensions that the trip in itself could have, and the suggestions that the elements of the trip could make to us. For Semprun, the trip to the camp is a round trip which contains within itself the camp experience ; the picture as we see it from his book is that of a trip which starts and ends the same way, into which the camp experience will be woven. He weaves his entire story around the trip, on many levels. Here, most effectively, the complete story of deportation is told, woven into the story of the trip. The trip is made to encapsule every element of the concentration camp universe. It begins with a description on a purely physical level :

Il y a cet entassement des corps dans le wagon, cette lancinante douleur dans le genou droit. (p. 11.)

This is a typical preoccupation of the prisoners both during the trip and in the life that they live as deportees thereafter : the preoccupation first and above all with oppressive physical elements, described with stinging precision. And then, the trouble our narrator experiences in counting the days and the nights. He counts too many nights for the corresponding number of days. Established things are no longer certain. The concept of time henceforth is subjective, not objective, showing a remarkable and clear parallel and influence with and by Proust.

All that seems definite is that the trip begins early one morning. It is worse than whatever they had imagined. The narrator closes his eyes and opens them to assure himself that this is not a dream. (He conveys this uncertainty to his reader.) As he plays at opening and closing his eyes, since both he and we need constant assurance that this is the reality of the situation and not a daydream, he becomes part of the scenery which surrounds him. The scenery enters his body through his eyes. A fusion takes place. The transformation of the man has begun, his self-image is transformed and he is transmitting this metamorphosis to us. He is filled with a strange happiness. Although in losing his sense of identity the narrator seems to have fallen into the trap of the Nazi archetypal vision, in reality his metamorphosis offers him the possibility of transcendence : 'Il ne faut pas me laisser distraire de cette joie sauvage' (p. 15). And this savage joy is his psychological defence against the situation, it is an avenue of escape, a transformation for survival. From this scenery, the valley of the Moselle, he makes other associations. He is reminded of the taste of the wine of that region and thus transcends the primary level of the voyage. It is the return trip that permits him to taste the wine for the first time in his life. He realizes that he is transcending present reality and that he must come back to it. He therefore states : 'Je ne connais pas le vin de la Moselle' (p. 18). He still did not want to talk of the return. He was disgusted by his repatriation, that night in Eisenbach when he first tasted the Moselle wine.

As we continue reading, the everyday things that we are so accustomed to knowing, and that the narrator and his fellow travellers are so accustomed to hearing, lose their significance. The whistle of the locomotive in this context seems absurd. As the narrator contemplates his situation and the relativity of his freedom, he comes to realize that he was never really free, and that others — even those not incarcerated — are not free either. In fact, paradoxically, he finds himself in this cattle car because of the exercise of freedom and that others enjoy greater freedom than he for the moment is only because they can partake of the fruits of the earth, whereas he cannot. Physically, he is enclosed.

... je suis dedans et... ils sont dehors. Une profonde tristesse m'envahit. Je suis dedans... et ces autres sont dehors. Ce n'est pas seulement le fait qu'ils soient libres, il y aurait beaucoup à dire là-dessus. C'est tout simplement qu'ils sont dehors, que pour eux il y a des routes... Ce n'est pas tellement le fait de ne pas être libre d'aller où je veux, on n'est jamais tellement libre d'aller où l'on veut... J'ai été libre d'aller où il fallait que j'aille... J'étais libre d'aller dans ce train... J'y suis librement, puisque j'aurais pu ne pas y être... C'est tout simplement une sensation physique : on est dedans. (p. 23.)

The feeling becomes more and more intense. In a later chapter, we realize that the feeling of *'dedans'* combined with other camp conditions robs the prisoner of his ability even to debate metaphysical questions. But, of course, the writer, writing in retrospect, after the event, is artistically free. Semprun affirms at the same time the feeling of *'dedans'* and his freedom as a writer to integrate the different moments of his life by a pattern of association which he has chosen : 'Mais c'est moi qui écris cette histoire et je fais comme je veux' (p. 24). The entire book stresses the opposition between his freedom as a writer and the physical feeling of being enclosed. We will see, that those who are able to think beyond their physical needs during the concentration camp experience generally revert to their literary experiences, especially their readings in poetry. But the technique is the same : thinking of literature or written ideas diverts oneself from the reality of the present moment. Not all were able to do this later. In Auschwitz the conditions were too oppressive to permit even this. But on the level of the trip, it was still possible. Because of the superb technique of the author, we realize that these mental wanderings do not last long, that he is rather absorbed with the different levels of the trip itself. There is a complicated time perspective involved here which shows a profound Proustian influence. Semprun recounts the trip, utilizing the time and space perspective of camp life and of the return trip. But, in reality, during the trip all this was unknown to him. So perhaps it was only an illusion that he did not dwell for long on the political considerations of which he speaks ; something must fill the gap in time that will be created as we remove all considerations other than those of the actual trip to the camp.

Semprun knows that we will find that the parallels with Proust are striking, even at first reading, and so he adds another literary dimension by integrating Proust directly into his narrative. 'Je guettais l'arrivée de Swann' (p. 88), he says, and Swann has thus become an integral part of the narrative. Every association that the reader can make is provided for and utilized to the fullest. And this reference to Swann reminds Semprun of an experience that he had with a Jewess. It is interesting to realize that here, in his trip, Semprun is sharing a condition with Jews, that Swann is Jewish, and that Proust was half-Jewish. The interplay and association of these facts embellish the reading of the narrative. There is a perfect unity not only of time but of Semprun's life with his literary inspirations. And he re-affirms that memory gives life its authenticity; an event cannot have taken place if no one remembers it. He is thus telling us that the train ride took place because someone, a participant, remembers it. The importance of memory is emphasized. In order to recover from this experience, he had to forget it for a long time, thereby externalizing it and objectifying it. We will speak of this later in another chapter of this treatise, when we deal with the concept of myth. An experience can only be concretized, for Semprun, as for Proust, when it is transformed by the memory. It is for this reason, because he is remembering, that the whole experience of deportation is real. The reality of the experience is found in its surrealistic transformation.

The author tells us that he is playing with dimensions of time. His thoughts wander. He contemplates the crematorium. But he returns constantly to the train, to the most minute details. The reality has been transformed into a surreal experience, into myth, but it never loses its base in reality. And Semprun reminds us constantly that his intention is two-fold : to stay within the temporal situation and to transcend it. A child is throwing stones at the window. The child is not guilty, yet he is. He is not a Nazi, but yet he is one. His parents stand by and permit him to play this game. The reactions of the outsiders to the passing train are contained perfectly in this small vignette.

The author is constantly taking a trip into the past. We are in prison. We are witnessing the execution of a comrade. The SS have decided to set an example, but they have succeeded only in setting an example of how bravely a man can die, and how dignified death can be. Still in the same time sequence, Semprun remembers that in prison he read Valéry whom he intensely dislikes. It was by reading Valéry that he could draw out the amount of soup allotted to him, that is, make it appear more by making it last longer, by making it last throughout the recitation of the poem. But he cannot deceive himself. There was never enough soup, no matter how well he played the game. And he always blocked certain lines of 'Le cimetière marin'. He is in his cell with his cell-mate, who has a surplus of food, thanks to packages. After eating the soup, he burps. And *le gars de Sémur,* Semprun's travelling companion whose name we do not ever find out (it is thus that the anonymity of the character is preserved, it is *le gars de Sémur* and it is any one and all of the 220,000 Frenchmen who were deported), tells us that he would have strangled him. Semprun replies that he would have done the same. By affirming this, he is making himself subject and object at the same time. He is detaching himself from himself. He is creating a *dédoublement de soi.* This is a re-affirmation of the writer's freedom as a creator. If Semprun were writing a novel, he would make his protagonist strangle his cell-mate in the above situation. But since this is a narrative, based on reality, he does not strangle him. He removes himself from the situation to make himself an object and to describe how the object would act in the given situation. But since here subject and object coincide, the cell-mate is not strangled. This capsulates Semprun's position ; it re-affirms both his limitations as a writer and his freedom as such.

It is sometimes the mention of an object that permits the author to free associate. We will discuss here one example which may remove us for a moment from the trip, but which is important in the illustration of the writer's style. He is in jail. He is talking about food. Then he is in camp, where a piece of bread equals the life of a man. And the moment of choice is there ; choosing to steal is choosing one's own life over that of another. It is the possibility for man to become sub-human, a possibility that we have seen elsewhere. The facts do not change with this author. There is no deformation of reality. The facts are merely transformed into an artistic creation that surpasses attempts at realism. The potential of man does not escape Semprun. He realizes that the animal is latent in all men. He accepts this and re-affirms his own guilt. But he also affirms that man is capable of altruism. The camp and the trip can produce either extreme. We have seen so far the past, the present and the future and remained in reality at all times. The surrealistic character of the narrative lends it scope.

The intensity of the unreal is felt particularly on the return trip. This is far more difficult for Semprun to adapt to than the trip to the camp. The things that he experiences have taken on a dimension of absurdity in the light of what he has just survived. The absurdity is not present in the trip to camp. It is so strongly felt in the recounting of the return trip that it makes us feel that the trip is unreal because we cannot accept that things so absurd can be taking place. Semprun communicates very effectively the double feeling of *dépaysement* on the trip to camp and on the trip back. The return journey is fused with the trip to the camp and his feelings remain constant. The absurd becomes a familiar part of his person. He tells us that he discovers his true being, his essence, on the trip. He must cling to reality, not to the reality of the past, but to the reality of the present world, of the concentration camp universe — in order to survive. And this is perhaps the key to survival that others were not able to put into words :

L'irréel et l'absurde devenaient familiers. Pour survivre, il faut que l'organisme colle à la réalité, et la réalité était précisément ce monde absolument pas naturel de la prison et de la mort. Mais le vrai choc s'est produit au retour de ce voyage. (p. 70.)

He preferred to cling to the past, to other thoughts, rather than confront the absurd world into which he was thrown, but, for his survival, this confrontation was mandatory. The fact that reality was constructed from the unreal and the absurd made the task difficult, but all the more necessary. This was not, however, the most difficult. For the deportee, strange as it may seem to the uninitiated reader, it was the trip home that was far more difficult to adjust to. Arthur Adamov, interned in a camp in France, Argelès, because he was a foreigner, although not deported, explains well what the deportee felt in *Je, Ils...* (Paris, 1969) :

Et cependant j'étais possédé par le sentiment... que mon existence méticuleuse de prisonnier, dans son humble simplicité, constituait la seule vraie vie, alors que la vie errante du dehors, celle des hommes libres ne m'apparaissait plus qu'irréelle, se mouvant dans la vanité d'une vague fantaisie abstraite. (p. 142.)

In the light of the years spent in camp, the outside world became absurd and the camp was more real, more valid. This is hardly what we would have expected, and it was simultaneously hardly what the deportee expected to feel during the long-awaited trip home. Hence, the shock that Semprun describes.

The physical preoccupations that dominate this literature in general also dominate Semprun's work. And he knows they are meaningless and most easily forgotten but that they were, at the same time, the cause of death of many thousands of men. The absurdity of the concentration camp microcosm is felt to the utmost when Semprun tells us of his first real meal on the return trip :

Un seul vrai repas, et la faim est devenue quelque chose d'abstrait. Et pourtant des milliers d'hommes sont morts autour de moi à cause de cette idée abstraite. (p. 85.)

The theme of hunger is always present. The absurd reaches its ulti-

mate with the above words by Semprun. The trip to the camp is the
beginning of hunger. The return is its end. Semprun's feelings continue to form a perfect circle. The same desperation characterizes
both halves of the trip.

Daybreak — but we do not know of which day — ushers in a
physical complaint : '... j'ai l'impression que mon corps va se briser
en morceaux' (p. 122). Semprun is taking us back into the past,
to the time when he had his hair cut. We recall the shaving and
haircutting experiences of camp life, and once again, the pieces fit
together perfectly, both in reality and in Semprun's subjective time
sequence. The balance of the book tends to weigh more heavily in
the direction of the return trip as our reading progresses. We have
made a gentle progression towards the future. Semprun's imagination
never permitted him to see what camp would be like before his
arrival. Therefore, it is a look into the future, not by the imagination,
but through a shift in time. He is not foretelling ; he is telling. As
he tells us of camp life, there is a preoccupation with the town surrounding the camp, with the people who lived in it. In short, he is
preoccupied by the same things that the other writers of this literature choose to discuss. Once again, his time sequence and style will
create the overwhelming difference. He is also preoccupied with the
idea that he should have recounted the trip in the time sequence in
which it took place, thus emphasizing his freedom and options. He
is haunted, at different times in his memory, by certain incidents : a
convoy of Jews that arrive in camp and the fifteen children in it that
are killed by SS dogs, the sign at the threshold of the camp *Arbeit
macht frei,* the effects of torture upon a man, and the possibility
that torture offers for a man to affirm his state as a human being
— (will he talk ?) —, a Jew who becomes a resistance fighter so that
he can fulfill his destiny as a Jewish deportee. There are also empty
moments in the narrative ; Semprun looks back on certain moments
of the trip without being able to remember what he thought of at
those moments. We are passing over certain incidents where he

speaks specifically of the life in camp or of the return because these subjects will be discussed in future chapters.

In the second part of the narrative, the narrator becomes a character. The narrative is no longer in the first person. Gérard is the principal character. We enter the camp of which we will not speak here. There are, however, several things we wish to point out about the first part of the narrative. As we have said, Semprun never mentions the name of his travelling companion. Moreover, he speaks in detail of only one travelling companion. We do have a rather precise idea of his origins, of his personality; we know him rather well, in fact. *Le gars de Sémur* dies during the trip and we know that he is going to die. We are therefore presented with the fact that the trip, in effect, endangers the lives of the passengers. The mortality of man is underlined by the anonymity of the character, by the closeness we feel towards him, and by the void which the author feels because of his death, of which we are reminded by the fact that our narrator tells us at times that he cannot speak of one subject or another because *le gars de Sémur* does not know about it. He had already died at the time. Throughout the first part of the narrative, the narrator remained a person, a subject, speaking in the first person.

It is quite significant that coinciding with the point in the objective time sequence at which the narrator enters the camp, he transcends his subjective personality and becomes the object of the narrative rather than its narrator. He is therefore no longer in control of his destiny. He can no longer re-affirm his freedom either as a writer or as a person. This trip is the transition between life as we know it and the life in camp, the loss of the personality. As long as Semprun was in his own time sequence, he could permit himself to retain his own identity. At the point at which he leaves his own time sequence, to enter the time sequence of the Nazi world, he is obliged to become just another victim, just another number, to deny his own freedom. He wants to die, to truly renounce his freedom, but he makes the last choice open to him : to stay alive. Time is no longer clear in his mind. He does not know how long the trip has lasted, nor when he left Compiègne. This because he is no longer free to establish his own time sequence. In the second part, there is no glimpse towards the future. There are some glances back into the past. Reminded by a kick in the pants administered by an SS officer, he recalls a scene in Compiègne. He no longer has the power to evade reality. The cold paralyzes him. There is an objective description of certain events, by the narrator, that take place in camp. It is no longer Gérard who is explaining. He is no longer the omnipotent narrator. He has renounced this world to become a subject within the Nazi world. The orchestra of the camp is playing and the trip is over. The introduction is finished. He has arrived at the other end of the world. He has taken his place in the world the Nazis created for him.

... il lui semble bien qu'ils arrivent par-là au bout du voyage, que c'est ainsi, en effet, parmi les vagues sonores de cette noble musique, sous la lumière glacée éclatant en gerbes mouvantes, qu'il faut quitter le monde des vivants, cette phrase toute faite tournoie vertigineusement dans les replis de son cerveau embué comme une vitre par les rafales d'une pluie rageuse, quitter le monde des vivants, quitter le monde des vivants... (p. 234.)

4

The Arrival and the Initiation

Just as the trip to the concentration camp is only part of a round-trip, the road to the camp, the entrance, is also the road from the camp, the exit. 'Rue de l'arrivée, Rue du départ', the opening poem in *Aucun de nous ne reviendra*, (Delbo, 1970) is perhaps the most effective introduction to camp life. The deportees arrive in a railway station.* In regular railway stations, there is an equal measure of those who are arriving and those who are leaving. There are different streets and entrances for those who arrive and those who depart.

> *Il y a les gens qui arrivent. Ils*
> *cherchent des yeux dans la foule de*
> *ceux qui attendent ceux qui les*
> *attendent. Ils les embrassent et ils*
> *disent qu'ils sont fatigués du voyage.*
>
> *Il y a les gens qui partent. Ils*
> *disent au revoir à ceux qui ne*
> *partent pas et ils embrassent les*
> *enfants.*
>
> *Il y a une rue pour les gens qui*
> *arrivent et une rue pour les gens*
> *qui partent.*
>
> *Il y a un café qui s'appelle A*
> L'Arrivée *et un café qui s'appelle*
> Au Départ.
>
> *Il y a des gens qui arrivent et il*
> *y a des gens qui partent.*
>
> (Delbo, *op. cit.*, p. 9.)

* It is interesting to note that in the region of the former Gare Montparnasse, there is a 'Rue de l'arrivée' and a 'Rue du départ'.

We notice that the balance is exact, even syntactically. This is the norm. But the station called Auschwitz, which did not even show the name of the station, was quite different. 'La gare n'est pas une gare. C'est la fin d'un rail' (p. 11). It was a place of arrival and a place of departure, but it was not departure in the usual sense of the word ; the people were not going to another place. Rather, they were taking the final step of departure from our world. Total incorporation into the Nazi world meant no return. They do not, then, arrive, they pass through the station. It is a transitional place ; it is not a definite arrival. And here, 'ceux qui arrivent sont justement ceux-là qui partent' (p. 9). Therefore, incorporated in the idea of arriving is the idea of departing — they are one and the same. In this opening poem, it is not departing from the camp that is suggested, it is the idea of final departure from this world, because '... ceux qui arrivent ne sont jamais arrivés,... ceux qui sont partis ne sont jamais revenus' (p. 9). To those who were there, it seemed that 'c'est la plus grande gare du monde' (p. 9). Perhaps it was. By this time, the travellers should know what will follow in a normal sequence of events, because they have been prepared by the train ride, but no : they expect hell, perhaps, but the only word that can be used to describe what they found is *'l'inconcevable'* (p. 11).

When they finally reach the camp, they are told to line up by rows of five. They are lost, they do not understand the language, but 'ils comprennent aux coups de bâton' (p. 11) ; the transition to the other world is complete. Their attitude, as described by Charlotte Delbo, is striking :

Et quand on leur dit de laisser les paquets, les édredons et les souvenirs sur le quai, ils les laissent parce qu'ils doivent s'attendre à tout et ne veulent s'étonner de rien. (p. 11.)

And they wait and quietly, still, they wonder. When they arrive at night, they have longer to wonder. When they arrive during the day, there is no waiting period. The women and children walk first and the men are relieved. Courtesy ? No : efficiency. In the winter, they are struck by the cold. They undress themselves, they undress their children. They cannot even react, they are already part of the Nazi world :

Et elles commencent à se déshabiller devant les enfants tant pis. (p. 16.)

This is all part of the *rites de passage* between our world and the other world. It is the disappearance of conventional manners and societal norms. It is the marking of a change in the very base of the society ; it is the passage from one society to another, and the passage was clearly calculated by the Nazis. In this case, some enter the other society, the camp, and the others go immediately to their death. These *rites de passage* prepare equally well for both. The victims are not disturbed by these rites, but they are disturbed by the fact that the shower may be cold, the children might catch a chill. This way of thinking is partly the camp attitude, but still contains remnants of their life before. They have become deportees, a part of the system. Even if they can understand what is happening, it serves no purpose, because they cannot warn the others. But they are still preoccupied by the same things that characterized their trip, and will characterize their life in camp :

Tous veulent se rappeler quelle impression ils ont eue et comme ils ont eu le sentiment qu'ils ne reviendraient pas. (p. 13.)

They feel, they have the *'sentiment'* that they will not return, but they cannot really imagine that they will not. They want to remember, and the underlying presumption is : to remember to tell.

There is an interesting *dédoublement* : the author, who herself passed through the 'Rue de l'arrivée, Rue du départ' is not describing her own arrival ; she is rather describing the arrival of another convoy (probably Jews), and of course, adding the dimension of the knowledge that her stay in Auschwitz permitted her to acquire.

Il y a une mère qui calotte son enfant de cinq ans peut-être parce qu'il ne veut pas lui donner la main... Elle calotte son enfant et nous qui savons ne le lui pardonnons pas. (p. 15.)

This is the initiation to camp life with the perspective of the camp, just as *Le Grand voyage* was the capsule of camp life with the dimension of the return trip. And from this poem we know what will happen in the camp : the girls' skirts will dress the band so that they can play Viennese waltzes on Sunday mornings. A Blockhova will make curtains for her windows from the rabbi's holy cloth and the Kapos will play bride and groom at night when the others have collapsed from exhaustion and they will wear the clothes that the newly-weds, who were snatched at the steps to the synagogue, brought to camp with them. And the food will be distributed to the German female prisoners who are sick and will not like it. And this will go on for eternity, the writer feels, and there is no idea, in the poem, of the end of this routine. All we are told is that it happens 'Et tout le jour et toute la nuit' (p. 18).

The poem is completely depersonalized ; it talks to all its readers, it tells the story as if the author had not lived it, but had simply seen it happen. But we know that she could have only known to tell if she had lived through it, because 'il n'y a que ceux qui entrent dans le camp qui sachent ensuite ce qui est arrivé aux autres et qui pleurent de les avoir quittés à la gare parce que, ce jour-là, l'officier commandait aux plus jeunes de former un rang à part' (p. 19). Why ? 'Il faut bien qu'il y en ait pour assécher les marais et y répandre la cendre des autres... et ils se disent qu'il aurait mieux valu de ne jamais entrer ici et ne jamais savoir' (p. 19).

We have already seen, in the first chapter, the details of the arrival and the selections that took place. The prisoner had only one choice left ; the only choice, that would be a constant companion during his stay in the concentration camp : the choice to commit suicide. During the first days in camp, therefore, after the prisoner has fully felt that he may not live long, that a horrible death awaited him ; inevitably, he debated with himself or with his co-inmates whether to take his own life. The beginning then, of the life of the deportee is a dialogue between life and death. The deportee still maintained the strength to discuss it, to think about it. It was only the first week (approximately) of his stay in camp. He had seen others around him die, at first the older ones and then some of the younger ones and when the younger ones began to die, he was truly convinced that soon, it would be his turn. And he saw that 'la mort n'a que des versions horribles ici' (Delbo, *Qui rapportera ces paroles ?*). The thought that he might survive did not enter his mind. He willed that someone must return to tell what has happened, but he could not conceive that it might be he. There is, therefore, an apparent dialectic which ensued between life and death. In *Qui rapportera ces paroles,* the crux of the matter is not only the dialectic between life and death, but also the responsibility of one woman towards the other. Françoise, the protagonist, was a resistance fighter. When she entered Birkenau, she was between 25 and 30 years old. Another deportee, Claire, approached her and told her she heard that she, Françoise, plans to commit suicide. Claire informs her that she does not have the right to do so. Françoise wants to use her last free choice, exercice her last extension of free will. She is sure that she will die in two weeks, a filthy death, a horrifying death and she prefers to maintain her pride, her self-image, her personality and die a clean death, a painless death and eliminate the suffering that will precede any death in camp. Claire informs her that she does not have the right, as a resistance fighter, to make the choice to die. 'Un combattant ne se suicide pas', says Claire. For Françoise, this does not hold true, given the context of their present situation. They are in a place where 'les vérités ont changé,... les vérités ne sont plus les mêmes' (p. 5). Françoise does not want to suffer to that limit that none of humanity has ever known before them, and she tells Claire that she should ask the others who have suffered that terrible death, that then she would be able to better understand why Françoise wants to commit suicide :

Tu me demandes... Pose la question à celles-là qui sont couchées raides dans la neige, pose la question à leurs visages qui ne sont plus des visages, à leurs orbites que les rats ont agrandies, à leurs membres qui ressemblent à du bois mort, à leur peau qui n'a la couleur de rien de connu. Ne sais-tu pas tout ce qu'un humain est capable de supporter avant d'en mourir ? Ne crois-tu pas que pour arriver à cet état de maigreur, de laideur, de convulsion, d'indénouable dans ce qui reste de chair et de peau, il faut avoir souffert jusqu'à la limite, la limite que personne ne connaissait avant nous ? Je ne veux pas souffrir jusqu'à cette limite-là. (p. 6.)

From all that we know about concentration camps, we cannot conclude but that Françoise is acting rationally, logically, lucidly and she herself knows it too. It is Claire who is asking for the irrational, the ideal. Death, personified by Françoise, debates for a long time with life, personified by Claire, and later by others. By the fact that there is basically so little difference between Claire and Françoise, in relation to their personalities, we see that there, in camp, there was little difference between life and death, to the inmates. Their life in camp, from the beginning, would be no more than a very slow, agonizing death. It was not life, it had nothing to do with life. It was death, in a variety of forms, all of which tarried much on the way. Every road ends in death : Françoise tells us there is only one sanction, death :

La mort si vous sortez du rang, la mort si vous traînez la jambe, la mort si vous ne courez pas assez vite, la mort si vous ne comprenez pas un ordre ou une insulte, la mort si vous ne tenez pas debout sans bouger pendant cinq heures, dans le froid, dans la nuit... (p. 14.)

They do not just wait for death, they expect it. Why fight, asks Françoise again and again. But Gina knows that in spite of all of this, they want to live, really want to. And we see another *dédoublement de soi* being created here :

Il me semble que ce n'est pas moi qui décide. Ce doit être que ce qui est encore vivant veut persister à vivre, sans raison. (p. 15.)

During the entire first act of this tragedy, there is only one question that is ever debated : to live or to die. There seems to be no point in discussing anything else, this is the only pertinent question. It is the question that poses itself each morning ; there is a fight to get up, to stand up, to stay standing, to walk. And at each step of the way, of the day, of the night, as the character is living, he can choose to die, to thus coincide with the destiny the Nazis have outlined for him. We must underline, in fact, that this debate, as such, continues only for the first act of the play, that is, when the deportees have been in Birkenau for only eight days. We will see, in our next chapters, how things have changed by Act III, when they have been there seventy days. What is the decisive factor, then, that prevents Françoise from committing suicide ? Or, what is the factor that makes her want to live, that makes her really want to fight to survive ? Mounette, a younger character, wanted to die when she first walked into the camp. She would have gladly volunteered to have been shot after having walked over cadavers in the snow, before having known and seen the rest. Now, knowing and seeing the rest, although she thinks it is for no reason that they persist in living, she is holding onto life, she is fighting. And Françoise is convinced, because of Mounette, and decides to *faire le pari* :

Tu aurais préféré être fusillée à l'arrivée [says Françoise to Mounette], et maintenant tu t'accroches. Je ne te laisse pas. (p. 16.)

Françoise has therefore decided to fight to live because Mounette will have a better chance to live if she and the others stay to help her, with no arm other than their simple presence, which raises the odds in her favor.

Once this verbal debate between life and death has ended, once Françoise has decided to bet, to *prendre l'engagement,* this phase of camp life has drawn to a close. It is no longer *l'arrivée* and the few days or the week that follow it. The introduction to camp life is over and the routine begins. The routine and the repetition of routine that formulate the daily drudgery. But before we discuss camp life as a totality, camp life after the decision to live was made, we shall examine several other presentations of the arrival and the first week or so in camp.

There are three levels from which Charlotte Delbo views the deportation : the anonymous characterizations that describe the total phenomenon on a depersonalized level, the sociological-historical level, and the personal level. In *Qui rapportera ces paroles,* we have the personalized reactions to the arrival, the feelings of the deportees, the passions that form the tragedy. In *Aucun de nous ne reviendra,* we have the overpowering description of the totality on an anonymous level. We are told that :

Tous étaient marqués au bras d'un numéro indélébile. Tous devaient mourir. Le tatouage identifait les morts et les mortes. (p. 24.)

It is precise, concise and anonymous. It describes the ceremonial *rite de passage* by showing its goal, its purpose and further demonstrates to the reader the anonymity and depersonalization of the deportee once he entered the camp. The only way in which he could be singled out or identified would be by his tatooed number. The same dialogue between life and death seen in *Qui rapportera ces paroles* is found in *Aucun de nous ne reviendra,* but it takes place on a different literary level. The persons' names are never mentioned. The scene is entitled 'Dialogue'. Two women — the author is one of them — are talking of their chance to live :

— Il faut lutter de tout son courage.
— Pourquoi... Pourquoi lutter puisque nous devons toutes... (p. 26.)

We have no idea who is convincing whom or who the second prisoner is. The dialogue is not individualizing or personalizing the phenomenon. The 'il faut' is significant : it shows, by the use of an impersonal verb, the tone the writer is trying to set. The 'je' enters for another single sentence and then is depersonalized further by a third person singular pronoun, it becomes 'on', the indefinite pronoun. 'Je lutte contre ma raison. On lutte contre sa raison' (p. 27). The author does not want to enter into the narrative for a prolonged period of time, nor does she want any other person to play a dominant role : she is conveying a depersonalized totality.

Let us now examine the sociological-historical treatment of the arrival, which is descriptive, realistic. The women are struck first by the smell of the camp : 'Une odeur d'étable mal tenue, une odeur de vaches sales...' (Delbo, *Le Convoi du 24 janvier*, p. 11). Lulu comments when she sees the other filthy prisoners, that they could at least wash themselves. But 'Qui soupçonnait qu'il n'y avait pas d'eau dans le camp ?' They do not know, but they begin to suspect, what the future holds : 'Cécile a dit : "Dans huit jours tu sentiras aussi mauvais et tu ne le sentiras plus".' Of course, as in the other effective narratives, the time sequence is not strictly objective. The dimension of the later-acquired knowledge is shown here, even in the sociological description. As they go through the gate leading to the camp, whose name they still do not know, they read the sign *Vernichtungslager*. The commentary : 'Eh bien, c'est gai' (p. 12). And they sing the *Marseillaise* : the only convoy ever to enter Auschwitz-Birkenau singing. They see the SS women for the first time. The description is realistic, exact :

Hautes bottes noires, longue pèlerine noire, haut capuchon par-dessus le calot. Des silhouettes au dessin précis sur le fond de neige. (p. 12.)

No reaction is recorded. The description continues :

Nous avons contourné des baraques... Il fallait enjamber des cadavres... On comprenait à les voir que la mort ici n'était pas douce. La vie non plus en l'attendant. (p. 12.)

The key word here is *'en l'attendant'*. It is definitive and leaves no question : death is awaited, it is the norm, the expectation. The same idea that we have seen before in Mrs. Delbo's writings ; only the literary technique has been altered, to fit the content. The next of the traumas described is the midday soup. It is the first confrontation of the prisoners with disgust and distaste that they have to overcome :

they have to eat that soup that revolts them. ' "On ne peut pas manger cette soupe. Elle sent la tinette" ' (p. 12), says one prisoner. And Madeleine Doiret, another, replies : ' "La soupe sentira toujours la tinette, il faudra bien la manger ou mourir de faim. Autant commencer tout de suite" ' (p. 12). We must point out that this act of eating the soup is more difficult than walking over the cadavers in the snow. It more closely attacks the person and the self-image.

Another phase of the initiation to camp will also be discussed by Charlotte Delbo, on each level. The deportees, shorn, shaven, naked, did not recognize each other. 'Nue et tondue, aucune n'était plus elle' (p. 13). Even dressed, they do not recognize each other ; this we see several times in *Qui rapportera ces paroles.* We therefore have to conclude that there is something other than the lack of clothes, or the absence of hair that prevents the prisoners from recognizing each other. It is the atmosphere of the camp which has deformed each one to such an extent that his looks have changed ; he has physically become dehumanized, depersonalized. And what clearer way of explaining it than to show that one did not recognize the other either by the voice or the looks. We must remember that this was still early in the life in camp, so it is not due to physical deformation, emaciation or illness.

We will dwell on only one more point of the *Convoi du 24 janvier,* Charlotte Delbo's sociological work, and that is the confrontation of the new prisoners and the old upon the arrival of the new ones in the camp. The latter are not able still, or shall we say yet, to understand why so many will die. A Dutch woman comes over to one of the women in the convoy and says that out of 230, they will be reduced to 30 within a month. The others, calculating that she has been given an order to demoralize them, do not believe her, because even after having taken the trip and seen the camp, they cannot imagine this. And when they are told that roll-call kills them all, they really refuse to believe it :

Nous avons cru qu'elle voulait nous abattre. Nous étions déterminées à ne pas nous en laisser accroire. Des heures debout ? Il n'y a pas de quoi en mourir. (p. 14.)

The suspension of disbelief is not, thus, quite complete. They refuse to understand, or do not understand, when they complain that the barracks where they sleep are overcrowded and the Blockhova tells them that soon it will be better. Thus they are in a transitional phase : they have taken the trip, seen what the camp is like, some of them have already been so overwhelmed that they have given up trying to live, they have not eaten nor slept ; they have let themselves die. Some have died of other causes, mostly the elderly. They are in the other world, but they are not completely entrenched in it. Only time will make this difference. It is not a visible transition that can be pinpointed. It is a gradual conditioning, that began with the first moment of the trip, that will affect different prisoners at different times. Here, as elsewhere, the key factor is time. It is impossible to say that the prisoners were one way the first week and different the second : their attitude depends entirely on what they bring with them to the camp — their lives before, their health, outlook, attitudes, mental armament.

The speech by the SS upon the entrance of the prisoners into Natzweiler, as reported by one of the deportees who survived, stresses the fact that the SS wished to demoralize the deportees as much as possible :

Vous êtes ici à Natzweiler, le camp de la mort, dont personne ne sort vivant. (Laromiguière, p. 78.)

This was typical of many of the inductions into camp life. They left the deportee without a clear idea of what his future would be in reference to daily life, but they definitely removed any hopes that might still linger with him. They also clearly defined for him the position of the SS so that he would be able to commence playing his role in the interaction.

The crematorium was the center of attention of the first walk through the camp. 'Pas bon monsieur', announces the SS man, in a rather large understatement, after pointing it out (Pineau, p. 19). This was indeed done to frighten the prisoners. The prisoner had never seen a crematorium before and would be aware of death's proportions here only as he pondered why the crematorium was there. Many were of course struck by the odor of burning flesh. Other reactions were characteristic of the background that the victim brings to camp ; a religious woman is traumatized when her rosary beads are taken away from her.

There was sometimes a feeling of loss of control over one's destiny. It was the dehumanization, the becoming an object that Semprun illustrates by the simple technique of change of the author's viewpoint from narrator to character that other authors (e.g. Catherine Roux, Simone Lahaye), not quite so skillful, will have to use words to describe. It was not yet a feeling of fear. It was the beginning of a feeling of humiliation, of lack of grandeur, of the lack of possibility for that feeling of grandeur to occur among the victims. It is described by one as a 'première mise en scène tragique et ridicule' (*Les Françaises à Ravensbrück,* p. 77). She is at the same time struck by the simulacre of honesty on the part of the Nazis and the attention to detail, the bureaucracy. She feels she has entered a dance.

One reaction must be singled out because it is quite typical of the author's point of view, style and also because it differs so much from any of the other *témoignages.* Catherine Roux, naked, stripped of all her possessions, maintains her pride, at least in her book *Triangle rouge* :

... prisonnière, désarmée, toute nue, je me sens riche comme une reine et je relève hautement le front. (p. 59.)

The reaction is unusual, atypical and tends to decoy the reader from focusing his attention on the horrors of camp life. It is in Ravensbrück that she is able to keep her head high : she avoids recounting sordid details and a certain naiveté pervades her book : 'Mon Dieu, je n'ai plus de vêtements sur moi !' (p. 57) she says after the traditional undressing scene. The maintenance of pride and calm is quite distinctive.

We must point out one other book because it is written by a non-deportee : Regina Wallet, *Celles qui ne voulaient pas mourir.* She places her story in Ravensbrück and her heroine, Valentine, aged 19, is quite naive and not at all prepared for camp life. Her first night in camp is more traumatic than her first day. This concept, that night is more terrifying than day, repeats itself many times throughout the literature of the deportation. Valentine's youth and naiveté dominate the novel. During this first night, she hallucinates and she cannot accept that she is really in camp. She is not at all sure at this time that she will survive. She wonders whether she will overcome the 'chocs multiples,... la faim et... les coups' (p. 65). These are, obviously, primarily physical preoccupations. This book is important because it shows the attempt of a non-deportee to capture a certain verisimilitude in reference to the deportee and his entrance into camp, but unfortunately, this verisimilitude, as we will see later, is not maintained.

This chapter would be incomplete if it did not speak at greater length of Elie Wiesel *(La Nuit)*. He arrived with his family in Auschwitz. It was a Jewish convoy. There was a selection to be made. Of course, the family wanted to stay together. The *camaraderie* of a stranger saved the father and son. They lied about their ages — the son was too young and the father too old — and they were sent to the left, the good column. The idea of the *camaraderie* of strangers, so important in the concentration camp literature, comes to the fore early in the narrative and its importance is thus underlined. Wiesel does not know that he is leaving his mother and sister forever. There is no inkling that it is not just a temporary separation. The SS prepares them for what will follow : he speaks to them as Jews and *Untermenschen* :

'Vous voyez, là-bas, la cheminée ? La voyez-vous ? Les flammes, les voyez-vous ?... Vous n'avez pas encore compris ? Fils de chiens... On va vous brûler... Vous réduire en cendres !' (p. 55.)

There is no equivocation, but still the people cannot believe. Wiesel thinks perhaps it is all an unimaginable (a word that occurs frequently, not only in Wiesel) nightmare. One man in the crowd wants to revolt ; he wants the others to know what has happened so far, he wants to escape to tell. The others still consider this to be a *bêtise*. The attitude witnessed on the train has not changed, yet. The SS plays a game ; no one knows which column leads to death and which one leads to life. Which is the good column ? Wiesel wants to know two things : is he awake and is he going to live ? And he wants to commit suicide, he too, if he has to die anyway. He doesn't want to wait, if he is waiting to be burnt alive. Around him, many are already reciting the Kaddish, the prayer for the dead. And it is at this point that Wiesel revolts against his upbringing and his present condition for the first time. He cannot accept that people repeat : *Viyis-gadal, viyiskadash shmé rabba* [Magnified and sanctified be Thy name]. He cannot praise the Lord for the horror that he is seeing. He cannot accept his religion. The concentration camp therefore incites the beginning of metaphysical questions and revolt that dominate his work. His relief is immense when he realizes that he is not going to die right then and there. And he holds tightly onto his father. And they remember Mrs. Schachter, the mad woman from the train. Wiesel tells us of the things that stand out in his mind, the things that he will never forget about that first night. The word 'Night' has a double meaning : it is the literal first night that he spends in camp, and it is also the beginning of that phase of his life that he calls 'la nuit', his stay in camp.

> *Jamais je n'oublierai cette nuit, la première nuit de camp*
> *qui a fait de ma vie une nuit longue et sept fois verrouillée.*
> . . . .

Jamais je n'oublierai cette fumée.

. . . .

Jamais je n'oublierai ces flammes qui consumèrent ma Foi. (p. 60.)

He quickly passes over the description of the barracks and the salient features which he emphasizes are the 'lucarnes bleuâtres' and the 'hommes affolés, tant de cris, tant de brutalité bestiale' (p. 61). At the time when all men become equal ('Pour nous, c'était la véritable égalité : celle de la nudité') (p. 61), he has only one desire — to cling to his father. They meet people who arrived in camp a week or so before they did and they use their last strength to cry. Cry at the joy that they are still alive and cry because they too let themselves be brought here. Gradually, Wiesel's feelings of fear dissolve and are replaced by overwhelming fatigue. We know that he has truly become part of the camp at this moment because this feeling of fatigue, produced by varied causes, is the feeling that dominates the narratives about the concentration camp *vie quotidienne*. They no longer think about the ones who are absent, and we are reminded of the character in *Qui rapportera ces paroles* who says : 'Il faut attendre d'être revenu pour se rappeler' (p. 55). Wiesel tells us in *La Nuit* that : 'Il était incapable de penser à quoi que ce soit' (p. 63), and this is the feeling we must underscore. Countless readers are under the mistaken impression that the camp inmates could lose themselves by letting their thoughts wander, by thinking about nature, by daydreaming. Wiesel realized early, in the first two days, and states here, that this was impossible. The oppressiveness of the Nazi system consists in the ability to make it impossible, physically or mentally. And Wiesel tells us that : 'L'instinct de conservation, d'autodéfense, l'amour-propre — tout avait fui' (p. 63). The parallel between Wiesel and Delbo is clear. Both tell us of the immediate loss of identity and of the desire for self-preservation. Only the literary form differs. In one case it is the narrative, in the other it is a dramatic dialogue. Wiesel writes :

Dans un ultime moment de lucidité, il me sembla que nous étions des âmes maudites errant dans le monde du néant, des âmes condamnées à errer à travers les espaces jusqu'à la fin de générations, à la recherche de leur rédemption, en quête de l'oubli, sans espoir de trouver. (p. 63.)

The feelings so poetically communicated here are the same as the ones which we find in Charlotte Delbo's play — the desire to forget and the feeling of being nowhere. The effective transmission of this feeling to the reader is far more important, and far more impressive upon the reader's conscious than is the more exact description of the rituals pertaining to the entrance into camp life. What is more important is this description of the metamorphosis of the prisoner's mind. They have already become automatons : 'Un ordre : "Courir." Et nous courons' (p. 63).

The deportees don't think about what they are doing ; they simply obey. All reflexes, except the one of obedience, are already gone. They have been in the camp only two days. The situations appear comical to Wiesel : 'Si la situation n'avait été tragique nous aurions pu éclater de rire' (p. 64). Wiesel can already see the change that has taken place, and is written on all the men, by seeing his father who shows all there is to show by the fact that : 'Ses yeux s'étaient obscurcis' (p. 64). And Wiesel remembers that he was incapable of finding anything comforting to say to him. There is also a parallel here with Semprun :

Tant d'événements étaient arrivés en quelques heures que j'avais complètement perdu la notion du temps... Quand avions-nous quitté la maison ? Et le ghetto ?... Une semaine ?... Une nuit — *une seule* nuit ? (p. 64.)

As Charlotte Delbo says : 'Des années d'une seule saison, des années d'hiver et de nuit' (*Qui rapportera ces paroles ?* p. 13).

The suspension of disbelief is still not complete. The integration into the other world has progressed quite a bit : 'C'était sûrement un rêve', writes Wiesel (p. 65). The same attitudes that are shown during the train ride and in the ghettoes are still coming to the fore here.

Wiesel falls asleep standing up and has his first dream. He dreams of a bed, the caress of his mother. We will remember this, that this is the dream of a boy who has been in camp for a day or two, and compare it later with the dreams of prisoners who have been in camp longer. This can be entitled an 'arrival dream'; the others will be referred to as concentration camp existence dreams. There is a sharply pronounced difference between the two.

Elie Wiesel heard the same type of initiation speech upon his entrance into camp that many others had heard. The SS man presented two essential choices to them :

'Ici, vous devez travailler. Sinon, vous irez droit à la cheminée. Au crématoire. Travailler ou le crématoire — le choix est entre vos mains.' (p. 66.)

Just as Charlotte Delbo tells us, there are no shadows, there are no ambiguities. There is only one penalty : death. There is nothing but life and death, and the two have little difference between them ; this is one of the convergent points between *La Nuit* and Charlotte Delbo's works. There is one factor which still maintains its element of reality for Wiesel, even at this point : the word 'cheminée', the image of death itself. 'Il [meaning the word] flottait dans l'air mêlé à la fumée' (p. 67). The first real trauma of camp life takes place when Wiesel's father falls to the ground because a gypsy *Proeminent* (see Appendix) slaps him, hard, because the former does not know, has not yet understood that he is an *Untermensch* and asks for the latrines. Wiesel remains motionless. Yesterday, in another place, anywhere else, he would have fought the gypsy. Here he is immobile.

The same element of irony that we found present in Mrs. Delbo's work can be found here. '*Cocasse*', says Charlotte Delbo in *Qui rapportera ces paroles* (p. 14) when she finds herself using the expression '*prendre froid*' in Françoise's long monologue about death. '*Dérision*', says Wiesel in *La Nuit* (p. 69), when he reads the inscription on the barbed wires 'Attention ! Danger de mort !' There is therefore an element of irony which later chapters will show even more clearly and which the prisoners are aware of from the beginning.

Wiesel is transferred from Birkenau to Auschwitz where *Arbeit macht frei* is the first thing that greets him. His first reaction is that Auschwitz is better than Birkenau :

Des bâtiments en béton à deux étages au lieu de baraques en bois. Des jardinets ça et là. (p. 63.)

There was water in Auschwitz, but none in Birkenau. Moreover, to welcome the prisoners, there was another induction speech, but this time by a Polish *Proeminent* who tells them not to lose hope, that they will see the liberation, that there is all possible hope since they have made it through the selection. He tells them to help each other, to remember that suffering is not eternal. We react neutrally to him and Wiesel records no reaction. The next day, they are still in quarantine, so they don't work. Their morale is better, they have better clothes, some food. They speak of everything but of the ones who have disappeared. Wiesel though, spoiled child that he himself says he is, cannot eat his soup. It disgusts him. His father swallows it. That afternoon, Wiesel is tatooed number A-7713. 'Je n'eus plus désormais d'autre nom' (p. 72). The days pass and by the third day, Elie Wiesel is hungry enough to eat anything. At night, some of the deportees sing Hassidic melodies and although Wiesel himself has ceased to pray he does not deny, at that moment, the existence of God, though he cannot help but doubt His absolute justice. Wiesel listens to the others talk of God and now and then he wonders where his mother and sister might be. Now, really knowing they were gassed, he pretends to believe that his mother is in another camp working with his sister. After three weeks, for the deportee still in quarantine, life is bearable ; it is better than the first days since now they are allowed to sleep. Then one day, they are sent off in transport to work. He is sent to Buna, a Kommando of Auschwitz. The same rituals of initiation and entrance take place once again and they have three more days of quarantine, before they are sent off to work.

Wiesel wants to get into a 'good' Kommando but he would have to give up his shoes as a bribe and he refuses. This shrewd sense of knowing what to do in a situation which one has never encountered previously is also seen in Charlotte Delbo's *Le Convoi du 24 janvier* and one wonders from where the knowledge came. They have just arrived in camp.

'Faisons bien attention aux chaussures. Essayons d'en trouver qui ne prennent pas l'eau, n'importe si elles sont trop grandes ou trop lourdes. Les chaussures, c'est ce qu'il y a de plus important', a dit Yvonne Blech. D'où tenait-elle tant d'expérience ? Elle a tiré posément, examiné méticuleusement. (pp. 13-14.)

They are sent to work and Elie's prime consideration, once again, is not to be separated from his father. And he finds friends, makes friends and begins to talk with them about Palestine, which is to play so important a role in his later life. His first concentration camp project is made : to go to Palestine if he survives.

Elie Wiesel is now integrated into camp life. His *vie quotidienne concentrationnaire* has begun. His long night has begun. There was no question of killing himself, perhaps because he was with his father, perhaps because of some religious taboos that still remained with him. Even though he ceases to pray, he still believes. The partial metamorphosis that the arrival in camp has brought about has begun to be effectuated. Wiesel's style, in *La Nuit* is one of simplicity, brevity, and clarity. It is realism, it is a rather skillful narrative. There is no attempt being made to transform the experiences. The goal of the author is clearly to recount, not to transform, the events. And he has captured the essential points of his own metamorphosis.

In the next chapters, we will see in detail how the deportee reacted once he became integrated into the camp system. We will not stress the idea of time in these chapters, except in contrast with the first chapters, because there is a striking difference between 'arrival reactions' and those of the later camp life, but there are few between, let us say, three weeks and ten weeks. Once the prisoner has passed through what we have just described here, and termed the 'arrival phase', he loses track of time and time becomes a concept : it is not days that matter, it is minutes : the day is reduced into its minutes and the minutes are real minutes, measured by suffering. The prisoner has a difficult time distinguishing between the real hours and the minutes that seem like hours.

4

The Life in Camp

Le temps pour nous ne passait
pas ; c'est nous qui passions ;
toujours plus las, sur ces jours
immobiles, remplis de souffrances,
d'inquiétudes, ou de monotonie,
mais immobiles ; sans que, le soir,
nous puissions les inscrire derrière
nous, dans le passé, puisque nous
ne connaissions plus la durée.
C'était vraiment du temps perdu,
et qui nous perdait avec lui.

L. MARTIN-CHAUFFIER,
L'Homme et la bête, p. 103.

The passage quoted above suggests 'out of time' existence within the concentration camp. The deportee, having left the 'arrival' phase of his stay in concentration camp, has become totally integrated into the camp. He can no longer distinguish moments in time, since time exists only as a static quantity which is reducing his life span.

A society was created in the concentration camps with all the attributes of a normal society. There was a plebeian class, a middle class, and an aristocracy. One could speak of an aristocracy among the prisoners, subservient to the omnipotent aristocracy of the SS personnel. There were few Frenchmen or women who were members of the aristocracy because, as we mentioned in Chapter One, the Kapos were primarily Poles or Germans. According to Nazi classification by nationality, the French were to find themselves in the lowest classes, and they were looked down upon, not only by the SS but also by the majority of the other prisoners. It seems that the reason for this is the following : the other prisoners, and perhaps the Germans too, could not respect a people who had so quickly capitulated and let themselves be placed under Hitler's tyranny, under Pétain. It is also that the French were a minority, and a minority who arrived late in the camp. The last two conditions would generally tend to incite prejudice in any kind of a situation. Also, we must remember that the French did not speak the same language as the majority of the others. This made their assimilation into the deportee group difficult. The capitulation of the French to the Nazis led to the generalization that all French-men were worthless, lazy and mentally incompetent, at least. There-fore, the Frenchmen in camps did not occupy privileged positions and were not well treated. It must also be noted that while of course they did contrive to get into 'good Kommandos', they did not seek posi-tions where they would be pitted against fellow prisoners of any nationality. In many ways, the position of the deportee was already created for him by the time he arrived in camp and the attitudes that others would have towards him were prejudiced. When the deportee arrived in camp, the society and the laws that governed it had already been determined. Invariably, to the surprise of the deportee who never believed he could become 'like that', he too soon became an integral part of that society and functioned in accordance with its laws :

Déjà nous réagissons les uns envers les autres selon les lois du camp. Sans nous frapper encore, nous nous traitons sans ménagement. La mauvaise hu-meur, la grossièreté sont de règle. Les termes orduriers dont nous agrémen-tons nos rapports sont une forme d'adaptation à notre situation. Nous trou-vons à les employer sinon du plaisir du moins une sorte de soulagement. (Pineau, p. 52.)

The camp routine, the routines of daily life, are described with infinite detail by almost every author who writes about deportation. The outstanding features of the routine, probably the most unbearable, that are found in each narrative, are roll-call, distribution of food, hunger, thirst, punishments, work and death. In some cases, we will also come across descriptions of nature in the camp. We must point out that although, for example, while the writers who speak of Auschwitz do not describe the beauties of nature nor the sky above, others writing of Ravensbrück which is not a *Vernichtungslager* for example, do so. We conclude that the explanation behind this is that conditions such as those that existed in Auschwitz did not leave the deportee with any inclination or possibility to find anything around him beautiful, and also that he was so totally integrated into the camp world that he could not escape into nature. He was so completely destroyed, had so completely disintegrated, that the world around him no longer preoccupied him at all.

The foremost preoccupation of the deportee was with what he would eat. His life centered around the hours of food distribution. These were the only hours in the day that he had any reason to look forward to. His conversations and relationships with others were often based upon food. Since food was invariably insufficient, the theme of hunger is a salient feature of the literature of the deportation. The camp aristocracy was distinguishable, in addition to differences in dress, by its obesity. This was equally true of the prisoner aristocracy and the SS. Both were well fed. The weapon of food and deprivation of food was a favorite Nazi tactic. Food was used as a reward ; the *Sonderkommando* was very well fed for three months, but after that, its members were killed.

It is interesting to note that a great part of the society, particularly of the men, was centered around the 'Aborts' (see Appendix). They had no place to exchange gossip, news or conversations where they were not watched. It was the only place where they enjoyed any sort of freedom and so it is their 'social hall'. Robert Antelme has interesting commentaries to make on this subject in *L'Espèce humaine* :

Les SS tolèrent également que l'on pisse et que l'on chie. Pour cela, ils nous font même réserver un emplacement qui s'appelle *Abort*. Pisser n'est pas choquant pour les SS ; beaucoup moins que d'être simplement debout et regarder devant soi, les bras ballants. Le SS s'incline devant l'indépendance apparente, la libre disposition de soi de l'homme qui pisse : il doit croire que pisser est exclusivement pour le détenu une servitude dont l'accomplissement doit le faire devenir meilleur, lui permettre de mieux travailler et ainsi le rendre plus dépendant de sa tâche ; le SS ne sait pas qu'en pissant on s'évade. Aussi, parfois, on se met contre un mur, on ouvre la braguette et on fait semblant ; le SS passe, comme le cocher devant le cheval. (p. 40.)

The society and its categories are defined by Francis Wetterwald in *Les Morts inutiles* as :

les puissants — strong because they were well fed ;
les capitalistes — those who had cigarettes ;
les pauvres — the oppressed, the weak, the scrupulous ;
les malins — those who flattered the gods ;
les désintéressés — those who died of hunger because they refused to debase themselves.

As can be seen, the classification is built around food. 'Les fauves attendent leur pitance... l'événement, le but et le moyen à la fois d'une existence que l'on semble voler au temps qui fuit' (p. 41).

For Gilbert Debrise, in *Cimetière sans tombeaux*, the conventional use of the word *bourgeois* carries over to camp society to represent petty capitalism :

Les petits bourgeois conformistes se lamentent à longueur de journées sur la perte de leurs valises. (p. 74.)

The distribution of food punctuated the different moments of the day. The first thought in the morning was always what they would get to eat and how much of it there would be. In many cases, the desire for food was so overwhelming, and the mentality of the deportee so debased, that they stole from other prisoners. To avoid descending to that level 'il faut atteindre d'un coup à la pureté du sacrifice total où les actes sont une arête de cristal...' (Simone Lahaye, *Un homme libre parmi les morts,* p. 32). Micheline Maurel writes, in *Un camp très ordinaire,* that the first time, when something was stolen from her, she let it pass. The second time it happened, she stole an equivalent item from a fellow deportee, unremorsefully. The deportee reached a point after a few days in camp at which he was ready to kill for a slice of bread. Fosty has a poem entitled 'La faim' in which the adjective used to qualify hunger is 'hurlante'. When he speaks of the past, as it appeared to him while in Buchenwald, it is 'le temps des bons repas' (*Anthologie des poèmes de Buchenwald*, p. 51).

Perhaps the most overpowering description of hunger is found in Elie Wiesel's *La Nuit*. The boy is with his father and they are eating, or drinking their ration of soup of the day. An SS passes by and forces the father to give his soup to his son. Wiesel tells us that :

Je n'attachais plus d'intérêt qu'à mon assiette de soupe quotidienne, à mon bout de pain rassis. Le pain, la soupe... c'était toute ma vie. J'étais un corps. Peut-être moins encore : un estomac affamé. L'estomac seul sentait le temps passer. (p. 87.)

We see therefore a distinct link between time and hunger ; one is the measure of the other. Wiesel is happy when the SS forces him to eat his father's ration of soup. He feels his hunger quenched. But of course, he feels guilty. And this happens many times, because of food and his father.

Je lui donnai ce qui me restait de soupe. Mais j'avais le cœur gros. Je sentais que je lui cédais cela contre mon gré. (p. 167.)

Later, when his father is dying, he is told by the Blockälteste that he must keep his father's food for himself, since his father cannot be helped anyway.

Il avait raison, pensais-je au plus secret de moi-même, sans me l'avouer. Trop tard pour sauver ton vieux père, me disais-je. Tu pourrais avoir deux rations de pain, deux rations de soupe... Une fraction de seconde seulement, mais je me sentais coupable. (p. 172.)

His hunger is overwhelming and he feels persecuted by guilt. We must point out that the idea of guilt as motivation is one of the principal themes of Wiesel and does not appear only in relation to food and his father. It seems to follow and haunt both Wiesel and his characters.

Hunger and food were the basis for all emotions; the degree of hunger from which a deportee suffered controlled his other feelings. He suffered more acutely from his exile, his enslavement, when he was less hungry. When hunger reached its peak, it prevented any other feelings or emotions from being felt. Very closely related to the thought of hunger was that of thirst. The deportee also suffered acutely from thirst. This presented, in turn, other problems to him. Drinking made dysentery worse and the worse the dysentery got, the more the prisoner craved liquids, which were poisonous for him. Elie Wiesel also describes this in relation to his father. His father craved water while he was dying of dysentery. Wiesel does not have the heart to refuse the dying man, but he knows that it will kill him. His father did not last long after this.

The description of thirst is not as frequent as the description of hunger. Thirst is most acutely described in *Aucun de nous ne reviendra*. Thirst in the camp is compared to thirst in the desert. But thirst in the camp, in the swamps where they work, is more burning, and it lasts longer. There is no miracle as there always is in the stories of the traveller lost in the desert for three days but found again. The deportee in the camp is not rescued by any Messiah. And 'La raison chancelle. La raison est terrassée par la soif. La raison résiste à tout, elle cède à la soif' (p. 114). There is no hope of finding an oasis.

Les joues collent aux dents, la langue est dure, raide, les mâchoires bloquées, et toujours cette impression d'être morte et de le savoir. Et l'épouvante grandit dans mes yeux. Je sens grandir l'épouvante dans mes yeux jusqu'à la démence. Tout sombre, tout échappe. La raison n'exerce plus de contrôle. La soif. Est-ce que je respire ? J'ai soif... soif à crier... Reste une idée fixe : boire. (p. 116.)

The desire to drink is so strong, so omnipotent that when the Blockhova sends her to get something, and she sees the soapy water in which the Blockhova washed, she wants to lap it up.

Au bord de la déraison, je mesure à quel point la soif me fait perdre le sens. (p. 116.)

But far worse than the thirst of the day is the thirst of the night, the thirst in their dreams :

... la soif de la nuit, la plus atroce. Parce que, la nuit, je bois et l'eau devient immédiatement sèche et solide dans ma bouche. Et plus je bois, plus ma bouche s'emplit de feuilles pourries qui durcissent. (p. 123.)

Then, there is the other dream, the quarter of an orange :

... j'ai le goût de l'orange dans la bouche, le jus se répand jusque sous ma langue, touche mon palais, un peu acide et merveilleusement fraîche. Ce goût d'orange et la sensation du frais qui coule me réveillent. Le réveil est affreux... c'est... la pâte de feuilles pourries en mortier qui pétrifie. Ma bouche est sèche. Pas amère. Lorsqu'on sent sa bouche amère c'est qu'on n'a pas perdu le goût, c'est qu'on a encore de la salive dans la bouche. (p. 123.)

As we will see again later, the sensations of the night are stronger, harder, than the sensations of the day. Whatever is relived in dreams is felt more acutely, more painfully.

The explanation for the fact that the night is worse than the day is found in *Qui rapportera ces paroles*. Mounette tells us that the dreams are worse than the reality because dreams are dreamt in solitude. There is no one to give moral support. At night, the prisoner is alone with his dreams. Each deportee realizes that, without the others, he would never have been able to come back. He would never have survived. It is the presence of the others, in itself, without their necessarily doing anything, that helped the deportees : this poem, entitled 'Aux autres merci' is indicative of the thoughts found in all the literature on this subject :

> *Un fantôme danseur de corde*
> *qui s'exerçait la nuit*
> *Sur les fils du télégraphe*
> *Il ne savait pas que je le voyais*
> *Il dansait*
> *Il s'était habillé en fantôme*
> *Et cependant*
> *Personne ne le voyait.*

> *Moi je n'aurais pas tenu*
> *Si personne ne m'avait vue,*
> *Si vous n'aviez pas été là.*
> (Ch. Delbo, *Une Connaissance inutile*, p. 35.)

There are many explanations of the need for others. According to certain writers, it was not solidarity by nationality that reinforced the prisoner's postion in camp, it is the religious affiliation or affiliations
with the communists or the marxists because these affiliations or
beliefs assured them of coherent explanations for the incoherent
world of the camps. It is this, according to Louis Martin-Chauffier
which prevented them from getting discouraged : 'Le sentiment
d'une durée extérieure à eux et qui les prolongeait' (*op. cit.*, p. 55). We
suspect that the explanation is not this, although it is part of it, but that
it is rather the presence of a strongly cohesive group of friends, held
together for any reason, that gave moral support, that made the difference. This discussion will be continued when we discuss relationships
within the camp.

As we mentioned in Chapter 1, the daily life consisted most generally of the roll-call, the work, the food, the afternoon work, the evening roll-call and the night. All the days were the same. Time was
measured only by the suffering endured. Otherwise, the hours melt-
ed one into the other, as the days, the months and the years did. From
all that we have read, we can state that although the work varied in
the different camps, and the conditions varied too, the roll-calls rarely
varied. It was a torturous experience which few people who have not
undergone can understand because it involved nothing more than
standing motionless. The prisoners could not understand it themselves when they heard, upon arrival, 'l'appel tue tout le monde'
(Delbo, *Le Convoi du 24 janvier*, p. 14). The roll-call was the easiest
way to kill off the largest number of people. It gave no trouble to the
SS and required a very minimal expenditure of both manpower and
energy on their part. It epitomized the effectiveness of the Nazi system.
It was one of the unique moments during the day when the entire

camp was assembled in the same place. In Birkenau, in 1943, there were 15,000 people. The number in charge was ridiculously low, comparatively. This indicates that the deportees were well controlled by very few, and that the atmosphere of terror was so pervasive that the discipline enforced by the Nazis was easily maintained even when they were present only to give a cursory glance. This is due to the extremely poor physical condition of the deportees, who were barely able to stand on their feet and therefore were easily dominated. The roll-call, whose purpose was to count the deportees, seemed eternal to them. The most usual ones were not the normal ones. The normal ones, that is, the ones without incident, were in the minority. So very often, the counts did not tally, and so the re-counting was interminable. Generally, the authors describe this in very matter-of-fact ways and tell us that the roll-calls lasted from one to fifty-six hours. But telling us the number of hours does not appeal to our emotions, it recounts facts that do nothing to our emotions. It does not really touch us because these are emotions that we cannot really know, and when they are told this way, we cannot feel them, either.

L'appel général est grandiose... Une heure après le réveil, ululé par une sirène à 3 h 30 du matin, arrivent dans la vaste *Lagerstrasse,* qui s'étend d'un bout à l'autre du camp, les colonnes rayées de prisonnières... La *Lagerstrasse* est remplie de ces colonnes sinistres que les policières rangent avec des injures et des coups qui ne sont pas simulés. (Quoted in *La Tragédie de la déportation,* p. 86. From Fr. et E. Michaut, *Esclavage pour une résurrection.*)

They are hungry at morning roll-call as they will be at evening roll-call, though in the evening the possibility of food is nearer. The roll-call is always dominated by its silence. No movements are permitted within sight of the *Proeminents.*

... il y a les mourants que l'on soutient et qui râlent ; ils ne passeront pas la nuit, la fièvre les ronge ; leur toux est le seul bruit permis,... avec, au-dessus de nous, le sinistre croassement des vols de corbeaux. Il y a les dysentériques qui se vident et qui sentent mauvais... (Quoted in *La Tragédie de la déportation,* p. 89. From M. Orset, *Misère et mort, nos deux compagnes.*)

These descriptions tell what the roll-calls were, but they do not penetrate our subconscious sufficiently for us to realize why they were so
deathly, why the inmates found them so painful.

After the roll-call came the daily work. This work was so varied
that it seems pointless to quote from many works to show the different kinds of labor details. What is important though is the fact that
it was useless work, designed to make the deportee feel that he was *de
trop* in the world and that his existence did not count at all. It had
nothing to do with what he was trained for or the career he had before
he came to camp, in most cases. It was impossible for him to judge
when a job was finished ; they all seemed endless. How can anyone
tell when a ditch is deep enough if he does not know the purpose for
which he is digging the ditch ? And even if he did... In *L'Arbre de
Goethe*, a man feels useless and talks to his friend. The friend replies :
' "Il ne s'agit pas d'être utile. Il s'agit de survivre." ' (Julitte, p. 178).
The deportee's mind was still using norms which he had brought
with him from the conventional society. The deportee's mind was like
a *palimpseste* — the *tabula rasa* desired by the Nazis had not been
completely accomplished, ideas remaining from normal life come to
the fore in many situations, even though at times it would have been
easier for the deportee if they had not. This feeling of uselessness, of
despair, led to the further disintegration of the deportee. Christian
Pineau describes the 'work' done in camp literally and his description
is typical of those found in most of our authors :

Transporter quelque chose d'un endroit à un autre sans utilité apparente,
c'est une des occupations typiques de Buchenwald. (p. 106.)

However, when he later feels a certain satisfaction over the comple-
tion of another kind of task, he realizes that he must not feel it
because it is work being done for 'them' and, in addition, it is falling
into a trap set by the Nazis.

Micheline Maurel speaks of 'la parfaite indifférence des Françaises
pour la discipline allemande' (*Un camp très ordinaire*, p. 83). This was

possible in Neubrandenburg or in Ravensbrück, and whenever it was possible (it certainly was not so in Auschwitz) it formed something which is not exactly a part of camp morality, nor was it exactly a means of psychological defence for the deportees. It was rather a way of gaining small victories. It hinted at defiance of German authority — not marching in step when it was commanded, singing a song other than the compulsory one. Punishments might follow such as roll-calls, varied races or calisthenics, but generally it was worth it to the deportee. It did not risk his life and it allowed him these small victories which he needed to feel fulfilled in some way, to remain human.

The deportee seemed most typically to be characterized by indifference. He became an automaton, functioning by commands and blows rather than by the pushing of a button, but there was very little other difference. When the conditions were extremely oppressive, he was robbed of his ability to think. We have seen that when they were less oppressive, he thought of his religion, of the past and of the future, and of things he had read but we must also comment on other possible and probable preoccupations of the deportee. The first was his surroundings, his physical surroundings. In Auschwitz, where the weather and physical conditions were as great an enemy as the SS, the deportee could not find anything to admire, anything encouraging, nature was completely hostile. In other camps (in Ravensbrück, for example, where the conditions were less oppressive), we find descriptions of nature in our readings. Christian Pineau describes Buchenwald for us when he has only been there a short time :

Ses pentes tapissées de hêtres et de sapins, lourds de neige éclatante, descendent avec des ondulations variées vers l'immense vallée qui s'étend pendant des kilomètres jusqu'à d'autres collines lointaines dont la silhouette se nappe d'une brume légère... la ligne de chemin de fer dont les rails tracent à travers les champs de fins sillons d'argent, tout semble appartenir à une nature reposée, à une humanité accueillante. (p. 37.)

This is certainly not an uncomplimentary, nor a negative description.

6

Pineau has been in the camp only a short time at the point in the narrative at which this description occurs, but since he is writing several years later, we must conclude that this is the description that remained with him. We find many descriptions of the different camps, but it is interesting to note that the non-derogatory descriptions of nature are those resulting from observations made while they are outside the camp, in transport to a Kommando or to work. The protagonist in Regina Wallet's novel is reminded of *Le Grand Meaulnes* when she admires the scenery on a three day work excursion outside the camp. In many of the descriptions of the interior of the camp, the crematorium, the smoke, dominates. Red is the most frequently recurring color. In Francis Wetterwald's description of nature, we find the following at the end :

Sur un tapis floral, dans un concert de mauves, de violets d'améthystes, de bleu de Prusse... au milieu des pensées comme une plaisanterie, jambes et bras repliés, bouche béante, yeux révulsés, s'étale, nu, grotesque, un cadavre. (p. 60.)

The latter is typical of many descriptions by the juxtaposition of beauty and horror of death. In René Salmé's poem, 'Krematorium', nature takes on the characteristics of the human beings that it is surrounding. The poem is about Buchenwald : '... des arbres criant, squelettiques/Dans le vent...' (*Anthologie de Buchenwald*, p. 100).

In camp, Micheline Maurel finds that : 'Le ciel, la seule beauté de Neubrandenburg, était superbe' (*Un camp très ordinaire*, p. 99). It is difficult to explain why, while most authors cannot bring themselves to an entirely positive description of nature while within the camp, in contrast to the times when they left the camp, for varied reasons, such as going to work on the outside, Micheline Maurel is able to appreciate sky, sun and grass. We must first point out that this is not Auschwitz, where there was never any grass at all. That Miss Maurel is able to find solace in nature, rather than being characteristic of the deportee, is exceptional, and here we must give place to her personality and presume that, in certain cases, her writing is the result of her personal formation. Since no archetypes can be formed, we will certainly not contradict ourselves by attempting to stereotype the authors we are discussing.

To some prisoners in Ravensbrück, even sunrise, a part of nature which most find very beautiful, becomes distasteful because it is associated with the roll-call and the beginning of the day in camp. One character in Charlotte Delbo's *Une connaissance inutile* tells us that she never wants to see another sunrise unless it is when she is returning from Les Halles after a good onion soup. For most writers, the characteristics of nature are too closely associated to the life and agonies of everyday existence to be appreciated or considered apart from the whole.

In a Kommando of Buchenwald, Porta Westphalica, André Bléton describes, in *Le Temps du purgatoire,* happiness : ' "Le temps est beau, la guerre avance, j'ai touché trente cigarettes. La vie est belle." ' (p. 79.) In this case, we tend to feel that appreciation of 'le beau temps' is not so much linked to nature as to the softening of conditions when it is less cold, or not snowing or raining. Time was passing, and since all the deportees were convinced that the 'right side' would win the war and that eventually concentration camps and the SS would be done away with, time was their worst enemy and the passing of it is a thing to be rejoiced over as an indication that perhaps if they have survived so long, they would see the end. Cigarettes meant more than food since they could be traded and smoked which was, for the prisoner, a coveted luxury. We must point out though that, judging by his *témoignage,* Bléton was a very solitary prisoner who did not seek out companionship as much as some of the others did and, therefore, his sources of happiness were different. Once again, there are no archetypes. While others talked all the time, to hear themselves talk and thus prove to themselves that they were still alive (and it is to themselves that they are trying to prove this), Bléton asks only that they leave him alone, and finds that he cannot depend on anyone but himself.

Death was the Final Solution that the Nazi concentration camps were to produce :

La mort est l'aboutissement logique, prémédité, de la déportation. La mort est la conséquence inéluctable des conditions de la vie quotidienne et du travail qui aboutissent à la mort 'naturelle', dit-on par euhémisme. (*La Tragédie de la déportation*, p. 353.)

We will not enter into a discussion of the most varied forms of death which the SS came upon to exterminate the *Untermenschen*. What is important to us here is not the descriptions of how people died, but rather the effects that death had upon the deportees because this was an important part of their psychological make-up. The deportees who arrived in *Vernichtungslager*, as we have seen by *Qui rapportera ces paroles*, found that death would be far easier, far preferable to the life in camp. But for varied reasons many chose to live, as we have already pointed out. Death however, remained a constant possibility and, in most cases, a probability, as Dominique Gaussen writes, in *Le Kapo,* that 'on s'habitue plus vite à l'idée de la mort qu'à la peur' (p. 74).

According to Laromiguière's *La Dame à l'ombrelle*, death caused the same reactions in concentration camps that it caused in normal life ; the young did not fear it, whereas the elderly did. We suppose though that a stronger feeling than the one that is found in everyday life was present among the inmates. For many, it was a very positive concept as exemplified by the following : '... aventure, renouveau, porte ouverte sur tout ce qui est au-delà du possible' (Hessel, p. 1080). This concept of death, of course, tends to give an idea of resurrection or of after-life. We do not know Stéphane Hessel's religious convictions but he obviously does not see death as an end. He sees it rather as an unknown but preferable alternative to what he is living through, but he does not see it as a *néant*. Even for those deportees, however, who did not think of life after death or the possibilities of resurrection, death offered a very positive alternative :

'La crainte de la mort n'était pas la pensée dominante des malades. Elle n'était rien à côté de l'obsession de la faim' (Tillard, *Mauthausen*, p. 61). In one of his poems, Fosty shows his indifference to the death of others, but unlike the other authors discussed, he is afraid of death. It is the only thing he can think of : 'A quoi peut-on penser si ce n'est à la mort/Car penser à la mort c'est penser à la vie' (*Anthologie de Buchenwald*, pp. 53-54). And when he thinks of death, he thinks of the past and he is somewhat remorseful. For most deportees, it was not enough to return, particularly when they thought about it in the earlier parts of their stay in camp : they wanted to survive whole. The general trend in the literature of the deportation is to show that death is a welcome possibility, it is not as dreaded as it is in normal life. When the conditions in camp are worse, it is more welcome. It is less painful than the life in camp, it is easier to bear, and it is the end of suffering. Never do we read of the torments of hell in a possible life thereafter ; nothing is ever considered worse than what is being suffered at the moment except perhaps a transport to a worse camp. The possibilities of the beyond are welcomed. The awareness of death in the concentration camp did not come immediately, though.

It was considered normal that the older ones should die, as they do in real life. It was when the younger ones began to die, the ones who were very strong the day before, that death becomes very real. Micheline Maurel writes that when the first person in her convoy dies, it is the beginning of a demoralization among the other prisoners, a realization that they would not all return. It is when they see death in great numbers, when they have experienced life in camp for a while, that the idea of the deportee about death is formulated. And it is at this time that the desire to live is still with him, lingering on, pulling him on. At the same time, the fright that death usually inspires is eradicated. There is much literature that is descriptive of the crematoriums, the gas chambers and the various other methods of putting the deportees to death, but the deportees themselves who have written are rarely haunted by the idea of death ; the punishments, the deaths of others that they were attached to, are far more acutely felt than their own fears. There is, then, another idea that is expressed : many of the women whose husbands were shot as hostages are glad that their husbands died a clean death, rather than face the possibility that they be deported, die in camp and become ugly, ravaged cadavers. It is far more difficult for the women to observe the men deportees, to see the condition they are in, than it is for them to see their co-deportees suffer. The deportee who writes this way shows us that the thought of the possibility of survival was not uppermost in the deportees' minds while in camp ; it is the length of time, the amount of suffering before death, particularly in the extermination camps, that weighed heavily.

Partly as a result of the closed society that was formed in the camps, relationships among the people involved developed, in the same way that they form in normal society but they were all the more crucial in the concentration camp context because they were quite often the means of and meaning for survival among the deportees. Christian Pineau writes :

L'organisation des camps a été conçue de telle façon que la haine se développe contre nos voisins de misère, non contre l'ennemi commun. Le berger dort tranquille tandis que s'affrontent entre eux les moutons transformés en loups. (p. 35.)

This is the pessimistic point of view. Actually, the relationships that developed among the deportees were quite positive in many cases and a source of strength. In the dialogue between life and death in *Qui rapportera ces paroles,* it is not because Claire feels that François has a responsibility to a party, or to any religion, that she tells her that she must try to live ; it is because she has a responsibility to history itself, and above all, because she has a responsibility to the others in general. Françoise decides twice in the play that it is worth it to go on living for the sake of the others. She does not have any hope that she will

survive, but she makes the decision to live because it may help another to be able to return and accomplish the mission : 'rapporter
ces paroles'.

The necessity of comradeship is also captured by the authors who
write about deportation without themselves having been in camp.
Regina Wallet's *récit* does so by giving a large place to the friendship between the heroine and Olivia, her best friend. Here, it is not
a group, but a pair of friends. The idea, though, is, all the same, the
necessity for comradeship, for at least one friend. In general, however, it is fraternity among one's compatriots that is sought. David
Rousset, in *Les Jours de notre mort,* a novel whose goal is to give a
panorama of camp life, therefore surpassing the level of his own
camp experience, stresses the importance of finding one's own. The
'others' for him are the Russians, Germans or Slavs, who are tougher,
and above all, not very receptive. The comradeship among Frenchmen is one of the dominant themes of all literature discussed here. In
L'Arbre de Gœthe, when the protagonist, a Gaullist, is invited to
speak to the Communists who are in charge of the camp on the deportee hierarchy level, the thing that he asks in return for the favor he
is doing them is that they place the French in separate barracks, under
the supervision of a French Kapo, so as to increase their solidarity
and, likewise, their chances for survival.

There is a fear of being separated from one's friends and compatriots, either by transport to Kommandos or elsewhere, to other
camps. The feeling of solidarity, it is our conclusion, is based upon
nationality. This does not exclude, of course, incidents of *camaraderie* among others.

Vercors, when presenting Clémentine to us, makes her dominant
trait the desire to be with and help others. For this reason, she is not
too unhappy in camp. We cannot help but conclude that although the
premise of the need for *camaraderie* is highly valid, the conclusion
that because of this Clémentine could be happy in camp is completely
false and unverisimilar. No one was happy in camp. No deportee has

ever written or said that he or she was happy in camp. Almost all stress the importance of others but we realize without any difficulty, and from the beginning, that the other conditions were far too oppressive to be eradicated by the presence of friends.

Tanguy, also written, as already mentioned, by a non-deportee, is an exception to the idea of *camaraderie* by nationalities. For Tanguy, it is *gentillesse* that counts more than nationality. Of course, we must point out that this is a unique case because it is being told from the point of view of a child who will, as is natural, take tenderness and friendship where he can find them. It is also true that the child is supposedly Spanish but lived for a while in France. This may be used to show that he is of somewhat mixed nationality. The child becomes friendly with a German prisoner, one who plays in the camp orchestra. But this is not exactly friendship as it is too one-sided to be called thusly. The child likes Gunther [*sic*] because of the things Gunther gives him. We suspect that Gunther, being privileged as a member of the orchestra because he sometimes gets extra food, feels a bit guilty about it. He has thus compensated by taking the child under his protective wing. Their friendship is rooted in food. The child likes those who manage to get him something to eat. Gunther is rather an interesting character ; he does not hate. He thinks that hate is only for those too weak to love and does not even hate his executioners. We will return to this point later when we discuss the deportees' concept of the 'others'. Tanguy is prejudiced against the Jewish prisoners. He finds *camaraderie* not so much in the other prisoners, but only in Gunther. When Gunther disappears because Gunther is shot, the child is left alone. This is the case of the child looking for the father whom he never really had, in the camp, rather than a true quest for friendship. In this respect, we offer no criticism of the book, and conclude that the faults lie elsewhere and that Del Castillo has captured the essential points in relation to Tanguy and his possible reactions and contacts with the other deportees. In a child's mind, the idea of nationality is perhaps far less definitely imprinted. Also, the idea of nationality implies a common cultural source, a common language and the possibility to converse. These later ideas are probably the basic reasons why prisoners grouped together not only by nationality, but by region. Two Parisians have more in common than a Parisian and a Tourangeau. They can remember the same restaurants, the same stores and evoke memories of them. For a child, this does not count as much.

Because sexual desires are not primary needs, there is almost no mention of them in the literature dealing with the camp experience. The only mention of them is found in the explanation for the reasons why they were not present among either the male or female deportees. They certainly did not preoccupy the female prisoners at all. The male prisoners tell us that hunger replaced sexual desires. There were bordellos in some of the camps. Most men did not desire to frequent them and in many cases, the visitation rights were restricted only to the SS and Kapos. The prisoners were too fatigued to desire this, and most did not have the money required by the bordellos in some of the camps (receiving of money was limited to certain nationalities or to certain positions in camp), or they did not want to betray their wives or girl friends. Whatever the case may be, there is little mention of sexual desires. There is also little mention of love stories among prisoners. Women were separated from men in the camps. In most instances, they were in entirely different camps. If the men say that they longed for women, it is that they longed for the comfort, the reassurance, the sympathetic company of women and this has nothing to do with sexual desires. It is the feminine presence that was sought, probably because it would make their world seem less foreign to them, more natural.

In all the French literature about the deportation, there are few love stories. We give the three following ones as examples, with the conclusion that they are probably unique in their genre and that they are typical of certain feelings, of what it was possible for a prisoner to feel, given his surroundings and daily life. The first two are written by deportees and seem completely probable. The third is written by a non-deportee and is so out of context, so unbelievably false, and so removed from anything that we have read, that we are forced to conclude that it is not authentic.

Lily was twenty. She worked in Raisko, a Kommando of Auschwitz, where she studied the *kok-saghyz*** with other prisoners under the direction of the SS. Every day, men from the camp come to work in the garden where the *kok-saghyz* was being cultivated. It was forbidden to talk to the men, but many of the girls had a fiancé or a friend among them. Lily had a fiancé. The men brought news and managed to transmit it to the women.

Ils étaient devenus fiancés en échangeant un regard, tandis que l'homme était courbé sur des plantes. Ils étaient devenus fiancés en échangeant quelques mots, sans se regarder, sans avoir l'air de parler. (Delbo, *Une connaissance inutile,* p. 76.)

And the fiancé managed to bring her little gifts, a cucumber, a cigarette, which he hid in the garden with a little note. They had not known each other before Raisko and the *kok-saghyz*. It was forbidden to communicate in any way with the men and since talking was difficult, Lily wrote each night, to her fiancé. And it made her very happy. One day, Lily's fiancé is sent to work elsewhere so he tells his friend to pick up the letter from Lily, but the friend gets caught. The letter is signed 'Lily'. The friend was tortured and Lily was not difficult to find in the laboratory. The friend said that the note was for him, but the real fiancé, not wanting him to be shot, gave himself up. All three were shot. The SS decided that the letter was in code and that it contained a political message.

Dans la lettre de Lily, il y avait cette phrase : 'Nous sommes-là comme des plantes riches de vie et de sève, comme des plantes qui voudraient pousser

---

* *Kok-saghyz :* a Russian word meaning '... une espèce de pissenlit dont la racine contient du latex' (Delbo, *Une connaissance inutile,* p. 74).

et vivre, et je ne peux m'empêcher de penser que ces plantes ne doivent pas vivre.' (p. 78.)

This love story, if it can be termed thusly, is a story, of the purest simplicity, of the relationship between two people which grows practically entirely out of letters. This development is in a way unreal, but is, of course, completely authentic. We see that Lily almost predicts their future ; she knows that nothing beautiful could develop or grow, under the watchful eye of the SS. The story is characterized by simplicity and cruelty ; the simplicity of the emotion and the cruelty of the ending is so unjustified, so uncalled for, but typical of the Nazi goal. This goal was to destroy any manifestation of human emotion. This story though, permits us to see the only type of love that existed, or that the prisoners could even want to find in such surroundings where all physical desire is absent. It is a relationship that gives comfort, that gives encouragement, that gives a reason to want to live, that promises. This is all that was possible there, but even this did not survive.*

Jean Lafitte, in his two volumes on camp life (*Ceux qui vivent*), and the life after camp (*Le Lac aux rêves*), tells a story of his love for a woman, also a completely platonic love when he is in the camp and she is on the outside. Because of Lafitte's orientation, however, the story takes on other dimensions. Marcel, Lafitte's protagonist, sees the woman for the first time when he is with another deportee. She gives the feeling to the men of 'la vision, depuis longtemps perdue, d'un être vivant que la souffrance, la méchanceté n'avaient pas déformé' (*Le Lac aux rêves*, p. 13). She gives some bread to the watchman who transmits it to Marcel, and she disappears. Marcel tells us that it is thanks to this act, and to the fact the woman is not visibly disgusted by the condition of the men she sees in camp that he can find again the human dignity which he had lost or which had

---

* It is interesting to note that this is the same Lily that Peter Weiss talks of in *L'Instruction*.

temporarily disappeared. It is interesting to note that Marcel tells us that the others who saw the beautiful woman bring the bread do not say anything at all about her beauty : they are rather more interested in the bread that she brings. They do not have eyes for anything else. But for Marcel, this woman is even more important than for her beauty and her bread ; she is a rare and unique contact with the exterior world. He wants to use her, first of all, to make known to others still in France that he is there in camp, deported. He throws a piece of paper to the woman. This all takes place not too long before the liberation and we will see, in the chapter on the return, that Marcel is haunted by this woman, that he is in love with her. Thus, this love, this feeling for the woman that started in camp, which started with a very tangible piece of bread, is permitted to develop later and the end is tragic. This book is entitled 'roman'. We do not know if it is a true story : we do know that 'Lily' is a true story. But given the camp context, Lafitte's story is plausible and appears authentic. We will return to his hunt for the woman after the liberation in a later chapter. Marcel's considerations during the time he is in contact with this woman differ slightly from Lily's. He wants not only the human dignity that he finds again when he discovers the woman, not only the bread, but he wants to make his presence known. Thus the idea of asserting one's being, the principal consideration of the deportees, is present even in this story of platonic love relationships.

The third 'love story' is the story told by a woman who was not deported and who was inspired to write the stories of deportation that she heard around her. Her heroine is a young girl named Valentine, whom we have mentioned elsewhere. The story takes place in Ravensbrück. A German officer saw Valentine and admired her during the occupation. He followed her to the camp and saved her from a beating by a *Proeminent*. He comes to the infirmary to visit her while she is recovering. He later makes her a Christmas supper — ham, biscuits, fruit. The two risk their lives, we are told. We must say that the detail of Christmas supper, although completely improbable does at least reveal a characteristic preoccupation with food. Ullrich, the German officer, is taken with Valentine and talks to her about the war and the problems of guilt and responsibility. Let us remember that, to further complicate the story, he is German and she is in a German concentration camp. Ullrich does not consider himself guilty, we will think of this later when we discuss Werner in *Ceux qui avaient choisi.* For Ullrich, when a man is a soldier, he is obliged to follow orders, even when he feels his commander is in the wrong. But Valentine feels guilty. She says that because she needed the tenderness of a man, she feels she is a traitor. This is perhaps because her husband died shortly before, and perhaps she feels guilty towards her fellow deportees ; because she is benefitting from something she does not share and also because France and Germany are at war, and Germany is the enemy of her country thus in her own eyes making her a traitor to her country. Ullrich leaves voluntarily for the Russian front while Valentine is still in the infirmary. She never speaks to anyone about that Christmas. It is a memory that she has no desire to share : we do not know if it is out of feelings of shame and guilt, or simply because it was something she felt she did not wish to share. Even this is not authentic : we think of the dialogue between Françoise and Lina in *Qui rapportera ces paroles*, when Françoise tells us that in camp, there are no secrets. In general this 'love story' is very unreal and it does not seem possible that it could have taken place in the context in which it is presented. While we maintain that a strict compliance with detail is unnecessary, we are convinced of the need to refrain from distorting the situation and of the necessity to take into account what was possible under the circumstances.

In Michel Borwicz' study, *Les Ecrits des condamnés à mort,* the 'we-they' dialectic is most thoroughly discussed in reference to the writings of the condemned to die. These include prisoners in camp and elsewhere, French prisoners and others. We agree with Borwicz in his discussion of the 'we' only partially, however. For Borwicz, the predominance of the 'we' concept is the idea of 'nous, peuple opprimé'. This is perhaps true of the literature in general, but when we limit the literature to just the French, 'we' seems to stand for the French imprisoned in the same camp, those that could be found, seen, together at the same time. As Borwicz states, there is an emphasis on the idea of 'we' : 'Un *Nous* positif et fortement accentué, c'est le Nous des amis' (p. 54).

We draw our conclusions from the literature which we have read which, of course, frequently uses the term 'we', the pronoun itself. We agree that 'we' is most generally the 'we' of friends together in camp, small groups of compatriots. It is rarely, in contrast to what Borwicz states, the 'we' of all humanity. Borwicz also stresses the importance of the 'we' of a certain barrack, the 'we' of a certain brigade. We find this far less prevalent than he does. It is far more difficult to define 'them'. As Borwicz's study points out, 'them' is at first the enemy itself : the SS and their assistants, the *bourreaux* :

Eux, c'étaient tout d'abord les bourreaux, les SS avec tous leurs services. Chacun d'entre *eux* représentait un ennemi implacable dont l'approche ne présageait rien de bon : beaucoup d'entre *eux* sont mentionnés nommément, et leurs noms suivis d'une description plus détaillée ou d'une énumération de leurs crimes... L'un d'entre *eux* martyrisait et assassinait ses victimes 'poliment', l'autre avec passion, l'autre encore en observant un système ou un rite à lui. C'était pourtant toujours du crime. (p. 155.)

Very often, though, there is no differentiation between Nazis and Germans, and both terms become synonymous with the word 'criminal'. But for Borwicz, 'them' is also the compatriots that have remained free. We were not able to find this concept in French literature. We must also point out that we have not differentiated, to this point, except when absolutely necessary, between Jewish and non-Jewish writers.

The concept, however, of 'we' and 'they' among the Jews is somewhat different. Just as the French themselves identify with the French as people, the Jews identify themselves with the Jews, and 'we' for the Jews is either 'we' as the Jewish people, the martyred people, or 'we' the Jews from a specific place. In this case, as an extension of 'them', we can find the use of the term to mean any non-Jews. But there is an extension of 'them' that is far more widely used, and that includes all the privileged prisoners, the hierarchy. Among the French, this is an easy distinction to make as very few of their own, the French, were members of this hierarchy. The 'we-they' distinction in the case of Kapos and Blockälteste, etc. is harder to discern in the literature of other countries and, of course, the German literature about concentration camps presents an obviously thorny problem in relation to the 'we-they' distinctions. We will not discuss this problem here. We can only conclude that when the deportee acted by collaborating in any way with 'them', he was considered as part of 'them' and not as 'we' by the others. In the case of the *Dolmetscher* and the *Schreiber,* this was not always the case, but as we go higher up, to Kapo and Blockälteste, these people are invariably part of 'they'. Since the *Vorarbeiter* is the *contremaître* and since he is a civilian, although he is never part of 'we', he is not always judged with as much severity as 'they'. As pointed out, there are many descriptions of the individual 'they', of Kapos, etc. We will not discuss all the reactions of the deportees to 'them', as individuals because this would not serve our purpose. However, it is very pertinent and important to show the reactions of the deportees as a trend because this daily 'we-they' dialectic forms an important part of the prisoner's life and of his chances for survival. There is also a realization, as life in camp progresses, of how difficult it is to resist the privileged positions called *'des planques'*. Paul Tillard points out that the young boys, chosen by the SS from among the prisoners to be their special companions, soon became as savage as the SS themselves. Few realized how contagious brutality was and how quickly the contagion would spread. Gilbert Debrise writes : 'La volupté de tyranniser son semblable est si contagieuse que tout gradé se révèle aussitôt un despote et une brute' (p. 140). Once the deportees obtained privileges, they were loathe to give them up, and the only way to keep them seems to have been to the detriment of one's fellow prisoners :

Stubendienste, larbins immondes qui, pour une gamelle supplémentaire, s'étaient changés en gardes-chiourme, car on ne conservait ces postes privilégiés qu'en frappant et en gueulant... (Laromiguière, p. 83.)

The Stubendienst in this case has become one of 'them', and Stubendienst is hardly one of the upper echelon : it is low in the hierarchy. Most deportees characterized the SS and at many times, the other 'they', by their unpredictability. Francis Wetterwald describes a scene between a deportee and an SS : the SS drops a cigarette and the prisoner is afraid to pick it up, even though he wants it. ' "Blöde Hunde ! Vous avez trop à fumer ?" ' shouts the SS, furious (p. 57). The reaction could just as well be the same even if the deportee had picked up the cigarette. It is impossible to know which is the good column, the right road, the correct thing to do.

From what we can conclude, then, the SS and other *Proeminents,* on occcasion, are typically characterized by their unpredictability. Gilbert Debrise writes : 'Cependant, à ses moments de bonne humeur, notre Blockälteste savait faire preuve de compréhension et d'indulgence' (p. 99). This is shown in 'Le Voyage' (Ch. Delbo : *Une connaissance inutile*). When Taube, the feared man, the despot of the camp, the man who inspired terror when he passed through, the man who put women to death for less of an offence than their untied shoelaces, bends down to help Carmen tie her shoelaces because her fingers are too frozen to do so by herself, the author remarks that they would have been less surprised if Carmen had been put to death for her clumsiness. When the *Proeminent* becomes a little nicer, tries to act good-naturedly, the deportees are at a loss to understand and they are more afraid than usual. They wonder if what lurks in the future is not something terrible. This means that with 'them', the deportee always had to be on his guard — even when 'they' are nice, it is not taken as a good sign because the deportees have so removed 'them' from themselves, from good, that everything that 'they' do is considered evil and foreboding. For Catherine Roux, who manifests the above feelings towards an *Aufseherin*, the difference between 'we' and 'they' is so important that she devotes a chapter to 'Nous' and another, the following one, to '*Eux*'. Our impression is that her 'nous' is all the prisoners in her camp, Ravensbrück at least the ones that she sees and knows. In 'Eux', she describes the Kommandant : '... incroyable sauvagerie et de désarmantes prévenances' (p. 135). The disarming manner seems to be very typical of 'them', particularly of the SS themselves. Her description of the Kommandant puts her on animal level ; a savage nag, beautiful and aggressive, very alluring, outrightly cruel. Her most outstanding characteristic is that she outlaws femininity among the deportees. The fact that the descriptions of the *Proeminents* vary little from a physical standpoint, is of minor importance. It is their attitudes, as seen by the deportees, that interest us. Outright cruelty is less feared than the unknown. Roux fears most of all a *Proeminent* whom she calls 'Mouche à miel', feeling her to be all the more frightening because she never strikes and therefore has not totally revealed herself. She sometimes acts kindly, but the expressions she uses so contradict her actions that Catherine Roux fears that her true character is terrifying.

Joseph Weinberg describes, in *Le Printemps des cendres,* Kola's letters (a camp *Proeminent*) to his mother. They do not surprise us ; they are gentle in tone though they recount terrible acts of cruelty. He tells how prisoners die and he explains to his mother that he would rather be a *Proeminent* than die. His mother never answers his letters. His clinging to writing to her is almost unreal, abnormal, undoubtedly a sort of catharsis. He is hardly a sympathetic character, but he is probably very typical of the SS. As we mentioned in Chapter 1 and as the autobiography of Hoess shows, the SS were normal in their family roles. They were almost completely different human beings from the ones seen by us in the camp literature. Kola appears to truly love his mother, to be truly capable of affection ; he even mentions somewhere in the letters that he loves a girl. Of course we can neither identify ourselves with him nor find excuses for him since he is not sufficiently explained or excused by the author to permit us to do this. He remains completely one of 'them' for us.

Anti-semitism among non-Jewish deportees was generally looked down upon. However, there were anti-semites among the deportees in the camps. Wanda's Madame Duthoit, Saveria's Madame Germain, and the other prisoners do not like these characters because of their prejudices. This does not include deportees who for one reason or another had gripes against other deportees, who might happen to be Jewish. The anti-semites do not place the Jews in camp with 'them' as we have used this term. They rather place them in a group apart and do not consider them exactly fellow prisoners, avoid them and then dislike them. This is anti-semitism without cause. It is anti-semitism that these people probably harbored before the war, prejudice without reason, which will probably not disappear after the war, either. While one might think that sharing the same conditions, or in many cases seeing Jews suffer more than non-Jewish prisoners for no other reason than that they were born Jewish, and suffering with them, might erase any prejudices, this is not the case. We can only conclude that certain habits, like prejudices, stem from personal likes and dislikes, much like preferences in food and other things, and were not eradicated or transformed by the camp experiences.

There is another 'they' that we have not as yet discussed ; this is the non-prisoner the prisoner came in contact with — those they saw and were seen by. We touched upon this subject in Chapter Two and return to it here momentarily to say that, generally, the reactions to the prisoners, by those outsiders who saw them, were divided into three groups, just as they were to the convoys in transit : apathy, hatred and pity. Most of 'them' were apathetic. They passed the deportees and they did not turn their heads. It was more apathy than hatred which infuriated the deportees and made them feel more sub-human. As far as the negative reaction of being spit upon and being detested was concerned and which happened to both political prisoners and Jews, we ask ourselves what could have motivated it. We can only presume that it was effective propaganda put through by the Germans, stating that these men and women in the camps were enemies of the Third Reich. There were people who passed by and tried to offer a piece of bread, or water or at least a kind smile. Sometimes the pity that they felt showed on their faces when they saw the condition of the deportees. Laromiguière tells us that once the peasants in the surrounding areas of the camp realized that they were political prisoners, the peasants became sympathetic. Their sympathy rarely, though, went as far as concrete acts ; although there are stories of bread and water being offered, they are in the minority. We must of course not forget that these camps were in areas that were controlled by the Gestapo, who inspired maximum fear. We presume also that the citizens felt a sentiment of helplessness in front of so much misery, therefore they chose to do nothing rather than not enough. Regina Wallet does write about the German peasants who share their bread with the prisoners, but this is after the liberation of the camps, when the Germans know they have lost the war.

The key to the prisoner's survival was not only his relationship with the others but also his relationship to himself. It is closely related to the idea of being a *musulman*. Once the prisoner lost his feeling of being a human being, his conscience of his own human dignity, when he would lower himself to doing things like eating garbage, a deed which destroyed his comarades' image of him and his own self-image because, even in such circumstances, the image of self is formed by the peer group, the prisoner was on the road to becoming a *musulman*, on the road to death. He would be able to continue fighting, to continue trying to live only as long as he held on to his own humanity. As soon as he began to look at himself the way the Nazis wanted him to see himself, he would be lost. It was an easy trap to fall into. The characters in *Qui rapportera ces paroles* tell us that they thought that a man, even if he was stripped of everything, would maintain his human dignity. Now, in Birkenau after a short time, they have changed their minds. But they realize that some measure of humanity, some intangible quality must remain with them so that they can face themselves and their comrades. Otherwise, they will either become 'they' or *musulman*. When he first entered the camp, the deportee generally saw himself as a healthy and apt human being. He looked around himself and saw all the others who had been there for varied lengths of time. He could not identify himself, or associate, with the deportees whose looks were so far removed from anything human that they frightened the newcomer. He could not even begin to believe that he could ever get to be this way, and the possibility that he might frightened him immensely. When Jeanne, upon arrival in Birkenau, said : 'Et dire que nous deviendrons aussi moches qu'elles' (anecdote recounted by Jeanne Serres, personal archives), the others did not want to believe it. At this time, the 'we' does not include those whose condition is so extreme, so atrocious that the newcomers do not want to include them in the realm of human beings. In general, these deportees are called *musulmans* or *Schmusstück* (see Appendix). This is the last stage of life, life just before death, although some did recover after having been at this point. Their description is most vivid in :

Ayant de loin dépassé ce qu'on appelle maigreur et près d'atteindre la période mortelle de la dénutrition (à l'autopsie on trouvait tous les organes réduits, le foie de la grosseur de celui d'un lapin), incapables de discipline intérieure ou sociale, ne se levant plus, ne cherchant plus leurs poux, vêtues de loques invraisemblables, couvertes de plaies suppurantes jamais soignées, de gale infectée, d'avitaminose, rouées de coups (avec ou sans raison) par toutes les Allemandes vigoureuses du camp (gardiennes SS ou prisonnières galonnées, les réflexes étaient les mêmes), se jetant à plat ventre dans la boue pour lécher par terre une gamelle de soupe renversée, sans amies, sans camarades, sans espoir, sans dignité, apparemment sans pensée, mues seulement par la faim et la peur... (Debrise, p. 62.)

This state of *musulman* is not physical, but emotional and mental, as well. The other prisoners, particularly at the beginning, cannot stand to be with, or see the *musulmans*. Madame Germain, in Jacqueline Saveria's *Ni sains ni saufs,* trembles with fear when she realizes that many can reach that state, that none are necessarily exempted.

There is a great difference in the camp hierarchy between the *musulman* and the deportee who collaborates but perhaps in reality, psychologically, the two are not far apart. Both have lost any concept, preconceived or otherwise inate, of what is right and wrong, and of what price is too dear to pay for life ; they have in some way lost their self-images. Some tell us that anyone has the capacity of becoming a brute, savage, in other words, part of 'them'. But we see repeatedly in literature that there are some people who refuse at any cost. In fiction, it is Claire and Gina *(Qui rapportera ces paroles ?),* in camp life, as told in *Le Convoi du 24 janvier,* it is Adelaïde Hautval.

We must dwell for a moment on Dominique Gaussen's *Le Kapo,* which is called a *témoignage* but which is somewhat different from these not only because it has more literary quality than most, but also because of its title. We notice, upon consultation of the bibliography, that most of the *témoignages* are told from a personal point of view. Either it is a title with 'We', 'I' or 'My', or it is a title descriptive of the camp. *Le Kapo* is perhaps unique in its title ; and the book is centered around Le Grand Georges, a Kapo, one of 'them', in Dora, one of the worst Kommandos of Buchenwald that eventually became an independant camp. Le Grand Georges had killed his mother. He was a huge man whom Gaussen compares to a gigantic spider : 'J'avais la sensation qu'une force occulte... se dégageait de cet homme' (p. 25). The Kapo's main desire is to have the power to decide whether a man should live or die. Gaussen writes :

Pour moi, les soldats portant l'uniforme avec l'écusson représentant une tête de mort sur deux tibias croisés étaient des êtres à part, sans âme. Leur poser une question ne m'était jamais venu à l'esprit et, chaque fois qu'il m'avait fallu répondre à l'un d'eux, j'avais reçu des coups. (p. 177.)

Gaussen's book is not only the study of the Kapo ; it is the study of life in camp, with many valid points and conclusions, but his title, *Le Kapo,* is distinctive enough in itself that mention be made of it here. The life in his book seems to center around the Kapo, around the *Proeminents* in general, the same way Antelme's *L'Espèce humaine* centers around food, thus showing that for certain prisoners, some enemies were more powerful than they were for others.

Before closing this discussion of basic relationships, we must discuss *La Mort est mon métier* by Robert Merle because it is one of the only works, if not the only work, of its kind. Based upon the life of Rudolph Hoess, and drawn from his autobiography, *Le Commandant d'Auschwitz parle,* this book is an attempt to present the story of concentration camps from the point of view of one of 'them'. It never attempts to excuse the Commandant for what he has done, and at the end of our reading, we do not really understand the psychological reasons for Hoess' conduct. However, this attempt at explanation, using the childhood as a basis, is most interresting. We are disappointed when we finish our reading of the work because we expect to find the explanation of what the henchman is, how his mind works, why he has become an executioner, but we find none of this. We find only that the executioner, be he Nazi Commandant or other, is an inexplicable character. What is interesting is the attempt that Merle has made and the fact that it is a literary work, with literary and artistic intentions, and that the work never borders on sensationalism, that it is, on the contrary, authentic, truthful and unpretentious. It begins with the childhood of Hoess and we find the first indications of an abnormal situation in the fact that the boy had a very strict father whom he held in deadly fear and respected. His father destines him to be a priest, but he loses faith at the age of thirteen because he thinks that a priest betrayed him. Both his father and mother are ferocious anti-semites. He is very much enthralled, particularly by the violence, and by chauvinism in general, when the First World War breaks out and he therefore joins a regiment. He is hated because of his strict discipline when he is in a position of authority. He maintains a war-like morality throughout his life. He is not touched by the death of people he is attached to. We do not wish to repeat all the details that Merle furnishes, but we choose those which we feel might give a clue to his future behavior, those clues that led us to hope that the book might contain the explanation we have long awaited of what makes a man become a henchman. Hoess works blindly, like an automaton. He does not feel an attraction towards women ; he only feels alive in wartime, in the army. Nothing else stimulates him. His father has long since died, but he sees him constantly, is haunted by his presence periodically. For him, the Devil is a Jew causing the ruin of Germany. Having read the *Völkischer Beobachter*, he joins the Nazi party. He seems to have a strange idea of morality and never looks for the easy way. His marriage is arranged and he is married without any desire. He is afraid of poverty, although he has no reason to be. At the time Dachau is organized, he is installed there with his family, and he definitely knows that it is a *Konzentrationslager*. The camp soon has more peo-ple than it can hold, and he writes to his superiors hoping to have fewer sent there in the future. Himmler then chooses him, because of his talent as an organizer and the qualities of his conscience, to direct the *Final Solution* in Auschwitz. He does, in fact, make inno-vations in systematic killing. There is no feeling of guilt, compassion or disgust that comes through at any point in the story. He tells his wife that everything he is doing is by orders, that, as a soldier, he cannot refuse these orders. His wife then asks if he would shoot his son if that were an order and he replies : of course. He wants only to obey. At the end, he denies nothing and only says that he obeyed. We are sure that Freudian interpretations of his childhood might reveal certain underlying factors that might further explicate this person, but we have not been able to find adequate explanations of what makes some men SS and some deportees *Proeminents,* whereas some would rather die. As Françoise tells us in *Qui rapportera ces paroles :*

Les bourreaux sont les bourreaux. Ils en ont le costume, les insignes, les traits. Ils ne cherchent pas à dissimuler, à passer pour des hommes. Ils sont les bourreaux sans hypocrisie. Jamais ils ne jouent à amadouer, jamais il ne singent un sourire. Ils ne nous voient pas. Nous les voyons dans leur différence toute nette. Les victimes sont les victimes, brutalisées, défaites, humiliées, dégoûtantes, pouilleuses. Et celles qui, de victimes, s'arrangent pour passer du côté des bourreaux, prennent immédiatement les signes qui les distinguent : brassard, bâton, ou fouet, gueule assortie. Nous aurons vu côte à côte la pire cruauté et la plus grande beauté. (p. 59.)

Let us return for a moment to the concept of time. French deportees usually spent three years or less in camp. Once they became integrated totally into the camp life, one day became like the next. Each hour became like the preceding and the following one. The deportees tried to keep track of the days. It was a difficult task since they had only the fact that Sunday occasionally was different from the other days to guide them :

Nous tenons le compte des jours comme pour empêcher la cassure entre nous avant et nous depuis que nous sommes ici. Jusqu'à présent, nous ne nous sommes pas embrouillés, du moins je le suppose. (p. 51.)

They are aware that there is a difference between subjective and objective time, and that they may also confuse the two :

Avec le printemps, il fait moins froid. Enfin, c'est façon de dire. En pleine nuit, quand nous sortons pour l'appel où nous restons debout des heures —

je dis des heures parce que ce sont de vraies heures, non un moment qui
paraît des heures. De trois heures du matin à sept heures du matin, cela fait
bien des heures. (p. 52.)

Time is long, very long, because each day is broken down into its
hours, and each hour is broken down into its minutes and the deportee knows that he must live minute by minute because each minute
brings another problem, another danger. His life may be in question
each moment. Then, at times, he cannot believe that he has lasted as
long as he has. It seems unbelievable, even to him. Here, subjective
time and objective time have become confused in the deportee's mind
and he is fighting against both. He fights against the idea of subjective time because this is one of the ways he will maintain his will
power, his strength to live. He fights against objective time because
his life depends upon it. He knows that it is all a question of time ;
he is sure that the Allies will win, but he continues to ask himself or
to doubt whether he will be there for the victory. When time seems
eternal to the prisoner, it is a subjective time sequence that he is for-
mulating in his mind and the time invariably appears longer to him.
This makes the fight seem harder and he is more discouraged.

The deportee was stripped of all means of combat when he entered the camp. He was alone with himself, his thoughts and his comrades, who were as naked as he was. Let us now consider the deportee
himself and see what devices he could employ, because a great part
of his chances for survival depended upon his internal measures of
self-defence. The religious prisoner called upon his religion. Micheline Maurel tells us that while others talked of the cold, of things to
eat, she talked with her friends, during that first year in camp, of
God, love, evil and the meaning of life. She maintains that she drew
her courage from this and prayer and tells us of it in her collection
of poems, *La Passion selon Ravensbrück* (p. 24) :

> *Si Tu peux quelque chose, O Toi !*
> *je T'en supplie*

Prends pitié de la guerre et daigne
        la finir,
Dans nos libres foyers laisse-nous revenir,
Et fais-moi retrouver les âmes de ma vie !

To amuse herself while eating, Micheline Maurel said the rosary. She prayed. She sometimes asked God that he let her die immediately.

There are some, however, whose beliefs were put in jeopardy when they looked around them. Wanda tells us that she no longer believed in God, supernatural intervention, faith, religion or any other metaphysical powers. Many priests were deported, and they remained from what we can see, believers. But for many, the internment in the camps posed religious questions. It was difficult to follow the dictates of one's religion there, at the end of the earth. Wiesel (in *La Nuit*) is surprised the first time he sees a man reciting the prayer for the dead over himself, something that is not supposed to happen according to Jewish law. Wiesel asks if perhaps it is not a first in history. He feels revolt growing in him. He cannot sanctify God's name ; he cannot thank Him because He is silent. Elie Wiesel stops praying. He identifies with Job ; he does not deny the existence of God but he does doubt His supreme justice :

Certains parlaient de Dieu, de ses voies mystérieuses, des péchés du peuple juif et de la délivrance future. Moi, j'avais cessé de prier. Comme si j'étais avec Job. Je n'avais pas renié Son existence mais je doutais de Sa Justice absolue. (p. 76.)

He hears great debates with the approach of Yom Kippour, the Day of Atonement when according to the Jewish religion, all adults are expected to fast. But under these circumstances, fasting could be a life and death question :

Fallait-il jeûner ? La question était âprement débattue. Jeûner pouvait signifier une mort plus certaine, plus rapide. On jeûnait ici toute l'année. Toute l'année, c'était le Yom Kippour. Mais d'autres disaient qu'il fallait jeûner justement parce que c'était un danger de le faire. Il fallait montrer à Dieu que même ici, dans cet enfer clos, on était capable de chanter Ses louanges. (p. 111.)

Wiesel decided not to fast ; first, because he does not want to hurt his father to whom he made the promise that he would eat his rations, and then because there is no reason to fast since he can no longer accept the silence of God. By eating, he is making his private protest against Him. The problem is an interesting one. According to the Orthodox Jewish laws, as recorded in *Shulhan Aruh* (Ganzfried, 1961), the law is the same for Yom Kippour as it is for the Sabbath. This means that :

Like all the Divine Commands, the Sabbath Laws are suspended when a human life is in danger. Hence, it is mandatory to desecrate the Sabbath for the sake of a person who is critically ill... For it is a grave sin to carry piety to the point of idiocy... (Vol. II, p. 133.)

The problem of fasting or not fasting that the Jew felt himself confronted by is rather strange. According to Jewish law, there really was no problem because the Jew is not supposed to fast if it in any way endangers his life. Why, then, did the Jew in camp become so obstinate and insist upon fasting when certainly it could put his life in jeopardy ? We think that the answer lies not in the religious overtones of the question, but rather in the psychological motivation of the prisoner. In order to maintain his self-image, in order to continue being the person he was before he came to camp, he felt that he must hold on to, or follow, some tenet, some precept, no matter how difficult. Since in the case of these men that are debating, the religious precepts are those ideas that are most basically engrained into their personality, they obstinately chose to fast because their own self-image is more important in their struggle, perhaps, than life itself. It is a tactic in self-preservation that is as valid as any other. Shortly after the Jewish New Year in camp, the deportees are subjected to a selection. Some pray, particularly the old men. Many lose faith, according to Wiesel, during that selection. He uses as an example the case of Akiba Drumer, resigned, empty. According to Wiesel, if Akiba Drumer hadn't lost faith at the time of the selection, he would have survived. If he could have seen in this selection a proof of God, he would not have been selected. But once he feels himself losing faith, his whole reason for fighting is lost and he begins to lament and to agonize. He is lost from that moment on. It seems, then, that we can conclude that according to some writers, the faith in God and in one's religion did give courage to some of the deportees. We wonder, ourselves, though, if it does not go a bit deeper than that, because there has to be a special reason why Akiba Drumer loses faith just at the moment when he needs it most, why he cannot sustain himself by his faith. We believe that there is something else, some other reason why he gives himself up at the selection, why he lets himself be selected. We feel that there is an inner strength, an inner resolution, that permits some to live whether it be by letting them keep their faith or by some other means, and that the keeping or the loss of the faith is only the apparent or outward manifestation of this inner strength.

What other means then did the deportee have to prevent himself from losing himself, from letting himself be overwhelmed by suffering? Since his primary problem was a physical one, a combination of extreme fatigue, hunger, thirst and filth, he had to find ways to mentally combat this problem. One of the ways that is mentioned in almost every work about deportation is the telling and collecting of recipes. The more hungry, the more famished the deportees became, the more they talked about food, the more they thought about it, and the more recipes they exchanged. This is true among the men as well as the women. Denise, in *Qui rapportera ces paroles* asks for the recipe for sole in whisky just before going to sleep one night. In 'Le départ' (*Une connaissance inutile*) the recipes that were collected during the stay in camp are ironically listed as part of the treasures acquired. Micheline Maurel tells us that at one moment, her favorite dish was rice in milk. And she regrets all the times that she was on a diet and all the times that she did not sufficiently thank her mother for the cakes she ate. It seems that to think of food, to talk about it, to imagine it, to have it on one's mind, somehow diminished the prisoner's hunger and comforted him in some way. The future plans that they made were to go and eat in each others' houses, to open a restaurant or a store to sell food. This seems in some cases to be a sort of delirium and at times it becomes a form of psychosis that is not restricted to the camp atmosphere. It seems that during the occupation, people who were not particularly hungry thought of nothing but food, ran everywhere in the vain hope of finding something for which they had a sudden craving : this even among prisoners of war and hungry students in a dormitory.*

But the prisoner needed more than this to keep himself intact, to keep from losing his mental strength. If the prisoner was convinced that he had a chance to return to those he loved, that is to say, if he was sure that they had not been gassed, or killed or arrested, then he sometimes thought of them. But, let us mention, as is the case of Gina and Françoise (*Qui rapportera ces paroles*), those who know that their husbands have been shot. They cannot think of the days when they were with their husbands because the memory is too painful, since they know that it is something they can never find again. Even if they return, they will not return to that happiness. They have mentally resolved not to think of it. For those, however, who have a chance to regain the happiness that they have temporarily been separated from, it is a source of strength. They think of their loved ones, at home, not in pain, not suffering and they are consoled by this thought. Some even dedicate poems to them as does Micheline Maurel :

> *Tout ce qu'un pauvre cœur anéanti de froid*
> *Peut encore pour un homme éprouver de tendresse*

* Translation of a letter written to us by Olga Wormser-Migot, February 14, 1970.

> *Je te l'envoie, afin d'apaiser ta tristesse,*
> *Car j'ai peur que demain ne soit triste pour toi.*
> (*La Passion selon Ravensbrück*, p. 47.)

Robert Desnos is often consoled by the thought of his wife who is well and safe at home. These cherished memories are only valid for those prisoners who have a chance to find them again. Nostalgia, such as we see in Desnos 'Porte Saint-Martin, Porte Saint-Denis/ Boire un café avec ses amis' (*La Tragédie de la déportation*, p. 445) is pitiful, because we know Desnos did not return. At the same time it was a positive memory for him. It formed part of a *communauté de souvenirs* that he shared with his fellow French prisoners and which heartened him because he thought he might find it again. Wiesel's father never thought of his wife because he doubted that they would ever be together again ; the chances were that she was gassed in Birkenau.

The thoughts of the prisoners go most often to their childhood years. They think of their mothers. They think of their childhood years when everything was simply : 'sans ombre ni mesure' (*Qui rapportera ces paroles*, p. 57). They think of their mothers to give them strength. Mounette, when she has a dream in which she is unable to recall her mother's face, loses her strength. She is convinced from then on that she will never see her mother again. Others, even though their parents have long since died, think of their childhood years because these are happy memories of things that have passed in the order of things, things that have disappeared, things that are naturally far away from them, not things that they were forcibly separated from. Yves Boulogne, in his poem 'Renouveau' (*Anthologie de Buchenwald*, p. 15) calls to his mother:

> *O mère, accorde-moi le geste fraternel*
> *Pour qu'au-delà des morts me sourisse le ciel.*

He calls to his mother whom we assume to be dead and asks for her to intercede in heaven for him. He remembers the softness of her heart, and for him, the fact that she is no longer there is an indication that the world is not right :

Puisque tu n'es plus là et que Dieu n'est plus Dieu.

It is of course, obvious that those who were interned with their mothers could not draw any strength from childhood memories ; their mothers had become different human beings and were no longer mothers to their children there, in camp. It is not a valid frame of reference in these cases because it could not offer encouragement. Several of the flashbacks in *Aucun de nous ne reviendra* are to childhood experiences : the naked dead that the author sees frighten her at first, they remind her of the mannequins that she saw naked for the first time to which she had the same reaction. A woman whom she sees, who is going to die, is dying such a pitiful and slow death that it reminds her of the death of Flac, her childhood pet dog and the memory of Flac is entangled with the present, with the woman who is about to die. There is even a physical resemblance between Flac and the dying woman :

C'était un manteau jaune, du jaune de notre chien Flac qui était devenu tellement maigre après sa maladie et dont tout le corps s'arrondissait en squelette d'oiseau du muséum au moment qu'il allait mourir. (p. 46.)

And one day, when she says to Lulu : 'Je t'assure qu'aujourd'hui je n'en peux plus. Cette fois c'est vrai', she cries for a few minutes on Lulu's shoulder and she is comforted : she can continue to fight to try to survive. She is comforted by Lulu :

... je n'avais pas honte d'avoir pleuré. C'est comme si j'avais pleuré contre la poitrine de ma mère. (p. 168.)

The simplicity of the feelings of childhood, the pleasant memories are a source of comfort. There were other sources of mental diversion, though, that are frequently mentioned. Those people who were cultivated, who had read, drew upon their memories not only when they wrote later, to make comparisons, but also during their stay in camp, to occupy their minds. We must point out that there were times when they could think of nothing but the moment ahead or the work to be done. This was particularly true in death camps such as Auschwitz. In 'Le ruisseau' *(Une connaissance inutile)*, Charlotte Delbo tells us clearly that when she washed herself for the first time in 67 days, she thought of nothing but which parts of her she could wash most effectively. Her mind was otherwise empty. But when the prisoner could think of something, he thought of plays, of novels, of literature in general. He sometimes sang or thought of songs. According to Micheline Maurel, the prisoners thought of all literature that was as far removed from prison experience and deportation as possible, first, because nowhere in folklore and nowhere in literature had there ever been such an experience, and also because the purpose of such thoughts was to distract the mind. Some deportees recited and reconstructed Racine or Baudelaire. Some sang songs of times when men left and the women stayed home to wait for them. They did not choose songs of captivity, nor of return and hope. Some recited Hugo, Lamartine and Musset, in short, the romantics. They preferred anything that spoke of themes foreign to their current situation.

We must point out that the literature written after the camp experience evokes many literary figures for use in comparisons. We find Kafka, Jarry's Ubu and Dante in predominance. It is easily explicable : Kafka and Ubu because they are symbols of the absurd, the grotesque, which is exactly the kind of world within a world that the SS tried to create in the Nazi camps, and Dante because his visions and descriptions of hell are so vivid. Rousset tells us, in *L'Univers concentrationnaire,* that in camp, King Ubu reigned in the person of the SS. Many have falsely said that Dante's line 'Lose all hope, all ye who enter here' was written at the entrance to one of the camps. While it never appeared in the camps, it is, of course, a quotation that fits the context very well. There was all reason to lose all hope ; it was the contrary that was unreasonable, beyond reason :

Ubu et Kafka perdent les traits d'origine liés à leurs histoires pour devenir des composants matériels du monde. (p. 185.)

In retrospect, Bourdet mentions in his poem 'Liberté' (in *Anthologie de Buchenwald*), Shelley, Hölderlin, Byron, Hugo and Lamartine because of their ideas of freedom. Ady Brille, in 'Poeme' evokes Victor Hugo. When Goethe appears, it is generally in connection with Buchenwald because of the story of Goethe's tree* located on the site of that camp.

We can at this point come to two conclusions. The first is in regard to those people who, when they returned and wrote, used other authors such as Dante and Kafka to support their own descriptions. Since concentration camps are unique in the history of man, since they are unimaginable to those who were not there, since they are unbelievable to those who were there, we do not consider that it improves the quality of the literary rendering of the experience if the authors use old metaphors or comparisons that are only partially relevant. Auschwitz is not Dante's inferno. And Kafka's castle is certainly not duplicated in Buchenwald. There is no comparison. We feel that it is because the people who wanted to write found it so difficult to describe, to communicate their experiences that they felt an urge to draw upon what others had written in an attempt to enter the reader's imagination. We cannot conclude that this embellishes their work. We also add that in those works which we consider to be the masterpieces of the literature of the deportation, *La Nuit, Le Grand voyage,* and *Aucun de nous ne reviendra,* ** this is not done. No other authors are drawn upon for metaphors. Wiesel mentions none, Semprun speaks only of *souvenirs littéraires,* and Charlotte Delbo makes no comparisons with any other literature and only mentions Molière's Arnolphe and Apollinaire, from whom her title comes.

Our second conclusion here is in reference to those authors who

---

* According to Olga Wormser-Migot (*Le Système concentrationnaire,* p. 110), concentration-camp tradition tells that Buchenwald was constructed around Goethe's oak, but in reality, Goethe's tree was a beech tree.

** Henceforth generally shortened to *Aucun de nous.*

talk about the writers they frequently thought of in camp. We use the following quotation in lieu of conclusion :

Cependant, objecterez-vous, chacun n'avait-il pas son bagage de souvenirs ? Non. Le passé ne nous était d'aucun secours, d'aucune ressource. Il était devenu irréel, incroyable. Tout ce qui avait été notre existence d'avant s'effilochait. Parler restait la seule évasion, notre délire. De quoi parlions-nous ? De choses matérielles et consommables, ou réalisables. Il fallait écarter tout ce qui éveillait la douleur ou le regret. Nous ne parlions jamais d'amour. (*Une Connaissance inutile*, p. 112.)

Since these literary *souvenirs* previously discussed were not the only source of support, since not only childhood is evoked, and certainly not only recipes, there remains something more. There were plans for the future. Some, like Wiesel, make a vow to go to Palestine. Some, like Gina, in *Qui rapportera ces paroles,* base their plans for the future on their present desire for edibles. Gina decides to open a tea shop :

Moi, si je rentre, j'ouvrirai un salon de thé. Les gâteaux seront exquis, surtout les éclairs, et je ferai un chocolat unique à Paris : crémeux, épais, avec une touche de café. Tu as essayé le chocolat au café ? On fait un café très fort... (p. 25.)

These future plans occupy a good part of the discussions of the deportees. They make imaginary plans for the return. The future is not painful to think of as long as it is only concerned with leaving the camp. But when they have to think of the readjustment to life, of the difficulty in telling others what they survived, in recounting to friends and relatives the death of the comrades, it is not with joy that they look towards the return. But these other plans, thoughts of what they'll read, what they'll do — what they won't ever do — such as marching in parades, etc., all of this gives them courage and more important, it makes the future believable, real to them. This is a constant source of strength. We find in David Rousset a point which we have previously mentioned as essential in reference to Semprun, which many authors overlooked, perhaps because they underestimate its importance :

Puis je compris que c'était précisément cette singulière faculté adaptative qui lui avait permis de survivre des années dans cet enfer : cette décision prise un jour de vivre dans l'univers concentrationnaire, de briser toutes les rêveries malsaines du passé (sans oublier jamais cependant qu'une lutte continue dans le monde et qu'elle devait avoir ses échos dans les camps) de se désintéresser enfin des métiers successifs qu'on lui imposait... (*Les Jours de notre mort,* p. 367.)

The same idea is found in *Qui rapportera ces paroles,* when Gina tells Denise that she must wait until they return to remember the death of her sister in camp, that painful memories or thoughts must be pushed aside because they prevent the living from surviving in such an environment. The inmate did not have the strength, the possibility to let himself weaken, even internally, because once he did, his chances for survival were considerably limited. There was a necessity to arrive at something rather difficult : a proportionate balance between the *bagage intellectuel,* memories, and the camp existence. If the past overweighed, in the very worst of the camps, it did not help the prisoner, whereas if the past played a dominant role in some of the other camps where life was a bit easier, then it was to the prisoner's advantage. It was important that the prisoner maintain his identity, call upon it at all times, or even establish a new identity which he grew later to adopt and believe in, but it was also important that he would not permit this identity to come into conflict with the camp morality, which as we will soon see, is very different from the Christian or other ethic that normal societies follow. The balance of all these elements is difficult to arrive at and to maintain. Pierre Julitte, in *L'Arbre de Gœthe,* tells us that he was happy when he could talk to others of the role that he played in the Resistance, because it permitted him to evoke an identity that was preferable to his identity of deportee number X. We are told elsewhere in the same work that the questions sessions by the SS were alleviated by the fact that they permitted the deportees to talk about themselves, to establish an identity. But this of course, was not always possible and often presented difficulties because some deportees were incarcerated under false papers, false names and fabricated identities. For these, nothing alleviated the questioning sessions.

The deportee wanted to maintain his identity. He wanted not to become a number, not to become just a part of the Nazi system, and in most cases he wanted to be as detached as possible from the executioners and the Nazi ethic. But generally, he could not retain his separate identity and he found that in order to live he had to adjust to the morality that he found being constructed, day by day, in camp both by the deportees in interaction among themselves and in interaction with the *Proeminents*. This ethic was valid only in the concentration camp universe. It was practiced only there : it did not exist before and does not exist today. It was part of the *bagage* from which the prisoner had to free himself in order to readjust to normal life.

There were always situations in which someone needed help, in which another could offer help. But generally, everyone was in need of assistance and there were not enough donors to go around. Whom to help first ? Francis Wetterwald describes a special kind of help : those who were in camp for the longest period of time remained a tightly closed group, helped each other and did not easily extend their help to others.

In general, the deportees helped their relatives first. Wiesel always helps his father first and the father helps and depends upon the son. Denise and Mounette *(Qui rapportera ces paroles)*, sisters, help each other first. Berthe helps Dédé first and vice-versa. *Le Convoi du 24 janvier* (p. 279) tells us that Lulu and Carmen, two sisters, never left each other, always went arm in arm to be sure to be taken together, whatever the reason might be. Friends helped each other first too, naturally. The solidarity and mutual help system has been discussed elsewhere. But the question here is whom to help. One helps one's own first : members of the Communist party helped sympathizers first, the others later. One helped first people from one's own town, one's own country and one's own religion.

Stealing was a commonplace occurrence in camp. The question is not whether this is right or wrong ; it is rather : when according to camp morality was stealing permissible and when was it not ? For Pierre Julitte, the definition of a blameworthy act is one that harms another. Stealing, then, from a dead man is not wrong since it harms no one. It is generally concluded that stealing from the SS was permissible. And when a group of prisoners was being punished and deprived of food, it was perfectly acceptable for other prisoners to steal a cauldron of soup from the kitchen to feed the punished prisoners. Of course, this might mean that someone else would eventually go without it, but one helps one's own first. This kind of stealling is never criticized.

There is however, another kind of stealing that is generally considered non-ethical and looked down upon : the stealing of things by one deportee from another. In camp, we must remember, there was no justice. There was no one the deportee could go to except other inmates, because he certainly could not tattle-tale to an SS or a *Proeminent*. His only recourse was to take the matter up with his fellow-prisoners who did not have much recourse either. The only thing that his fellow prisoners could do was to look for the robber, a task which was difficult because all camp items looked alike, and steal back the article, or console the prisoner and share their own similar articles with him. It was exceedingly rare to steal from one's own group, and this was looked down upon. Stealing from one's own group could lead to exclusion from the group if the culprit was caught ; it is a form of being a traitor. If a robber was caught stealing cigarettes or vital utensils from a fellow prisoner he might be placing his life in jeopardy. He was also in danger of a beating or other kinds of physical punishment unless of course the deportee from whom the object was stolen was quite saintly and decided that such drastic measures were not necessary. The fact that one prisoner would steal from another shows the effectiveness of the Nazi system. It shows that the system could indeed dehumanize because as we mentioned once before, one of the goals of the system was to pit one prisoner against another. It succeeded.

But there is another part of the system which is perhaps even more difficult for us, the non-deportees, to understand. The basic premise involved here is the following : save and help first those who have, relatively, a better chance to survive. If two people have to be taken for any reason that may cause their death, let it be two who are going to die shortly anyway. There is not sufficient reason to help someone if the assistance which you offer will not save or prolong sufficiently his life and may endanger your own, or may make your own more difficult.

Part of the camp morality incorporates the ways of looking at 'others'. In this case, the others are the wounded German soldiers, returning from the front, who can be seen by the prisoners either when they themselves were in transport, or from the camps. In 'Berlin' *(Une connaissance inutile)* we find the expression 'bien fait pour eux'. There is no sympathy for the wounded men. Though they are soldiers, not SS or Gestapo men, the author cannot sympathize with them. They are German fighting men. They are part of the enemy.

The camp morality was not a constant element of camp existence. It was constantly changing. In the beginning of life in Auschwitz, for example, when tasks consisted of clearing the marshes, demolition work or gardening, the idea was to work as slowly and as little as possible so as to economize one's strength. But there was no reason to do any more of it than was absolutely necessary to avoid being beaten or put to death. It was one of those small victories, like looking straight in the eyes of the SS when they passed, instead of shrivelling up. It is for this reason that there is such a sharp criticism of the Russians, who were peasants deported from the Ukraine to Auschwitz, in *Un Métro nommé Lénine* (Delbo, unpublished). They worked as if they were working for themselves, as if there were some reason to work speedily, to work efficiently, when, according to camp morality, there was every reason to do just the opposite whenever possible. Although suicide is considered a cowardly way out, as seen in the discussion between Claire and Françoise in *Qui rapportera ces paroles,* it is preferable for Gina to commit suicide rather than to work in the Kommando that helps kill little children, the 'white handkerchief Kommando '.

There was not just one moral code that governed all the prisoners in all the camps. Some of the religious prisoners, Christian or Jewish, had ethics involved with their religion as in the case of Akiba Drumer, discussed previously. It was generally considered wrong, though, to prostitute oneself in any way, to kow-tow to any of the *Proeminents.* In many cases, particularly among the males, the lives of the prisoners could be made much easier by accepting to enter into homosexual relationships and become a 'pipel' of a Kapo, the favorite, and thereby avoid punishments, sometimes receive extra food and be, in a certain way, privileged. But this involved becoming friends, more than friends, with someone that is disdainable according to the camp ethic. Even for the man who was a homosexual before, there was a difference between entering into a relationship for the pleasures that would be derived from it and entering into a relationship because of the privileges it would afford. According to camp morality, homosexuals were generally looked down upon, in any case by non-homosexuals, but the homosexuals who indulged in these activities with 'them' were snickered at and considered part of 'them'. The most fearful punishment in camp was not death itself; it was the way in which one would die. It was sometimes the torture, the punishments, the way in which they would leave the camp — black transports. But, as Gina tells us in *Qui rapportera ces paroles,* there is always a choice : death. Besides, as Marie-Claude Vaillant-Couturier points out, refusal, as in the case of Adelaïde Hautval, did not always, lead to dire consequences and Mrs. Vaillant-Couturier criticizes her fellow deportees strongly for not refusing often enough, because the dreaded punishments, for some illogical reason, did not always follow. The illogical way in which the camps were run makes it difficult to foretell the dangers of one's acts.

There was nothing wrong with selling one's possessions, but it was wrong to sell oneself, in any way. None reproached Danielle Casanova (see *Le Convoi du 24 janvier*) for profiting from the fact that she was a dentist. When she first declared that this is her profession, she did not know, as a matter of fact, what effect this might have on her future. She is criticized for not having taken advantage of her privileged position to have done more for her fellow deportees.

The rule was to share everything that could be shared. This included packages whenever they were received, extra food when it could be obtained. Eating something in secret, even an onion from the garden, was deplored. Of course, some items could not be shared : toothbrush, toothpaste, a nightshirt. The prisoner would probably be content to use these articles and since they were his, as long as he did not steal them from another prisoner, he would not feel guilty over having them when others did not. But for some, the thought that they might have something more than the others, something that could not be shared, was a weight on their consciences.

Those for whom life was more important than retaining their human dignity did not necessarily have to kill or steal. It seemed sufficient to speak politely to the SS, click one's heels loudly, share packages with the Blockhovas and the Kapos, give well-placed gifts. This too was looked down upon by the other prisoners. It was kowtowing and giving in, unless, as in *L'Arbre de Gœthe,* it is a group effort benefitting all.

One of the intrinsic parts of the Nazi system involved the pitting of one man against the others, by giving some privileges, or by collective punishments. Among the deportees who refused to cooperate in any way with the system, and it was possible to do so (see Danielle Casanova, in *Le Convoi du 24 janvier*), these things were considered wrong. They were not jealous of the prisoner who was well-placed, and the latter, in turn, hopefully, did not forget his comrades. If these positions were to be gotten through favoritism, through doing things that were distasteful, like sleeping with the Kapo, the deportees refused to compete and therefore, according to camp morality, remained men. It is when men started to act like animals, when they fought each other for a slice of bread, that the breakdown of the human morality system began and the de-personalization took place.

For Robert Antelme, the culmination of the system, the epitomy of the moral problems is, of course, centered around food (this theme dominates his entire *L'Espèce humaine*). For him, the final breakdown of societal norms is expressed in man's eating of peelings, in other words : garbage.

Mais l'expérience de celui qui mange les épluchures est une des situations ultimes de résistance. Elle n'est autre aussi que l'extrême expérience de la condition du prolétaire. Tout y est : d'abord le mépris, de la part de celui qui le contraint à cet état et fait tout pour l'entretenir, en sorte que cet état rende compte apparemment de toute la personne de l'opprimé et du même coup le justifie, lui. D'autre part, la revendication — dans l'acharnement à manger pour vivre — des valeurs les plus hautes. Luttant pour vivre, il lutte pour justifier toutes les valeurs, y compris celles de son oppresseur, en les falsifiant d'ailleurs,... Celui qui méprise le copain qui mange les épluchures... le méprise parce que ce copain 'ne se respecte plus'. Il pense que ce n'est pas digne d'une politique de bouffer des épluchures. (p. 101.)

Another intrinsic part of the camp value system is found in the ability of the prisoner to bear pain silently. This can be noted in Antelme but it is found all over, in women and men equally because the camp system grants complete equality to men and women ; there is no different treatment. The ability to bear pain in silence is not only respected but considered necessary for the maintenance of one's respect and the respect of others. In 'Jusqu'à la cinquantaine' *(Aucun de nous)*, the man faints, but he never screams. Nor does Elie Wiesel when he is administered a form of the same punishment. In *L'Espèce humaine*, we do not respect Félix because he uses his extra food to try to take advantage of a starving boy and make him indulge in homosexual activities. But when Félix is punished, and when during the entire punishment, a very severe one, he curses the SS but never screams from pain, one of the political prisoners in his barrack, when he comes back that night, shakes his hand. For his conduct, he has gained the respect of the readers too, and he has gained a small victory over the SS, as do all those who bear pain in silence. In a way, it is not giving in to 'them', it is not permitting them to have complete power ; Félix has not let them have the satisfaction of having completely destroyed him. Bearing pain in silence is distinctly part of the camp ethic. It is also that, as another writer puts it : 'Il fallait se garder de toute sensibilité qui rendrait perméable aux maux qui nous étreignaient en si grand nombre, que les admettre, c'était y succomber' (Lahaye, *Un homme libre parmi les morts*, p. 35).

There is also a fine line of demarcation, forming part of the camp morality which is difficult to show ; it is most clearly perhaps found in the case of the *Dolmetscher* (see Appendix). The translator was always a prisoner, picked because he or she knew his native language and German and could translate the Kapo's and other *Proeminent's* orders to the prisoners. Robert Antelme clearly points out the possibility that the job offers and we know, according to deportee ethic, which one of the two interpreters is 'okay'.

Pour Lucien, ça consistait à traduire les ordres des SS et des Kapos, mais en les prenant progressivement à son propre compte. Lucien n'était pas seulement celui qui répétait en langue française ce que les autres disaient en allemand ; il était devenu avec habileté l'auxiliaire de langue française de ceux qui commandaient dans la langue allemande. Il ne fut que l'interprète des Kapos et des SS, jamais celui des détenus.

...

Gilbert, à l'usine comme à l'église, fut l'interprète des détenus, c'est-à-dire qu'il ne se servait de la langue allemande que pour tenter de neutraliser les SS, les Kapos, les Meister. Il fut assez habile d'ailleurs pour régler pas mal de conflits entre nous et le Meister et assez courageux pour justifier ou *excuser* certains camarades, devant les SS. Il remplissait son rôle de détenu politique, il prévenait, il couvrait les copains, il leur servait de rempart. Alors être interprète n'était plus simplement une planque, c'était aussi un risque supplémentaire. Car en agissant ainsi, Gilbert était devenu l'ennemi des Kapos. (p. 133.)

There is no question that there is a choice. The choice is completely up to the deportee. Part of the camp ethic revolved around the use of the German language. For non-German prisoners, in this case French deportees, there was no reason to use the German language and thus facilite the job of the SS and the *Proeminents*. If the deportee needed to use the German language at one point or another to save his own life, this was of course, permissible. But if it was to ingratiate himself, to make things easier for 'them', use of the German language went against the deportee ethic. The exception was the interpreter : he was a necessary functionary, necessary for the survival of his comrades. He should not however, use his position to ingratiate himself or better his standing in camp but rather to ameliorate the lot of his co-deportees. He was in a position in which he could change passive resistance to active resistance.

More frightening than the daytime, more frightening perhaps than death itself, were the nightmares of the deportees. 'Le crépuscule est plus triste encore que l'aurore quand il n'annonce pas la tranquilité de la nuit' (Martin-Chauffier, p. 133). The deportee was more frightened at night because he was alone. He could not look for consolation ; he could not talk. He was alone with his psyche, and with his nightmares. These dreams and nightmares take on many forms. We wish to preface our remarks by stating that there is a study by Jean Cayrol entitled *Lazare parmi nous* in which the author analyzes and compares prison dreams, concentration camp dreams and other dreams of the same period. We discredit this study because, first of all, of its tendency to categorize and draw conclusions, and also because of its emphasis on the prophetic value of dreams. We prefer to state categorically that dreams as an index of the future or an index of the dreamer's extra-sensory perception do not interest us and that we are interested in studying dreams only because they are an intrinsic part of the psychological problems of the deportee and often reflect these problems. We also wish to state that even twenty-five years later, many former deportees are still haunted by their camp experience in their dreams, as they are during their waking hours. We will not enter here into a discussion of these dreams except to say that they are experienced by a great many deportees and that they are part of the results of having undergone this experience. They often relive the horror, review the atrocities of camp life in their nightmares.

There are several kinds of concentration camp dreams which are discussed in the literature of the deportation. In camps where conditions are very oppressive, such as in Auschwitz, the deportees dream perhaps the most terrifying nightmares. They relive what they have experienced during the day, the actual experiences, accompanied by the same emotions, the same fears that were with them during the day. In *Aucun de nous,* we find one of the most frightening dreams of the deportee. Here, it is as if the deportee were not alone dreaming this. It is as if all the deportees were dreaming the same thing, simultaneously. Octopi are strangling her and, at the same time, them :

... de leurs muscles visqueux et nous ne dégagions un bras que pour être étranglées par un tentacule qui s'enroulait autour du cou, serrait les vertèbres, la trachée, l'œsophage, le larynx, le pharynx, et tous les conduits qu'il y a dans le cou, les serrait à les briser. Il fallait libérer la gorge pour se délivrer de l'étranglement, céder les bras, les jambes, la taille aux tentacules prenants, envahissants qui se multiplient... Nous étions près de succomber quand nous avions soudain l'impression de nous réveiller. Ce ne sont pas des pieuvres, c'est la boue. Nous nageons dans la boue, une boue visqueuse avec les tentacules inépuisables de ses vagues... Nous sommes contractées de dégoût, la boue entre les yeux, dans le nez, dans la bouche... Et ce serait peu de nager dans la boue si nous n'étions pas obligées de porter des tragues remplies de mottes de terre, si pesantes que la charge entraîne irrémédiablment au fond... Maintenir cette trague au-desus de la tête coûte un effort surhumain et la camarade d'avant s'enfonce, disparaît, s'engloutit dans la boue. Il faut la tirer... (pp. 87-90.)

They fight to get out of the mudbank, they pound and then they realize that they are pounding on the boards on which they are sleeping and that the others are their comrades, asleep next to them. The literary transmutation of this dream (which we know is an authentic concentration camp dream) is so skillful that we feel the collusion of reality and the dream world at the point when they are carrying the tragues (see Appendix) of mud and they are in mud over their heads. And when the author is half-awake, and realizes that the jumble of bodies which she is fighting with to get out of the mudbank, is her sleeping comrades, she momentarily personalizes the experience when she sees vaguely Lulu's moving leg, Viva's head and Yvonne's arm. And then we return to the collective sleep, the collective dream. The only hope is that this time it will be more bearable and the nightmare will be less horrible, perhaps the one, she says, in which she returns home. Each deportee had thought her family anxiety-ridden over the lost children because the author here returns to her mother, but the mothers do not turn around to greet their children. They have become silent, indifferent strangers. And the returning deportees tell them that this time it's a real return, it's not the dream-return ; it is real because they are touching the mother's sink, a comforting image, but at the same time, a cold porcelain, white image, and an image which is not fluid, that in itself is not warm and welcoming. It is comforting only because of its associations. The coldness of the stone of the sink awakens the dreamer, and the deportee realizes that her sink is a loose brick, transformed by her dream. She tries to cling to the brick, to hold it tight to her heart. This is again a transfer from every day routine of camp life when they must carry cold bricks tight against their hearts from one pile to another. The Kapos shout and the dogs follow close behind the prisoners. And the author tells us that the night is worse than the day since at night they will die in solitude and they will be found dead the next morning when the others awake. They must be carried to roll-call and

chaque morte est aussi légère et aussi lourde que les ombres de la mort, légère tant elle est décharnée et lourde d'une somme de souffrances que personne ne partagera jamais. (p. 92.)

The same haunting that is found so many other places in the literature of the deportation comes to haunt even the sleep of the deportee — the suffering that none will ever share — because no one will be able to understand it. Night is as endless as day for this author. It is nothing more than an infinity of nightmares that are so closely related, so similar to the day, that we do not know when they end, as our author does not. The dream of the return is an interesting one, as it shows the psychological state of the deportee. The fact that the mother does not turn around does not have to do with fact that she is unhappy to see her offspring. It is rather, we think, that she thinks she is seeing a ghost, and the deportee realizes that if she returns, she will have come back from the dead, and people do not, or refuse to, believe in ghosts and do not acknowledge their presence. Far more distressing than the reaction of the mother is the fact that the child realizes that if she returns, she will have come back from death.

The same nightmare is found, somewhat transformed aesthetically, in Mounette's dream in *Qui rapportera ces paroles,* because it is a tragedy, and because plays, tragedies, involve feelings on an individual level, the dream is the dream of one deportee portrayed as such, and thus individualized. It illustrates, with the character's own words, more simply, more starkly, the idea that the author shows in *Aucun de nous* : that night is worse than day in Auschwitz because when the reality of an individual life becomes so unbearable, so deeply anguishing, the deportee cannot escape even during his dreams and his dreams become merely a repetition of his daytime suffering. Mounette tells us that she is afraid to sleep because she is afraid to dream. If she has carried bricks during the day, then she will carry bricks in her dreams and they will be colder against her breasts than they were during the day because she is all alone. And the bricks bring back a childhood memory of the brick that her mother used to give each night to warm her bed. She carries the bricks on an interminable road. And when it is not the bricks that haunt her, it is the dogs. She uses every trick, every calculation, to try to escape but they do not work and the dogs' breath against her cheek is so strong that it awakens her and then she realizes that it is only the breath of those sleeping next to her, Renée and Agnès. She knows that she has to go back to sleep but she is afraid that this time she will dream the mud dream, the same one described in *Aucun de nous,* except that in the latter, it is a gifted author who describes it, whereas here it is a simple girl who is part of a play. And there is the mother again : the mother who does not turn towards her. This is a happy dream until the dreamer awakes to find herself once again next to Renée or Agnès, their hands in hers. As we have seen, the reality of Auschwitz was too oppressive, too stifling, to permit the mind to escape even in dream. This is very important for the physical and mental state of the deportee. To dream these dreams is as physically exhausting as doing the activities dreamt. It meant the deportee would awaken without having really rested, ill-equipped to face a new day. It also means that he was afraid to go to sleep, yet he must in order to regain his strengh. Sleep is not restful, a welcome escape, as it is in real life ; it is more torturous than the day : a difficult concept to understand. There are many other dreams described in the literature about concentration camps, perhaps none of them as frightening as this, nor as skillfully described.

We will discuss certain dreams because they exemplify salient features of the psychology of the deportees. Micheline Maurel describes a nightmare which seems not to be a recurrent one, although we cannot be sure. She dreams that the man she loves, a parachutist, is caught and she sees him in a concentration camp. It is a nightmare that expresses her preoccupation with her loved one and her opinion of the camp. She sees the camp as the worst thing that could possibly happen to him : worse than death. This also shows, though, that the routine of her daily life is not so oppressive, she is able to dream of other things, rather than relive the horror of the day.

In *Ceux qui vivent,* Jean Lafitte also describes a dream, probably not a recurrent one, in which he sees himself in a huge bed, lying down. He contemplates the knots in the wood of the bed. And he sees a familiar face. A woman calls him gently — the one who used to rock him to sleep long ago. This dream shows the desire not only to escape from the reality of the camp but to return to infancy, not even to childhood but to infancy, to the comfort of the mother, to the peace and tranquillity that only the infant knows, that he will never know again. He is awakened from that pleasant escape by '*Aufstehen*' the reveille command. Elsewhere in the same book, Lafitte describes another dream, troubling, typical of the concentration camp universe, rooted in camp experience. He dreams that he passes in front of the crematorium and that a man jumps up from the pile of the dead to tell Lafitte that he (the other man) is going to die soon and wants to be consoled. This shows a preoccupation with the thought of being burnt alive, a preoccupation that haunted many deportees, coupled with the desire not to die alone.

In *Un homme libre parmi les morts,* Simone Lahaye describes a dream that she had in camp :

J'étais dans un bateau à la proue effilée qui fendait une eau verte dont je vois encore le remous argenté. Le bateau filait poussé par le vent, d'un mouvement silencieux, sans le heurt des machines et aboutissait à un port aux ruelles pittoresques, semblable à certains ports d'Angleterre. (p. 41.)

She can interpret her own dream ; it is a dream of liberty, of the desire to escape from the camp, to tranquillity, 'poussé par le vent', where nature is the guide rather than other authoritarian forces.

Pierre Julitte, in *L'Arbre de Gœthe* recounts a dream he had in Buchenwald. He dreams that he found friends with whom, for the entire day, he could spend his time at his favorite game : bridge. In this dream he cannot see as far as liberation and freedom. It remains within the camp situation, but seeks amelioration of it, by companionship, and by the opportunity to remain pleasantly occupied. It is almost as if he longed to be in prison, rather than in camp.

Dreams and daytime reality show that death in camp is not the greatest fear nor the most oppressive possibility. A single day in camp is terrible, but the repetition of these terrible days is mortal. In order to understand the cumulative effects of camp life, it is necessary for us to analyze an entire work about the deportation, in addition to those individual topics and passages that we have just treated. For this, we have picked the one we find to be superior as a literary creation, *Aucun de nous ne reviendra*.

*

> Et on demandera encore :
> 'Mais de quoi sont-elles mor-
> tes, toutes ?'
> (*Qui rapportera ces paroles*,
> p. 53.)

The rhetorical question posited by Denise suggests the chorus of ancient tragedy. She herself answers : '... elles sont mortes de la vie ici.'

Each day in the life of the deportee was very much like the preceding one and the following one. The deportee's memory is one of painful monotony, of the repetition of daily events, of days which were difficult to distinguish from each other. It is the multiplication of the hours, the days, the weeks, the months, that the deportee spent in camp, that together form his experience in the other world. It is rare to find one day that stands out in his memory. And if we find one day that he remembers more distinctly than the preceding one, it is because that day was so much more horrible, so much more traumatic, so much more deathly than the others and because, on that particular day, the toll that death took was greater than average. The norm is monotony. The abnormal, the different, is the day in which there was an outstanding event, the day in which the deportee, who was usually surprised by nothing, had to take notice because the horror of the events shook his numbed conscious. In *Aucun de nous ne reviendra*, we are made aware of the answer to Denise's question.

From the beginning, there is a tone of gentle irony. The people

9

arrive 'Rue de l'arrivée, rue du départ'. We see masses of people but we see no individuals. People will die before we ever get to know them. 'Peut-on jouer une pièce avec des personnages qui meurent avant qu'on ait eu le temps de les connaître ? Moi non plus, je n'ai pas eu le temps de les connaître', writes Charlotte Delbo elsewhere (*Qui rapportera ces paroles*, p. 48). None of the details given — whether it be winter or summer, whether it be night or day — matter at all. Whenever they arrive, the formalities are the same, and certain civilities, at least for the sake of appearance, are observed by the SS. 'Car on fait passer en premier les femmes et les enfants' (*Aucun de nous*, p. 12). We must point out that just as we never see the SS in *Qui rapportera ces paroles* we never see them here either. They are referred to at this point only as '*on*'. This '*on*' troubles us ; we want to know its identity. As yet, no one knows these SS, nor has anyone as yet penetrated their psychology or become aware of their capacity for brutality, and thus for the readers they must remain as anonymous as the crowds. '*On*' shows how impersonal they are, shows us that they have no individuality — that one is the same as the other. The unspoken dialectic is between '*ils*' and '*on*'. The anonymity that characterizes the book commences here. In the beginning, there is no differentiation between the men and the women, just as the Nazis do not really differentiate. But at the point at which the SS force them to separate to form two columns, there is a differentiation made, by Mrs. Delbo, between '*ils*' and '*elles*'. Later, the dialectic that evolves includes the reader. The dialectic evolves from '*ils-on*' to '*ils-vous*', that is, it becomes a conversation, almost a lecture to the reader, the universal '*vous*'. And we feel that the author is dissatisfied with us.

The people look around, so that later they can tell how it was. But the author knows that they have the feeling that they will not return. They know already that 'il faut se défier des sentiments' (*Aucun de nous*, p. 13). The people do not speak because just as they themselves are *de trop* in the situation, so too their words would be superflous. When the schoolmarm says 'Soyons sages les petites'

(p. 14) to her schoolchildren, we are told that it is useless because 'Elles n'ont pas envie de n'être pas sages' (p. 14). And it is a cliché that has no meaning in their present situation ; it is left over from a former life that is irrelevant here. The author shows that it is a situation where words are useless, where the mind, and therefore the tongue, are muted and stripped of the power to speak. None will return to 'rapporter ces paroles'. Words will not serve immortality and thus they have no function.

There is a distinction made between those who 'know' and those who act without 'knowing'. But at the same time, the feeling of the absurd penetrates ; it would not matter if they knew, however they act, whatever they do, it is the wrong thing, now, here :

Il y a une mère qui calotte son enfant de cinq ans peut-être parce qu'il ne veut pas lui donner la main... Elle calotte son enfant et nous qui savons ne lui pardonnons pas. D'ailleurs ce serait la même chose si elle le couvrait de baisers. (p. 15.)

It is *'une connaissance inutile'* but perhaps now they understand, they 'know' when they are made to undress in front of their children, but it makes no difference. It is useless knowledge since they cannot warn the others. The absurd world of *Aucun de nous* is slowly being created. It is the *'inconcevable'*. The absurdity and the illogical features of the Nazi world are already clear :

On distribuera aux Allemandes malades des olives noires et du lokoum mais elles n'aiment pas les olives de Calamata ni les olives en général. (p. 18.)

Auschwitz is not a city because 'city' implies metropolis. There is no way to describe Auschwitz. The only way to bring it to the reader is to evoke its *néant*. Charlotte Delbo speaks little about it. It is a desolate plain, at the edge of a city. The plain is iced over, and the city has no name. This description suffices to evoke the camp. It is desolate, because of its lack of human inhabitants, because the victims are no more than shadows and the SS are not human beings. It is stripped of human inhabitants and nothing grows there, not even a thorn on a garbage heap. Auschwitz is at the edge of a city ; just as it is at the border of human frontiers. The people are stateless, they have no rights, because with the idea of city and state comes the idea of citizenship. The word city, *civitas,* implies relationships, implies rights granted to inhabitants. Here the deportees are stripped of natural and societal ties, once they have passed through the *rites de passage.* Out of necessity, other relationships will evolve, as we saw, and this is the basis upon which the society maintains itself, but this society is an unnatural one which has nothing to do with *civitas* and civilization. It is, in fact, the simple negation of both concepts. This place has no name because many who died in Auschwitz never knew its name. Since it was such an unnatural place, they could not themselves give it a name and no name was told to them. Others lived to find out its name, but the concept of the name goes far deeper than this ; the camp only has a name today, only exists today because of its survivors. As we will discuss in the conclusion to this book, immortality and survivors give their true names to the camps. That it was called Oswiecim in Polish and Auschwitz in English does not matter.

The dimensions of time in camp are brought to our awareness. The endlessness of time — 'Et tout le jour et toute la nuit' (p. 18) — time which is not differentiated by an awareness of its elements, sets the tone of the life there. The deportee is not able to distinguish in time. Time is a totality ; seconds upon seconds are added but the sum total remains constant. The chimneys smoke 'tous les jours et toutes les nuits' (p. 18). The repetition of 'tous les jours et toutes les nuits' suggests endlessness. The only activity that is described here is the passing of the ashes to find gold from the teeth of the victims. What more monotonous, more unchanging activity exists ? In the spring, they scatter the ashes over the swamps and fertilize the earth with human phosphate. The wind blows the ashes back over their faces so that at night they are all white. There is no risk of running short of fertilizer :

... il en arrive tous les jours et toutes les nuits, toutes les heures de tous les jours et de toutes les nuits. (p. 19.)

It is the repetition of '*tous*' and of the certain other key phrases (e.g. '*arrivés*' and '*départs*') that sets the one of the opening of *Aucun de nous ne reviendra*. It tells us that this is an unceasing, never-changing torment and Charlotte Delbo, by her style, conveys to us the monotony of the torment.

For two thousand years, we have lamented the death of Christ, Mrs. Delbo tells us, but he agonized (according to her) for only three days and three nights. We pass over her interpretation of the Agony of Christ. What tears will we have for those who agonized more than three hundred nights ? The repetition of 'trois cents nuits et beaucoup plus de trois cents journées' (p. 20) twice in the same sentence reinforces the length of time. The bitterness is apparent. 'Ils ne croyaient pas à la résurrection dans l'éternité / Et ils savaient que vous ne pleureriez pas' (p. 20). This is a dominant theme, not only of *Aucun de nous* but also of *Qui rapportera ces paroles* : none shall cry for those who suffered. This phenomenon is beyond understanding. It is easier to accept that one man suffered on the cross and died to redeem humanity than it is to accept the '*inconcevable*', that six million died and four million returned after a trip to the other end of the earth. The futility of their suffering is contained in 'Et ils savaient que vous ne pleureriez pas'. If their suffering would change nothing, would bring about nothing new, then they were suffering for nothing, and they were aware of the futility of their suffering.

The leitmotif of those who 'know' is one of the dominant themes of *Aucun de nous*. We are surprised that there are so many things that can be learned from life in camp : that hunger brightens the eyes, that thirst dims them, that one's eyes can stay dry at the death of the mother that one loved, that in the morning one wants to die, that at night one is afraid, that a day is longer than a year, that a minute is longer than a life, that the heart, the eyes and the nerves are the most durable parts of the body, that stones do not cry, that there is only one word for terror and one for anguish.

Here, Charlotte Delbo is illustrating part of her technique. If there is only one word for terror and one for anguish, then there is no need to look for synonyms. The repetition of the same word conveys the repetitions of a suffering that never changes, of a terror that never relents and that never is metamorphosed. Familiar words do not have the same meaning because the frame of reference from which they are being drawn is so different. The author will therefore recreate this frame of reference, at the same time fully realizing that she cannot at any time leave it to our imaginations because life in Auschwitz is beyond imagination.

The induction to the concentration camp world implies certain *rites de passage* because, just as the reader finds difficulty in assimilating this world into his psyche, the deportee was originally in the same position and it is only because of these certain *rites de passage* that he is able to pass into the other world. We will analyze a *rite de passage* that is typical of the initiation into camp. The first person that we encounter is the mother. It is the mother of all the deportees. This is the first remembrance, as we mentioned previously, of the deportee : childhood and mother. But the mother is immediately depersonalized.

> *Ma mère*
> *C'était des mains un visage*
> *Ils ont mis nos mères nues devant nous*
> *Ici les mères ne sont plus mères à leurs enfants.* (p. 23.)

At first it is her mother, then the mother. Then it is the universal mother, represented by her hands and her face, the symbols of the tenderness of a mother. And then the mother is no longer mother, because when a mother is naked before a child, the relationship is no longer the same. The mother can do nothing for the child here, and the child can do nothing about this humiliation except to share it.

The loss of her normal role is felt for the first time. The mother, symbol of the beginning and end of all life, is no longer a mother. All life then has ceased, for without the mother, there is no earth, there is no life. The *rites de passage* continues the process of depersonalization. 'Tous étaient marqués au bras d'un numéro indélébile.' The scars will be there always, even for those who return.

Until now, we have seen very few men in *Aucun de nous*. We do not know if the SS are necessarily men, probably not, and except in the opening poem, it is the female deportees that are being discussed. Here, in 'Les Hommes', the women see the columns of men, Jews and non-Jews. The Jews are always in poorer condition. The women feel sorry for all of the men because they have to march in step and they can hardly manage. For the women, the men are much worse off than they themselves are.

One morning the women take them some of their bread, the bread of the women who have given up living and can no longer force themselves to eat. When the columns meet, on the way to work, they throw the bread to the men who, like animals, fight over it. This is one of the only times that we will read about the male deportees in *Aucun de nous,* undoubtedly because of the acute pain that their presence caused to our author, and also because there is nothing more to say. The women never get to know them and were left, more than likely, with only sparse memories of them. It is interesting to note that Verdet *(La Nuit n'est pas la nuit)* describes this same scene from the male point of view. The men are ashamed when they take the bread, he tells us, and most do not want it ; they want the women to keep it for themselves.

As we have already seen, roll-call begins the day. Its description is that of waiting : waiting to be counted, waiting until the SS pass. The outstanding word of this passage is 'attendre'. And 'attendre' is really a symbol of the entire life in camp. It is a passive wait, interspersed at varied times with activities that were sometimes easier than standing still, sometimes worse. 'On attend ce qui arrive. La nuit parce qu'elle succède au jour. Le jour parce qu'il succède à la nuit' (p. 37). It is a physical and a mental waiting because there is nothing else for the prisoners to do. The whole fight is reduced to the necessity to wait out each minute. And the roll-call is the most pointed symbol of the waiting period. It is long, tiresome to the point that it often becomes mortal.

Each day is the same as the next. But there are days which are distinguishable in the mass of time which is piling up, and they are distinguishable by the painful events that stand out. A certain roll-call is described, one which stands out in the author's mind. It contains the description of a woman who broke roll-call rank and went to a ditch and now is trying to climb up out of it.

Charlotte Delbo tells us that whatever there is to see, it is difficult to distinguish it from the snow. There are forms arranged one next to the other, one pressing against the other. The snow makes their whiteness appear blue. Their heads are shaven. We know they are frozen cadavers.

Les cadavres sont gelés. Blanc avec les ongles marrons. Les orteils dressés sont ridicules à vrai dire. (p. 29.)

The same things that would make this story funny if it were not so tragic, the same ridiculous details that we found in the opening poem, the same light tone of mockery appears here too. And then the author makes an immediate association back to her childhood. She is waiting for her father in front of a department store. Men are moving naked dummies around and placing them side by side on the sidewalk. She looks at the naked dummies as she looks now at the cadavers. The word 'regardez' along with 'savoir' is a key word. She looks and she is troubled. By the nudity of the dummies, and by their bare heads. She is troubled because she never realized that dummies could exist outside of the window, naked, without wigs. She was as troubled then as she is now at seeing the naked cadavers in the snow. And these bodies lying in the snow are described by the word 'mannequins' because they are the same as the store-window dummies. But they had diarrhea yesterday, and yesterday they were beaten. Yesterday they could still stand at roll-call. They worked. They were hungry, they had lice, they scratched. It is interesting to note the details that Charlotte Delbo chooses to distinguish the living from the dead. They had diarrhea yesterday, and yesterday they were beaten. Yesterday they had suffered and yesterday they wanted to die. But death does not bring them serenity, because here even death is robbed of its usual powers. The day before they had been in Block 25. At night they had screamed, during the day they had been silent. Even this is a reversal of normal order ; one would expect the contrary. The author feels guilty ; isn't it she alone who is being sought out by the eyes of the woman in the ditch for help because she is still strong enough to help ? We are told what is in the mind of the woman : she wants to know why all the others in the rank are staring at her. She convinces herself that they really do not see her, otherwise they would come and help. But the other women are '... réduites au seul battement de nos cœurs' (p. 43). No one knows why she broke rank, but yet when she does it, we are told, she does not seem crazy. It seems that she knows why she was doing it. We do not know yet. She cannot control her own movements. The author wants to look elsewhere, but there is nowhere else to look. Her eyes fall again on Block 25 : a place that keeps returning to haunt us throughout our reading, just as it haunted the deportees throughout their lives in Birkenau. And in front of Block 25, she sees a body wrapped in a blanket. She thinks it's a boy, but it's a woman, and the woman is dancing. 'Un squelette de femme qui danse' (p. 45). And the author tells us that '... maintenant je suis dans un café à écrire cette histoire — car cela devient une histoire' (p. 45). We return to the roll-call square and the author is attempting to tell what time it is. They have lost all track of time. She asks if it is the afternoon. The woman is still in the ditch. And Charlotte Delbo tells us that she now knows why that woman broke rank — she wanted clean snow for her lips. Since daybreak she had been attracted, seduced by the clean snow, untrampled in the ditch. But the snow does not assuage her thirst ; it is like a handful of salt in her mouth. And the woman's yellow coat reminds Madame Delbo of her childhood pet, Flac. The woman in the ditch thinks all the others in the ranks are dead and when a woman moves to help her, it is a dead woman. A dummy. She drags the unconscious woman from the ditch to the ranks and she lies there for a long while. Suddenly she shivers. She is going to die, just the way Flac did. She moves towards the SS — we never know if he calls her or if she imagines that he does. And the SS dog silently strangles her. She screams once. And each one of the others in the ranks thinks that it is she herself who screams because each feels the fangs of the dog in her throat. They scream, but it is a silent scream. It is over. The woman is dead. And Flac dies too. With a death rattle that sounds as if someone has strangled him. They are still at roll-call and it is night. Nothing has changed, the woman in front of Block 25 is still dancing. And they are standing still at roll-call. And now, says the author '... je suis dans un café à écrire ceci' (p. 49). She herself cannot believe her memory, yet she knows it is true. She cannot believe that she survived and she tells us that this is becoming a story, which can only mean that it is becoming a literary creation apart from her, because she can no longer believe that it actually took place and that she lived through it.

Let us examine the progression of vignettes. We went from 'Appel' to 'Un jour' and now we consider 'Le lendemain'. The time sequence here is most revealing. It shows the monotony, the length, the repetitiveness of time. We have the feeling that we are reading the story of perhaps a week in camp, but this week repeats itself into eternity and this is how, at the end of the book, we arrive at spring, when we clearly began in winter (we know because of the snow). The next day begins with roll-call, the monotony begins to become painful to the reader, but it is painful because of its effectiveness. At no moment does this repetition exceed aesthetic demands, and

at no moment is it uncalled for, unnecessary or distasteful. The day
is the same as the night. 'La nuit était claire et froide... le jour est
claire et froide' (p. 51). And we are told that the deportees are passing
time but '... du temps en dehors du temps' (p. 53). They are
motionless. Nothing changes, not even the light. A woman sits
down in the snow; the other tells her that she will catch cold
and the author seizes the ridiculousness of the statement. The
author thinks of childhood and childhood pets once again. She
thinks of animals that make a bed in the earth for themselves
to die in. A truck passes by, loaded with women, who once
again resemble boys (not men). The truck is silent too. Silence
is another leitmotif of this work — there are silent nights,
silent days, silent deaths, silent screams. The women cry out as the
truck passes by, but the author and her companions hear nothing.
There is again a *jeu* of silence. 'Chaque corps est un cri. Chacune
est un cri matérialisé, un hurlement...' (p. 56). The truck moves
silently too. The snow serves as a blotter. The atmosphere of death
and cold absorbs all humanity, so that only silence is left Another
truck appears. It is just like the first (there are never any changes).
Then another. The women in the ranks cry out this time, but again it
is a silent cry. Or perhaps they are struck mute, suggests Charlotte
Delbo. Again, we do not know. The trucks contain naked, dead
women, piled up, mixed with some who are still alive. The living in
the truck do not want to touch the dead. They shriek. The women
in the ranks watch with their eyes; their eyes cry out, silently and
they do not believe. And for eternity, those who have seen the truck-
loads are marked, precisely by the faces they will never forget and
by the mute cries. That day is endless and we approach another chapter entitled 'Le même jour'. The women are completely motionless,
without feelings or sensations. They return to camp. To get there,
they walk over the cadavers that the day has produced, but to them,
these bodies are ordinary, everyday obstacles, says Charlotte Delbo.
They cannot feel anymore; they are silent and stripped of feeling.

They are told they must run. And they run. It is idiotic, it is absurd, but to them, it is not even grotesque. The author runs, and it does not occur to her or anyone else not to conform to the absurd, nor do they even realize it is absurd. And they run to the accompaniment of belts, whips and straps. The author tells us that she is suddenly (because it was a time of unusual crisis — unusual even for Birkenau) aware of regaining all her faculties to the extent that she can protect herself on all sides. It is the miracle of the human mind and strength that come to the fore when called upon. None of those who ran that day could see how sad, how absurd it was. This would have required objectivity. But now, writing in 1946, the author notes that it was senseless, absurd and even funny. During the 'race', we see nobody but the author because she is aware of none of her companions, only of herself, and the others, 'them', that is, the SS and others who are sorting out who shall live and who shall die. And Mrs. Delbo remembers Drexler, a particularly sadistic female SS officer, hooking one of the women through her collar with her cane. As our author returns to her Block, she regains consciousness of the others. Death must have taken more than its usual toll.

The one who takes the longest to die is Alice. Alice's leg is lying in the snow. It is a wooden leg, which has become detached from Alice. Dismemberment, the separation of mind and body are principal themes of *Aucun de nous*. The person, dead or alive, is no longer whole, neither mentally nor physically. How can an artificial leg be alive and sensitive? Since we are beginning to 'know', we find the answer. The human beings in the camp are so deprived of sensitivity that wood is more sentiant than they are. Alice, symbolized by her leg, was still alive to the deportees who go to visit her leg, lying abandoned in the snow. They are powerless to do anything; they do not want to look, but something much more than curiosity, something which we do not yet understand, is forcing them to look. Alice has been dead for a long time but her artificial leg keeps appearing, as if to haunt them and us. After it disappears, they presume that a gypsy woman must have taken it for firewood and there is a light pejorative tone : '... personne autre n'aurait eu le courage' (p. 68).

The vignette that describes the plains of Auschwitz is significant because of the equation that it makes. The plain is covered with marshes, with implements and with men and women. There is no differentiation made between the roles of the implements on the plain and the roles of the human beings. In fact, it is indicated that the implements belong there far more than the human beings. The men and women are servile not only to the plains and the marshes, but to the implements. They are less than the shovels, they are only tools of tools. They are on the same level only as the *'cailloux',* which are also there to serve the shovels and the *'wagonnets'*.

There is never any thought of escaping, says Charlotte Delbo, because escaping would require thinking and thinking necessitates strength. They pay attention only to their feet. They walk endlessly, it seems. There is no scenery, nothing to see. And then they work. The work is futile. 'Tout hurle.' It is not only people that yell, it is the entire *ambiance.* The prisoners fill things up, and then empty them. The same dialectic discussed earlier between screaming and silence is again present. There are screams, 'jusqu'aux confins du marais' (p. 77). The insects are mute. We ask ourselves what is screaming. Perhaps the Kapos. At times, the SS begin to scream, and they strike too, without knowing why. And then silence begins again. The author asks what is longer than a day and tells us that time passes because the fog lifts. Now they are standing in mud and this is our first clue to the change in seasons. The eternity of the day is captured not only by the repetitions but by : 'C'est le jour pour jusqu'à la fin du jour' (p. 79). The insects — these insects are the deportees themselves — grow exhausted, their eyes filled with terror. And the work gets progressively more difficult as the day goes on because the body is more exhausted. 'C'est le jour pour toute une éternité' (p. 79).

The slow progression of time continues. At first, it is just days, but now that we have read further and time has become more acute, more painful to the deportee, his day is being broken down into minutes, and each will be as long as the days themselves were in the beginning. The vignettes convey that idea. The first of this series is night, because night is more terrifying than day. The second is morning (logically following night). Morning begins with the lash of a whip to make those who do not waken quickly enough stir and come out of their boxes. And then there is some tea, which smells, repulsively, which the Stubhovas 'servent chichement à nos soifs de fièvre' (p. 101). It is a fight just to be served, but it is a non-aggressive crowd. Then there is roll-call again. We do not want to become repetitious so we will not dwell upon the iterations that Mrs. Delbo makes, except to state once again that they are most effective, since the true image of camp life will be derived from them. This sketch of roll-call is different from the preceding ones, though. The previous incidents at roll-call either involved the entire group or else they involved other single individuals and the reactions of the entire group to these individuals. In this case, it is the personal tribulations of the author as she tries to survive roll-call. We enter her psyche to understand the psychological means that the deportee utilizes to remain standing up and alive and we realize that each moment involves the same question which has to be answered over and over again : shall I stand up or am I ready to lie down and die ? Is it worthwhile to stand up or am I going to die anyway ? No one thinks this, no one asks it, though, not even of himself. Charlotte Delbo explains that it is an inner mechanism that is involved. The women do not say to each other, nor to themselves : you must continue standing up, you must stand up again. They do not ask each other, nor do they question themselves. As the author is standing there, she thinks of how she will explain it if she returns, and she knows it will be false if she says that while she stood up she thought of any relationship between her standing up and the possibility that she might some day return. At that time, there is no relationship in her mind between the two. She thinks of nothing ; the surroundings, the physical factors, are so oppressive that they rob her power to think. She looks at nothing. She sees, in her mind, her mother's face covered by a mask of resolution. She sees her far away and cannot look at anything or think. Suddenly, she feels very good, as if a stone — she thinks it is her heart — has dropped from her. She feels she is surrendering, and feels a moment of bliss. She is happy. She awakens

... au choc des gifles que m'applique Viva sur les joues, de toute sa force, en serrant la bouche, en détournant les yeux. Viva est forte... Elle dit et dit encore mon nom qui m'arrive de lointain, du vide — c'est la voix de ma mère que j'entends. La voix se fait dure... (pp. 105-106.)

And at this moment she feels herself choosing, but she is choosing because Viva is forcing her to choose and although she wants to give in to that bliss, she does not because she obeys Viva's order. Viva is one of the heroines of *Aucun de nous*. We hardly see much of her, she is not spoken of often, but when Charlotte Delbo mentions her, it is with indebtedness and love. Later, when the cortège of the dead passes, the bodies go out feet first ; the author stiffens. She watches the bodies pass by. And then she knows that she does not want to die. She is not frightened by death, she is not afraid ; she is rather reassured by it, but she does not want to pass by on that stretcher, naked, covered only by a ragged blanket, feet dangling from one end, and head from the other. She knows about death, she calls it a kindred spirit. And she tells us that those who paint it with repulsion have not known it. We find here one of the few literary allusions of the book. She tells us that she speaks to her heart as Arnolphe speaks to his, and it is fitting that Charlotte Delbo, who was secretary to Louis Jouvet, loves the theatre as much as he did, should think of Arnolphe. She talks to her heart and tells it to keep on functioning, and she waits for the end of roll-call to go to work. Again, the waiting, for something that is no better and is perhaps worse. We are told that what they find at work is what had been haunting them in their dreams at night. And this is told in such a way that we wonder whether they are worse off in the day or in the night, and since the dreams of the night, in which they are haunted by the day, haunt them in the day, we cannot help but conclude that dreams are more oppressive than reality.

In the evening, when they return from work, there are some who died during the day. Since they were counted at morning roll-call, they must be counted at evening roll-call and this means that they must be transported back to camp.

Il faudra les porter. Aucune ne bouge. Involontairement, chacune baisse la tête, voudrait se fondre dans la masse, ne pas être remarquée, ne pas faire signe. (p. 129.)

It is left to the *Anweiserins* to choose. They pick the strongest looking and the ones with the best shoes. Each woman carries the body by a limb. It takes a long time until they can manipulate the bodies and finally carry them. They are, at first, carrying the bodies of two women, their former companions. Then the women become nothing more than very heavy burdens. They walk to the accompaniment of the SS playing a harmonica. The SS laugh when death surrounds them, probably because they feel so safe and removed from it that they can be amused ; it shows their own power, even over death. The SS plays the harmonica and the women are discomforted. For them, it is like hearing happy music during a funeral procession. The women carrying the body call for others to relieve them, but no one comes and there is no blame placed on the others by the author. She realizes that they do not have the strength to put forth either. One of the women, Carmen, tries putting the women on boards. The SS wait patiently while this is accomplished. And Carmen remembers her mother's words :

Ne touche pas à ce bois sale. Tu vas te mettre une écharde et tu auras un vilain mal blanc. (p. 131.)

A truck appears to collect the soup canteens. The driver is about seventeen, the age of the author's younger brother, she notices. She asks if they can put the cadavers on the truck to transport them back to camp. He laughs hysterically. And the others, 'them', follow suit.

Son ricanement nous insulte et il éclate de rire. Il rit et trouve cela d'un drôle. Il est tout secoué de rire et l'autre l'imite et la fille, qui me donne une gifle en forçant son rire... (p. 132.)

Charlotte Delbo is ashamed, ashamed to think that she could ask 'them' for anything, for any kind of favor. And we see here a very important part of the highest morality of the camp. It is not right to *mendier,* to ask 'them' for favors. It is better to suffer, to fall alone then to ask, to lean, to debase oneself by accepting a consideration, a favor from 'them'. It is a question of pride, but it is also a question of morality. The SS decide they have been lenient enough and the dogs are pulled to attention, the harmonica is put away and the whole tone becomes far more serious, far more deadly. The dogs are trailing close behind, so the deportees must walk quickly. They can no longer bear to look at the cadavers whose eyes are still open. Tears stream down their faces, but they are not crying. They feel the dogs' breath. They are tense. And when they finally reach the gate of the camp :

... nous nous sommes redressées. Nous avons serré les mâchoires, nous avons regardé haut. C'était un serment que nous nous étions fait, Viva et moi. La tête haute devant Drexler, devant Taube. Nous avions même dit : 'La tête haute ou les pieds devant.' O Viva. (p. 135.)

We see the men as a group, once again. They are silent, in a small group, and they appear completely resigned. The SS treat them as, by now, we would expect that they would — with no regard, with no apparent logic. We are told that they wait and they 'know', and by the use of the word 'know', doom is foreshadowed. They are colorless and they have a far-away look. They enter the barrack and one by one they come out and those who come out avoid the eyes of those who are still waiting. Charlotte Delbo says 'we', and by this word we presume that she means the women who observe this scene, and they cannot describe the humiliation and distress in the men's eyes but this inability does not matter since 'aucun d'eux ne doit revenir. Puisque aucun de nous ne reviendra' (p. 153). And the leitmotif of these words which we have not seen since the title page, is being constructed, because now we see that none of them were supposed to return, and we see that the camp world was constructed on that premise. We postpone offering possible interpretation of this title. At this time, we wish to point out only that the section we have discussed, entitled 'Les hommes', is striking by its shame and its modesty.

One day the deportees take a road on the way to work and they see a house they have never seen before. It is decorated with white curtains and they wonder who lives in it. In the window, there is a tulip. While they are working all day — it is the middle of winter and wet snow is pouring down upon them — at the bottom of a ditch, they think about the tulip and they tell their comrades in camp about it. They never return to work in that ditch and when they learn that it is the house of an SS that they passed, they hate their memory and the tenderness that has not withered away within them. When we realize, at the end of the sketch, that it is the house of an SS, we realize that not even the briefest brightness will be permitted in *Aucun de nous* because in Auschwitz, there was none.

There is only one person to whom a whole chapter, a whole sketch is devoted. She is, in a way, along with Viva, one of the heroines of the book. The women have been working in the bottom of the ditch since morning. At first they are three, then the author is left alone. And she is terribly afraid, because, in camp, loneliness and solitude were perhaps the most terrifying emotions. When they were together, at least two of them, they could talk and, as we have seen previously, this was one of the principal methods of survival. Loneliness brings only despair. The protagonist wants to hurry up and finish so she can join the others, and she wants to give up and die at the same time. And then one of the Kapos leads her back to the others. Viva, whom we hear for the last time, says : 'Viens ici, face à piler le riz' (p. 166). And then our author is next to Lulu. She cannot even smile. Lulu is worried and asks if she is sick. She assures her she is not, that it's just that she cannot take it any more. For her, it is the end. Lulu tries practicality first : they exchange implements. Perhaps Lulu's is lighter. It doesn't help. Charlotte Delbo wonders : how shall we ever get out of here ? Lulu smiles, pats her hand. It doesn't work.

Lulu regarde autour de nous, voit qu'aucune Kapo n'est près pour l'instant, me prend le poignet et dit : 'Mets-toi derrière moi, qu'on ne te voie pas. Tu pourras pleurer.' Elle parle à voix basse, timidement. Sans doute est-ce justement ce qu'il faut me dire puisque j'obéis à sa poussée gentille. Je laisse retomber mon outil, je reste là appuyée sur le manche et je pleure. Je ne voulais pas pleurer, mais les larmes affleurent, coulent sur mes joues. Je les laisse couler et, quand une larme touche mes lèvres, je sens le salé et je continue de pleurer.
Lulu travaille et guette. Parfois elle se retourne et, de sa manche, doucement, elle essuie mon visage. Je pleure. Je ne pense plus à rien, je pleure... (p. 168.)

There are times in camp when the orchestra plays. It is an orchestra composed of deportees. It is unbearable for the deportees to hear the waltzes ; it only brings painful memories. The musicians and the orchestra leader — all women — are grotesque as we read their description. They come from something out of the past. The conductor was once a female orchestra leader. She knows how to conduct only the way she did in Vienna and here, in camp, it is absurd. Charlotte Delbo tells us not to think, not to listen, especially when they play waltzes, particularly the *Lustige Witwe*. While they are playing, naked men are being beaten with straps because they have too many lice. Charlotte Delbo tells us not to think of all the Yehudim who brought their violins with them to camp, so that they could be left to the violonists in orchestra. It is to us that she is saying this and to her comrades too.

None ever believed that anyone would return. They never thought of giving a deathbed message to their companions. And when the deportees returned, their task was complicated because their friends and relatives, who did not know any but the conventional way of dying, could not understand why there were no last words and hungrily asked again and again for them. But it seems that before dying, in the *révir,* nearly all said : 'Cette fois-ci je vais claboter' (p. 172). They did not want to weaken, not even then, nor did they want to undermine the courage of those around them. And since there was no reason to say anything more, that was all they said. And here Charlotte Delbo is telling the world not to ask for last words, because in this context, there can be none because they had no hope that any would ever return. Even spring, when it comes, brings no hope. It brings only pain. Pain because of the memories that come with it : memories of other springs, springs that cannot be rediscovered here in camp, because spring here means only carrying mud instead of frozen earth, means only sitting on dust instead of snow. It means nothing that spring means to the living world. There is nothing green, nothing grows, and the author is left only with her memory. She wishes ardently that it would leave her. A woman near her is dying and at the moment at which she dies, the author tells us that they, the others, have lost their memory. We are left with nothing. Both memory and life have disappeared. 'Aucun de nous ne reviendra. Aucun de nous n'aurait dû revenir' (pp. 182-183). The last two lines of the book are a total negation of the fight to live, of the concentration camp universe, of life itself. They leave us with nothing because the author, even at the time she is writing this, less than a year after her liberation from camp, is completely stripped of everything, including life itself. We choose to take the words 'aucun de nous ne reviendra' in the sense that Claudel used 'revenir' when he wrote : 'Nous ne reviendrons plus vers vous.' The author makes us feel that she has not totally returned to the living, that she cannot. We are left with an emptiness, an absence of life.

The memory of the characters whom we have scarcely gotten to know has faded. We are left with a dehumanized impression, with almost no details. We are left with feelings about the experience, rather than a knowledge of it. The work is an impressionistic creation, one of tenderness, of compassion, of love and of human strength, all shown on the background of the most extreme contrasts. We have been confronted with a *collage* to which we are responding. Our conscious is responding through the author's. The experience has been universalized and personalized simultaneously. We have not stood off and objectively looked at a mass of gory detail. We have rather been drawn in by pieces that form a totality and leave us with overall impressions, feelings. We have felt the weariness, the eternity of time because our author has broken down each moment for us and we have put the pieces together to achieve a total impression. We have felt the weariness, the thirst, because they are broken down into their smallest, most individualized sensations and we have unconsciously reconstructed them to transmit to our subconscious the total feeling. We know no details about Birkenau, nothing numerical or graphic, but we have felt the agony for as much of it that it is possible to transmit to the reader who has not undergone the same experiences. For as much as it will be possible for him to feel, he experiences it reading this work far more profoundly than he would by consulting statistics or reading *témoignages* from which he perhaps learns more but feels less. This is not a form of catharsis, nor a literary exercise which the author permits herself to indulge in. On the contrary, it becomes an individualized recounting only when it is absolutely necessary for our own identification with the work. From this, its universality, its modesty. The author is certainly not attempting to exorcise the experience from her psyche by writing about it ; she is rather attempting to have it enter ours, so that we may not forget.

5

Liberation and Readaptation to Normal Life

J'ai rêvé tellement fort de toi
J'ai tellement marché,
tellement parlé,
Tellement aimé ton ombre,
Qu'il ne me reste plus rien
de toi.
Il me reste d'être l'ombre
parmi les ombres,
D'être cent fois plus ombre
que l'ombre,
D'être l'ombre qui viendra et
reviendra dans
ta vie ensoleillée.

DESNOS

This is Desnos' poem, written just before he died, to his wife Youki. He was at the end of his life ; he had become a phantom, *'l'ombre'*, the last step before his death. Nothing of his essence was left, not even his fondest memories. Youki became just a shadow to him because of his exhaustion and then, as the life in camp destroyed him further, he became a shadow himself. He lived to see the liberation, but liberation came too late, as for many of the deportees. Time here is crucial ; one could say that if the liberating forces had reached the camp where he was (Theresienstadt) just a few days earlier, he might have lived. But he died, near the camp, from exhaustion, several days after the arrival of the liberating armies.

When the troops finally arrived, Soviet, American, or mixed European, they either liberated the camp or found that the deportees had already been liberated by the SS and that they were still in camp. In either case, the deportee realized that he was free and that he would shortly be transported out of the camp. But for many, grace came too late. The numbers that died in camp at the very end were enormous perhaps for the reasons mentioned in Chapter 1 : that the camps were overcrowded at the end and that there was less food than ever before. Or perhaps, the prisoners, aware that the battle was over, stopped fighting a little too soon and did not conceive that they still needed all their strength to return to normal life and begin anew. It was, of course, very true that they were progressively weakened during the successive phases of their captivity and that by the end, many were just not strong enough to last another minute.

As we have seen before, the first considerations of the deportee were physical. Wiesel tells us in *La Nuit* :

Notre premier geste d'hommes libres fut de nous jeter sur le ravitaillement. On ne pensait qu'à cela. Ni à la vengeance, ni aux parents. Rien qu'au pain. (p. 178.)

And even when they were no longer hungry, the desires were still on a physical level : clothes and women. His case is ironic. Food poisoning three days after the liberation left him very sick : two weeks in the hospital in critical condition. When his strength returned, he remembered that he had not seen himself in a mirror for years. And he looks and finds that :

Du fond du miroir, un cadavre me contemplait. Son regard dans mes yeux ne me quitte plus. (p. 178.)

The liberation, in many cases, had tragic overtones : it provoked such fear among the Germans who realized impending doom that they wanted to rid themselves of all traces of the crime, including the deportees. They wished to transport the deportees away from the camps that might be liberated first. This resulted in long marches during which many of the deportees died. In Buchenwald, the camp interior resistance force was strong enough to force the SS to flee and thus to prevent the evacuation of the last 20,000 deportees for whom the death march might have proved fatal.

There are many variations on the theme of liberation. Many had the strength to be happy when they were found. For some, the greatest moment was when they saw the SS take off their armbands, as if to deny what they had been :

... ce qui m'est encore révélé restera à jamais gravé dans ma mémoire, cinq ou six SS tiennent conciliabule et l'un d'eux, sous mes yeux, arrache nerveusement de sa manche l'aigle à croix gammée. Un SS enlevant les insignes sacrés de sa mystique et sa puissance ! Un SS se reniant lui-même ! Est-ce Dieu croyable ? (Bonifas, p. 148.)

Some, though, did not have the strength to be happy. They had looked forward to this day for a long time, hoped for it, expected it and expected that it would be full of joy when it finally came. On the contrary. Some of the French who were in Ravensbrück were liberated on April 23, 1945, by the Swedish Red Cross and transported to Sweden from where they were repatriated to France during the last week of June. Among them, Charlotte Delbo, who writes the story of her liberation 'Le matin de la liberté' in *Une connaissance inutile*. The Swede who is in charge of the liberation is the most beautiful man they have ever seen. The deportees look at him without knowing why they find him so beautiful. He sees this column of women which advances slowly towards him, motionless, silently. Their faces cannot show what they think of the man because they are so used to not showing their emotions, and also because :

Les visages ne sont marqués en gros et en profond que par une longue ancienne lutte. Il semble que la volonté et la douleur se soient planquées sur les visages — peut-être à leur entrée dans cet endroit-ci, au passage du seuil où se tient l'homme — et y aient durci pour toujours. (p. 175.)

The column advances, the door of the camp is open ; the bar is lowered. The women realize for the first time that the entrance is also an exit. The column stops at the bar. The women look at the man and they wait, and the man waits. They watch the man :

de leurs yeux qui ne disent pas qu'ils voient, des yeux qui ont dû depuis si longtemps ne rien exprimer, ne rien laisser paraître. Et peut-être n'y avait-il en chacun de ces êtres aucune émotion — à force de se raidir et de se dominer, on ne sent plus rien. (p. 175.)

The women realize that the man is trying not to show his emotions. The same anonymity that dominated *Aucun de nous* is present here. We are told about the women, but none are mentioned specifically, by name ; even the liberating captain and the crew have only imprecise designations.

The deportees were still in the world of the concentration camp even at the moment when they finally left it. They had been so conditioned by this world that they were merely passing through the door of the camp for the last time : this did not free them of the conditioning. We will see shortly that another fight, another immense effort, which many could not put forth, was necessary to achieve the final goal : the true liberation from the hallucinations of the night, the haunting of the camp. It is the physical liberation that is our concern here. The latter part of this chapter will deal with the liberation of the mind from the camp experience.

The man speaks to the women, and his accent, so different from the Slavic accents that they have grown used to hearing, surprises their ears. He announces that they are going to Sweden. The reaction :

Nous allons en Suède et rien ne répond dans la longue bande de taches claires où les regards font des trous dans l'ombre. Aucune animation, aucun tressaillement. (p. 178.)

Just a few moments ago, the women had been evacuated from their barracks by the SS and they had feared that they were being evacuated rather than liberated. Now they know they were being liberated. Now they know they are going to Sweden, but : 'Rien ne répond dans les regards, mais nous retrouvons notre faculté de voir' (p. 178). They remain mute. They show no emotion whatsoever. This is hardly the reaction that we expect, and it is equally hardly the reaction they expected. There is no surprise, no joy. They believe it, they believe they are going to Sweden, but they show nothing :

Nous attendons, silencieuses. D'un calme qui nous surprend nous-mêmes. Nous qui croyions que ce jour-là, s'il arrivait, nous défaillirions de bonheur. (p. 180.)

At the moment when the long rows are ready to pass over the threshold of the camp, one voice asks for a moment of silence for those who will not return. 'Et cette voix qui demande le silence rompt le silence' (p. 181). It is night, the camp is asleep. The night has not yet ended, not even for those who are freed at that moment. The women smile for the first time when the man in charge smiles and tells them 'Fini la Gestapo' (p. 182).

Charlotte Delbo tells us that she knows now (May, 1946, at the time she is writing this story) why *le capitaine M.* was beautiful on April 23, 1945, and why the flowers were beautiful and the children too that she saw in the little Danish station where they arrived. She also knows why the human voices were 'troublantes et belles' : 'La terre était belle d'être retrouvée. Belle et déshabitée' (p. 182).

The deportee was thus free, but he had another struggle before him. He had to readapt to daily life. After all he had suffered, after all he had seen, after all the friends or family that he had lost, this last struggle is very trying for him, and he does not always completely succeed. For the pious Jew, there is sometimes a problem of loss or questioning of faith, as we will see. For others, there is a moral problem. The deportee, as we saw, had lived by a different moral code which he now had to forget. Many had lost lovers, husbands or wives, parents. They returned to find that they had no homes, or that the people vital to them had been exterminated. Some did not even want to return to their home countries, or could not. Most of the French did, however, return to France shortly after the liberation. No one returned unscathed. They all had a mission : to bear witness. They had to recount to the families and loved ones of those they had seen die how they died, what they said, and how they lived in camp. For most, the task was difficult if not impossible. Few of their audiences understood. The prologue and epilogue of *Qui rapportera ces paroles* (p. 70) explain the problem :

> *Parce que je reviens d'où nul n'est*
> > *revenu*
> *Vous croyez que je sais des choses*
> *Et vous vous pressez vers moi*
> *Tout gonflés de vos questions*
> *De vos questions informulables.*
> *Vous croyez que je sais les réponses.*
> *Je ne sais que les évidences*
> *La vie*
> *La mort*
> *La vérité.*
> *Je reviens de la vérité*
>
> . . . .
>
> *Alors pourquoi dire puisque ces choses*
> > *que je pourrais vous dire*
> > *ne vous serviront à rien...*

The deportee cannot communicate with those who have not lived through what he has survived because even the words that he uses do not mean the same thing to him and to his audience. He sees things in a light which does not illuminate his audience. Generally, he bears no ill will because he knows the others cannot understand : he only wishes that he himself could understand how he succeeded in returning :

> *Nous sommes revenues pour vous dire*
> *et nous voilà devant vous tout empruntées.*
> *Que dire...*
> *Comment dire...*
> *C'est que là d'où nous revenons les mots*
> > *ne voulaient pas dire la*
> > *même chose.*
>
> . . . . .

Nous voulions nous faire entendre,
nous voulions nous faire comprendre
et
Ne croyez pas que nous en ayons
       du dépit
Nous savions que vous ne comprendriez
       pas,
Que vous ne croiriez pas
car cela est devenu à nous-mêmes
       incroyable.
Pourquoi iriez-vous croire
à ces histoires de revenants
de revenants qui reviennent
sans pouvoir expliquer comment ?

This is a perfect explanation of the frustrations that the deportee encountered from the very first : the fact that others could not understand him. Some were bitter about this, some said they knew it would be thus and resigned themselves. And in other cases, there is a strong bitterness against those who know : they know everything else, but they cannot 'know' this, and some cannot feel what they do not know. Charlotte Delbo realizes this and realizes that others will not be able to cry over the sufferings of the deportees because they cannot sufficiently understand on a conscious level, and because the ramifications of the holocaust have not entered their subconscious.

These are part of the mental frustrations of the deportee. He unfortunately also encountered many frustrations of a far less metaphysical nature. He had to find work, medical aid, money, a place to live. In many cases, he had to begin to search for his family to find only that they had all disappeared in the Nazi ovens. Many women were married and had children ; it seemed the best way to replace what they had lost, to regain their appreciation of life, to make a new life for themselves, to fulfill themselves. But many found they could not be happy. They still carried with them the shadow of those they had left behind. They continued to dream of the nights and days in the camp. In brief, they found they could not liberate themselves. They found that the people around them could not help them enough, did not understand, could not do enough for them. Simone Alizon (*Le Convoi du 24 janvier*) tells us :

... je me suis entendu traiter d'anormale, de malade. Aucun membre de la famille n'a pris la déportation au sérieux puisque j'en étais sortie vivante. Les mille difficultés de la vie quotidienne ne nous ont pas été épargnées ; elles se sont ajoutées aux souffrances passées. (p. 30.)

Many felt that their immense sacrifice had been for nothing, and had to fight constantly against this feeling. Most have lasting physical ailments which are a direct result of their life in camp. This does not, of course, help their readaptation to life and makes it difficult for them to work, and in some cases, to have a family. Most think very often of camp life. There is a certain fraternity which is maintained among the former deportees. Many of them remained friends and societies have been formed to help them, morally and physically. But many still find that the others, those who were not deported, are *vaches* : they are not sympathetic, they do not do enough for the compatriots who sacrificed themselves for the freedom of all. Some of the women have readapted thanks to the men who fell in love with them and are able to lighten the burden by removing financial and other menial preoccupations. But this is not true in all cases. The women who married to feel like the others, to live as if the deportation had not left its mark, to feel alive, found this did not necessarily suffice. One deportee, when she gave birth to her first son could not rejoice ; in the back of her mind were all the women who had died in Auschwitz without knowing the joy of childbirth. Others are exasperated by the injustices of society which the holocaust did not rectify : the revolts in the underdeveloped countries, the imperialism of capitalist societies. Many deportees do not have the strength to continue living. They are alive, but they cannot operate efficiently in the face of the obstacles of daily life :

On dirait que Rolande, comme Yolande Gili, comme beaucoup de revenantes, a usé en quelques mois à Birkenau toute la somme d'énergie, toute la vitalité qui lui avaient été impartie à la naissance pour durer toute une vie. Elle est vivante, mais le ressort de la vie est cassé. (p. 97.)

This is the general condition of most of the deportees who returned. The literature shows us that there was a necessity to adapt to a new life in camp, but as Semprun tells us 'Mais le vrai choc s'est produit au retour', the readaptation to the life after the camps is even harder, because so much of the strength had been left in camp, because of the *'connaissance inutile'* that the deportees had acquired.

The majority of the eyewitness reports about concentration camps ends with a description of the return to normal life which is, at best sketchy. But now, more than twenty-five years later, several definitive and comprehensive works have appeared. We mention one of the first, Micheline Maurel's *La Vie normale*, which deals entirely with this subject. The protagonist, Laurence, after the war, finds herself all alone, in London, working and poorly making ends meet. She is physically exhausted and must go into a hospital. These circumstances are entirely due to the fact that she was a deportee. In the hospital, though, begins the story of a love affair, the dominating theme of the book, which ends very unhappily for Laurence. The defect of the book is the following : we begin by seeing a situation in which she finds herself due to post-camp complications. However, from the point at which she enters the hospital, when she is a patient in the hospital, were it not for the fact that she thinks back, at varied times, to her experiences in Neubrandenburg, and evokes the memories of her comrades there, we would never know that she is a former deportee because the problems described in *La Vie normale* are not restricted to persons having been in camp. Any woman could have a love affair of this sort, and it does not end unhappily because of the fact that she was in camp. The end, as a matter of fact, is completely out of her hands. Therefore, the book is not a clear portrayal of the problems of readaptation to normal life because the situations that it depicts could happen and probably have happened to many women who were not in camp. What is interesting to note is that Laurence thinks how her comrades in camp would tell her to act before she makes a decision, and that she sometimes tells herself that she must get the most out of a situation, enjoy it to the fullest, because other-wise, if she were to find herself in camp again, she would have no pleasures, no blissful moments to look back upon, no experience in love. Laurence feels that she should not have been treated the way she was by life and her lover because she was deported and is therefore entitled to a better life. There are no other clues, other than the fact that the author specifically mentions it, to point to that fact that we are dealing with the problems of a young woman trying to readapt after deportation. This novel is not, then, a great contribution to the literature of the readaptation to normal life, because its problems are not limited to former deportees and are not sufficiently particularized. The destiny of the protagonist does not appear to be in her own hands : her reactions to her problems matter little. It is not even pro-per to conclude that her reactions to her problems are the result of the fact that she was deported.

Christian Pineau has seized, in a very small vignette, an essential part of the problem of readaptation. His son, who hardly knew him when he left, is a complete stranger to him when he returns. The child thinks he will make the father happy when he brings him home a box of sardines, a precious and rare commodity in the post-war times, and purchased on the black market. The father — this is one day after his return home — is still living by the moral code of the concentration camp :

Le pauvre gosse reçoit une gifle trop vite partie par un réflexe qu'il ne peut comprendre. Des larmes lui viennent aux yeux. — C'était pour te faire plaisir, papa, dit-il en reniflant. Je ne croyais pas que c'était mal de penser aux autres. La vie pour lui, n'a pas changé. (*Pineau,* p. 312.)

The generation gap is widened in these situations and of course, it is even more complicated for the child to adapt to the parent because if it is difficult for an adult to understand what happened in camp it is certainly more difficult for a child. And the fact that, in many cases, the parent was in camp during the time when the child was at a crucial age may make the two remain strangers for a long time to come. And the child does not understand why, when the parent places a dish of food in front of him which he rejects, he is told that in Auschwitz he would have eaten it gladly. Nor does the child understand why the parent hovers over him excessively and displays fears for him, beyond the normal worries one has over a child, or when the same parent tells him that the shoes he is wearing would have made anyone in Auschwitz overjoyed. All the child sees is that other children do not have to live by this code, and so, although he realizes that there is something special, someone to be especially respected, in his parents who have suffered so much and survived, there are many things that annoy him, which he would rather not hear, and which are completely alien to his world. Unfortunately, though, the parent cannot forget and so cannot change his frame of reference.

The problem of the necessity for readaptation to a new moral code is clearly seen by Elie Wiesel. In *L'Aube*, set in Israel, Elisha is placed in the role of the executioner. He is told to kill a British soldier being held as hostage. Elisha is a former deportee. The story takes place not long after the war. The execution is set to take place at dawn ; the story begins at night, the evening before. As we have seen, the time terminology is very significant in Wiesel's work. '*La Nuit*' is over. It is dawn, but the sun has not risen yet. 'Dawn' is perhaps also the intermediate time in the deportee's life when he makes the readjustment between night, his life in camp, and day, '*la vie normale*'. This book is the story of the transplantation of situations that take place in camp, slightly transformed, and placed in normal life, and the reactions that the deportee has. We see again that camp morality cannot be transposed to normal life ; as Françoise of *Qui rapportera ces paroles* feared, all that was learned in camp was useless. Camp morality is not a valid frame of reference for normal life situations.

11

Elisha the Jew rationalizes that he and his people have been the victims for long enough. The Commandment 'Thou shalt not kill' was not respected by anyone but the Jews for centuries, he thinks. Yet it is always the Jews who have been martyred. He feels that it is time for all this to change. He will help to kill those that make him a murderer. He will kill to help himself and others become men again. But he is horrified by his own personality to the point where he says : 'Je me voyais avec les yeux du passé. Je m'imaginais en uniforme, en uniforme gris foncé, en uniforme SS' (*L'Aube*, p. 42). He cannot dissociate executioner and SS in his mind. Whatever acts of violence he commits, he judges with the eyes of the deported Jew. And his association is always with the Nazi situation ; in his victims, he sees the victims of the SS cruelty, of which he was one. And now he sees himself as an executioner, an SS and '... la nausée me contracta soudain l'estomac' (p. 44). He recalls a scene from the ghetto when victims tried to flee from the SS. And of course, throughout the book, his memory reverts to things that happened in camp, to experiences that took place right after the liberation. He is haunted and cannot free his mind of these associations. They are a constant frame of reference. The idea of being an executioner frightens him and he fears that the dead will always remember him as such, that he will never be anything else for the rest of his life because it is the eyes of others that define his role. Elisha's frame of reference is entirely structured around the camp experience so that when he is told that the man he is to kill, John Dawson, knowing that he is going to die, wants to eat, he finds it unbelievable. In his camp experience none wanted to eat before they were to die. Elisha succeeds in killing the hostage. But he does not succeed in liberating himself from his past :

Je regardai ce morceau de nuit et la peur me saisit la gorge. Le morceau noir, fait de lambeaux d'ombres, avait un visage. Je le regardai et je compris ma peur. Ce visage, c'était le mien. (p. 141.)

Many of Wiesel's books show haunting preoccupations with camp incidents. In *Le Jour* which, according to Wiesel's own time classifications, should indicate the end of the camp experience, the return to normal life, the protagonist is still haunted by people he knew in camp, by his memories. The fact that this takes place in the book called *Le Jour* shows us that for Wiesel, *'la vie normale'* will never be without memories and nightmares of camp. He cannot forget the dead. The protagonist is with the woman who loves him. She tries to encourage him to eat. But :

Je pris un morceau de viande et le portai à ma bouche. L'odeur du sang me fit tourner l'estomac. Une envie de vomir me prit soudain. Un jour, j'avais vu un homme qui dévorait avec appétit une tranche de viande sans pain. Affamé, j'avais observé un long moment. Je suivais, hypnotisé, le mouvement de ses doigts et celui de ses mâchoires. J'espérais qu'en m'apercevant là, devant lui, il me jetterait un morceau. Il ne m'avait pas vu. Le lendemain, ses camarades de baraque l'avaient pendu : il mangeait de la chair humaine... En voyant ce corps se balancer dans la baraque des toilettes, j'avais pensé : 'Et s'il m'avait vu ?' (p. 13.)

The theme of physical needs is still with us, but, of course, here, it is mixed with other considerations. Now, free at least physically, eating has become a luxury, something his mind can dwell upon, and given the opportunity to do so, he of course remembers the camp experience. This frame of reference does not leave him. The protagonist (the book is in the first person) is in an accident, a critical one, and the doctor informs him that he is lucky to be alive, and that he must thank God. He replies that he does not know how. And he also replies, to himself that 'le regret d'être revenu de si loin ne m'avait pas encore quitté' (p. 23). This is ambiguous, but we can take it to mean either the regret that he has survived the accident or the regret, more probably, of having survived the camp experience. And Wiesel tells us that he is ashamed at having chosen to remain alive, to survive. The idea of the guilt of the survivor, of the one who was chosen to return when so many did not, is a striking feature of Wiesel's work.

While the protagonist is in a coma in the hospital, and even after he is out of the coma, he is haunted by the name 'Sarah' and we learn that it was for two reasons : his mother (killed by the Nazis) was named 'Sarah' and he does not want to ever forget her name, and because there was a woman named Sarah who started her career as a prostitute when she was twelve years old, in a concentration camp, as she was forced to make love to an SS officer who wanted her as a birthday present.

There is, of course, a leitmotif of *Le Jour* that must be mentioned : the protagonist is loved by Kathleen. He may also be in love with her, but we are never sure. In any case, he cannot let himself be helped by her, even completely surrender to her love because he is haunted by the past which prevents him from accepting her. His mind constantly travels back in time and he does not permit himself to be in love or loved. This is, of course, a direct psychological result of the experience in camp. He feels that he is, in a sense, being unfaithful to the past, to his mother, to the Sarahs whom he has known, to all those who played that role in camp, if he permits himself to love Kathleen.

The problems that the male or female deportee faces, on a psychological level, or in relationship with the other sex are sometimes presented as they are in *Le Jour*, by themselves, with no central themes other than the conflict of the love and the haunting of the camp experience. However, in Charlotte Delbo's *Ceux qui avaient choisi* (unpublished play) a similar situation is further complicated by the fact that Werner, the man whom Françoise meets twenty years after the liberation, in a café in Greece, is a German. *Ceux qui avaient choisi* is, in a way almost a sequel to *Qui rapportera ces paroles*. The same character who remains to recite the epilogue of the latter play to us, Françoise, is the protagonist of *Ceux qui avaient choisi*. The play takes place after Françoise has been leading '*la vie normale*' for some twenty years. We learn that Françoise's husband was shot at Mont Valérien and that she had seen him several hours before he was to be shot, and we see a scene, entitled elsewhere *Une Scène jouée dans la mémoire** the farewell between husband and wife. Françoise relives the scene for the first time, at the café while she and Werner are chatting. The situation is further complicated by the fact that it is not just a male-female meeting, but by the fact that Werner was in Hitler's army although not in active combat. He was rather something like a cultural attaché in Greece during the war. But he was not one who chose, as Françoise and her husband were. He was a victim of the choices made by his government. It is more for this than for the reason that he was German, we feel, that Françoise cannot find herself completely at ease with him. She tells him about the farewell scene with her husband, but then cannot speak of it again to him ; it is too painful a memory for her. When Françoise refuses to see Werner again, or to let him get in touch with her, we are convinced that it is at least partially because of the fact that she was deported for having been in the Resistance and that he claims that during the war, he was completely oblivious to what was transpiring in his own country. He was too young to have voted in the elections, so he claims he is not directly guilty. But he was entirely apathetic during the war, buried in his studies and we see that, for Françoise, this implies a certain degree of guilt on his part. She weakens at times : we realize that she is in some way attracted to Werner, but she cannot reconcile her feelings and her past. Her past wins out : she would always be able to get in touch with him, but we feel that she will not and he has no way of finding her.

We have thus so far seen both physiological and psychological effects that the deportation has left on its victims, even in present times, twenty-five years later. On a religious level, the reactions are as varied as they were on other levels. For one man, Aimé Bonifas, the answer for what to do afterwards is to join the clergy :

Pour moi, il vaut la peine maintenant de travailler à édifier l'église de Jésus-Christ, ce peuple composé d'hommes qui se savent petits... Cela n'exclut pas

* This scene, extracted from the play for radio performance, is now an independent work with the above title.

notre engagement dans les affaires de ce monde... Et sachant aussi que tout le désespoir de la terre n'a plus de prise définitive contre la grande espérance d'une 'nouvelle terre et de nouveaux cieux'... où il n'y aura plus de bagnes... (p. 179.)

For others, the experiences in the Nazi world led to the doubting of one's religious tenets rather than the reinforcement of them. Elie Wiesel, in *Le Chant des morts*, is confronted by the problem of prayer. Tomorrow is the anniversary of his father's death. He remembers that on the day of his father's death in Buchenwald, he did not recite the Kaddish, the prayer for the dead, first because no one would have said *Amen* and second, because he did not know the prayer by heart, and third, because, most important to him, it would have been blasphemous :

Reciter le Kaddish dans cette baraque étouffante, en plein royaume de la mort, c'eût été le pire des blasphèmes. Et je manquais même la force de blasphémer. (p. 12.)

He decides to recite the prayer to commemorate the anniversary of his father's death, but not for religious reasons or out of conviction, because he cannot reconcile the idea of Auschwitz and the presence of God, but because :

Tout compte fait, je crois que j'irai demain à la synagogue. J'allumerai les bougies, je réciterai le Kaddish et ce sera pour moi une épreuve supplémentaire de mon impuissance. (p. 14.)

The feeling of '*impuissance*', now, more than twenty years later, is the same feeling that overcame him when he saw his father die and could do nothing for him.

There are, of course, special problems related to the aftermaths of the deportation : for example, the cases of children left with one set of parents while their natural parents were in camp, and the question, afterwards, of who had a right to keep the child. Also the question of children (Jewish) not circumcised, children born of mixed marriages, the guilt of those who tried to disguise their origins to avoid persecution, the attempts by others, who collaborated, but who were part Jewish and wished to use their Jewishness to hide their collaboration. All this is dealt with by Weinberg, who informs us that most of these problems were resolved by a *Din Torah,* over which he himself sometimes presided, according to ancient Jewish tradition. We will not dwell upon these problems as they are not salient features of the French literature of the deportation.

There are many for whom the camp was more authentic than were their lives afterwards. They return to it rather than adapt themselves to daily life, mentally. There, life was arranged for them ; there were no decisions to make, there were no problems. Wanda, for example, tells us that she and Yolande, the friend from camp whom she lives with after the war, think about starting to do the gymnastic exercises that they had done during their stay in camp. This shows that they have not adapted to their new lives, and that they are secure only in the past and must cling to memories of it. We must point out two facts here : first, that this is an aberration from the norm and that rather than showing any merits whatsoever of camp life, it rather demonstrates just how terrible camp was by the fact that it left such an enduring mark. We also wish to state that nowhere does this reaction occur to a deportee from any of the *Vernichtungslager.*

Two authors previously discussed, who were not deported but who write on the holocaust must be spoken of here. They both speak of the readaptation to normal life of their protagonists. Vercors' Clémentine does not make the adjustment to normal life at all effectively. When she returns, she continues to work with deportees in the *'Amicales'.* She learned the joy of helping in camp and this is the only satisfaction that she seeks in life afterwards. But even at this level she is constantly frustrated by bureaucracy, by rudimentary obstacles. The women come to the *'Amicale'* and seek her out to find again the solidarity they knew in camp. This is a withdrawal into the past ; normal life does not present situations where such a degree of solidarity is necessary. When Clémentine looks for work, she cannot find any and she is told that people prefer not to hire a former deportee because it gives them a bad conscience. She meets a man, younger than she, whom she would like to keep, but he cannot agree to this. They are both arrested because the boy is a minor. She is later sentenced to death for assault and battery, but the sentence is reduced. The judge attempts to absolve himself of any guilt in the matter. We find that the goal of Vercors in recounting Clémentine's life (*Sur ce rivage*) is clear : to prove that the ills of society are not at all cured yet, and that they are indeed appalling.

De me dire que Clémentine a été plus heureuse dans les camps de la mort que parmi nous, j'en ai froid dans le dos. (p. 249.)

Del Castillo does somewhat the same thing as Vercors. He shows the life of Tanguy in camp and then devotes two-thirds of his book to the later life of Tanguy, during which we see that the child suffers as much, if not more, than he did in camp. He studies under the Jesuits in Spain where he is treated miserably. He is unhappy wherever he goes and finds a great many people who resemble 'them' : nasty, mean. He finds happiness only for short periods of time with his father, with friends. But he cannot find true happiness. Del Castillo leaves us without any conclusion as to his future and tells us that it will depend on whether he finds more of 'them' in this world, or more people whom he can love and trust. We suppose that the purpose of this novel is political and sociological : to prove that our society is as bad as the Nazi system, and that it does not function properly since it does not afford chances for happiness even to children as innocent as Tanguy. There is an implicit critique of the church here ; the brothers whom Tanguy studies under and lives with distinctly remind us of the SS. There is no war going on, yet Tanguy's life is as bad as it was in camp. It is after the war, in our society, that Tanguy first learns to hate. In camp, he is rather apathetic. He eventually loses this hatred when he decides that the world is divided into 'good guys' and 'bad guys' — almost 'we' and 'they'. But he will not be happy and we are not convinced that it is because the camp has so distorted his way of looking at things that it is impossible for him to find happiness. We do not believe that this was the author's intention in creating the character. We find, rather, that the elements of society that Del Castillo presents us with and his way of comparing and paralleling them with the life in camp bring us to the conclusion that Tanguy will not be happy in our society.

We find that in the above two mentioned books, there is a danger for the uninitiated reader because they present concentration camps in a distorted context. While we agree that there are elements of our society that are badly in need of change, we also find that there is nothing worse than what camps were and we find also that to show otherwise is to diminish the horror of the holocaust. The use of the phenomenon of concentration camps to further political doctrines, or sociological ones, is not restricted to the two above mentioned authors. We will discuss this further in our conclusion, but in relation to the readaptation to normal life, we bring to our reader's attention Jean Lafitte. An ardent, militant member of the Communist party, Jean Lafitte tells us of a love story, discussed previously in this book which ends when he is liberated and returns to normal life. He finds his beloved, after a long search for her, at the 1949 Communist Party congress. The idea that the Party congress should be the place for the reunion clearly shows the orientation of the author. He finds bliss in love only in the part of his life, his world, that is oriented towards his political happiness. He is uniting his readaptation, his future happiness and his political considerations without any distortions, though, that would lead the uninitiated reader to untoward conclusions. He views the concentration camp somewhat as Del Castillo and Vercors do : the caricatural reduction of the world in which we live, rather than as a closed society, which is our concept of it. It is a most pessimistic viewpoint and gives little hope not only for the readaptation of the deportee but for the future happiness of all : deportee and non-deportee.

Elie Wiesel's *Entre deux soleils*, a collection of selections dealing with his experiences as he tried to readapt to normal life, shows the same haunting themes that previous books of his have already described. An attempt to return to the fold of the faith is shown to be uppermost in the author's mind in he opening selection, 'Itineraire d'une fin'. The existence of God is affirmed for what may be the last time in this context (for Wiesel states that he will no longer write about the holocaust) as the author tells us that without the concept of God, Auschwitz is inconceivable. Elie Wiesel closes his work with a parable : when it was Rabbi Yishmael's turn to undergo torture by the Romans, a celestial voice spoke to him and told him to be silent, for a single tear would suffice for Him to return the world to nothingness. And so Rabbi Yishmael didn't cry. Despite his pain and his anger, he did not destroy. This is perhaps Elie Wiesel's message to those who wish to cry out in rage and desperation at the thought of Auschwitz : it is a call to passivity.

Perhaps the most surprising and important books on the subject of the return to normal life are Vercors' *Les Armes de la nuit* and *La puissance du jour*. In the first, probably the superior of the two, Vercors describes Pierre Cange's return to the woman he loved, Nicole, to his home town (a small village where he goes primarily to escape from reality as does the schoolmaster in Solzhenitsyn's *The House of Matrena*), his mother and the narrator. Pierre Cange cannot communicate : he is questioned constantly, by the narrator in particular, in an attempt to force him to verbalize the reasons why he cannot really 'come back'. He is finally able to tell the story of his role in the *Sonderkommando* and the shame that he cannot overcome of having participated in this work, but the reader realizes that Vercors has captured something far more important than the return of a *Sonderkommando* worker who survived — it is the feeling of each deportee who returned, no matter what work he did in camp : the inability to love again those who care for him still, because he thinks that they cannot understand him, the impotence when faced with the problem of vocalization of one's feelings and the difficulty for others and for oneself to understand and overcome these feelings. Pierre Cange, despite his physical and emotional problems, through political activity in Spain, through the patience of those who love him and contrive in every possible way to bring him back, through his involvement in a situation utilizing possible reprisals against a collaborator, will succeed in returning. Vercors has successfully captured Pierre's inability, at first to re-orient himself, to make a successful contribution to life, to return to life itself. *Les Armes de la nuit* is one of the finest works on the aftermath of the camp.

We close our discussion of this subject with a look at the most recent work on the return : Charlotte Delbo's very beautiful masterpiece, *Mesure de nos jours.* In a series of monologues, some in poetry, some in prose, successfully unified by the presence of the narrator, the author has shown us both typical and atypical reactions : 'Loulou', which the reader has difficulty believing (although we know it to be a true story) is the tale of a young man who preferred being kept in a psychiatric home rather than face the world, who never left it for twenty years, until his friends rescued him. 'Marie-Louise', perhaps the most tragic of the monologues, is the story of a young woman who returns to her husband and her home after the camp and who is taken care of in every way by Pierre, her doting husband. But, in his desire to know all that happened to her, to understand, he has not liberated her from the experience : it is now, twenty-five years later, as if he were the deportee — he knows as much as she and this *communauté de souvenirs* forms the singular basis for their existence and the reader is overwhelmed by the sadness, the tragedy, the reticence and inability of both the man and the woman to leave the world of 'la nuit'. Mado, who doesn't think she is alive, Poupette, who would have wanted a little more consideration from the others because she was deported and deserved it but never got it, Jacques who has to prove he was not a traitor, Denise, the woman who loves him, who has no time to concern herself with her own problems because she has to help Jacques, Gaby who can never get warm again, all of these tell us their story and each is different but each touches upon some inexplicable part of the return, and together they do not explain, since answers cannot be found, but each throws light upon why 'le vrai choc s'est produit au retour'.

This concludes the study of the life of the deportee in camp and his return and attempts to re-adapt to normal life. In the next chapter, we will discuss, rather than the experience itself, its literary and aesthetic facets. As it is reflected in literature, the theme of deportation has given rise to certain transmutations which, from a purely literary point of view, are highly interesting. Because of a lapse in time, the experience has become myth ; it has transcended itself to become part of a greater reality and to become an aesthetic consideration.

6

Myth, Symbol and Transcendence

> *C'est alors que je revis le sourire de mon chauf-*
> *feur : m'avait-il dupé aussi ? Ma déception fut*
> *de courte durée. Le chauffeur ne le savait pas,*
> *mais j'ai vu Babi-Yar. Car Babi-Yar, le vrai,*
> *est autre chose qu'un nom, autre chose qu'un*
> *emplacement. Babi-Yar, poème de deuil, nie*
> *toute géographie, et la dépasse. Babi-Yar se*
> *situe pas seulement à Babi-Yar. Et le chauffeur,*
> *malgré lui, me l'a montré.*
>
> E. WIESEL, *Les Juifs du silence*, p. 49.

In *Les Juifs du silence*, Elie Wiesel describes his trip through the Soviet Union. He wants to visit Babi-Yar, the mass grave, site of many Nazi executions, to see it and to say the Kaddish, the prayer for the dead discussed elsewhere in this treatise in relation to Wiesel. He can find no one to take him there and he finally takes a taxi. The driver points out the spot to him :

Je descendis de la voiture. Pour regarder. Pour chercher. Pour murmurer le Kaddish, la prière pour les morts. Mais il n'y avait rien à voir. Du massacre, rien n'a subsisté. Les morts ont emporté leurs ombres, leurs traces. (p. 48.)

For an hour, he remains there, glued to the spot. A week later, when he is back in Moscow, he speaks to some friends in the diplomatic corps, who recount the story of their trip to Babi-Yar. They could not find anyone to drive them to the ravine either, and they went by taxi. But they wonder if perhaps it was a fraud : they are not sure they have really seen the place where it happened. But Wiesel realizes a far greater truth than the one involved in a possible fraud. He has created myth for us, and defined it, simultaneously. Babi-Yar has now become more than a historical site. It surpasses all concepts of reality and becomes myth : a poetic recreation and transmutation of a deep and significant reality. Only time has the power to create this dimension ; no other element has the power to produce it. The by-product, in literature, of this dimension is the element that we choose to call myth.

We refer to Jerzy Grotowski's *Exemple d'un traitement de texte : Acropolis* for the definition of myth. When he speaks of the profane and the sacred, without using the word myth, Grotowski is furnishing us with at least part of the definition of myth as we choose to use the term here :

Ainsi, il nous faut... un texte classique qu'à priori, en quelque sorte, nous profanons, mais auquel simultanément nous rendons sa vérité... (p. 19.)

The idea of the profanation of the sacred is perhaps akin to the idea of those authors who choose to create myth in their contribution to the literature of the concentration camps. We can successfully substitute for *'le texte classique'* the *témoignages,* the historical reality, the details. The profanation of these details is simultaneously not only keeping but *returning* their authenticity — *returning* because these truths are in a way lost in the historical reality, in the detail. This is the creation of myth. This separation from the detail, from historical reality is possible only with a time lapse, when the psyche of the person involved has not altered them, but has changed the perspective in which they are seen, in his own mind and therefore, before the eye of the reader. 'L'interprétation littérale et la métaphore s'y [in myth] entrecroisent comme dans une rêverie somnolente' (p. 31). This is a description of *Acropolis,* Grotowski's adaptation of Wyspianski's text about concentration camps. It is the *'entrecroisement'* that is important ; the two concepts meet on equal levels. It is the element of time that is both cause and effect in this relationship. Time permits the author to interlace the literal interpretations and the metaphor which together form myth and time and adds, in itself, a perspective to this meeting which is retained within it and remains a part of it, thereby becoming one more dimension of it.

André Schwarz-Bart, in *Le Dernier des Justes*, has a curious combination of the use of Jewish mythology, folklore and the creation of myth. Our attention here is drawn towards his creation of what we choose to call the mythology of names. Just as Babi-Yar is more than a simple place of execution by the Nazis for Wiesel, Schwarz-Bart has succeeded in creating more than just the story of Ernie Lévy for us. He has immortalized, by a prayer — almost a song — the camps by immortalizing their names. It is somewhat the reverse of the modern structuralist trend ; here, the item precedes the name, but the name survives the item. The camp preceded its nomenclature, but its name survives. Schwarz-Bart, on the last page of his book weaves the names of the sites of Nazi atrocities into the ritual of Jewish prayer services, almost all of which begin 'And Praised Be...' :

> *Et loué. Auschwitz. Soit. Maidanek.*
> *L'Eternel. Treblinka. Et loué.*
> *Buchenwald. Soit. Mauthausen.*
> *L'Eternel. Belzec. Et loué. Sobibor.*
> *Soit. Chelmno. L'Eternel. Ponary.*
> *Et loué. Theresienstadt. Soit. Varsovie.*
> *L'Eternel. Vilno. Et loué. Skarzysko.*
> *Soit. Neuengamme. L'Eternel. Pustkow.*
> *Et loué...*

When Louis Aragon writes in *Le Musée Grévin* (p. 72) :

> *Auschwitz, Auschwitz O syllabes sanglantes*
> *Ici l'on vit, ici l'on meurt à petit feu*

it is an extension of the idea of myth. The myth of concentration camps is also a linguistic myth, transmitted by literature. It has now become sufficient, because of all that has been written about camps, to utter the name of Auschwitz for the place to rise within the mind of man. Aragon has shown us that it is possible to do just this by his poem in which the painful syllables evoke the atrocious memories. André Schwarz-Bart is aware of the power of the name, and of its immortality. Eluard, for example, rather than writing hagiographic literature, realizes that he might further immortalize his heroes by the roll-call of the dead and so he writes in one of his poems (*Poèmes pour tous,* p. 184) :

> *Visages clairs souvenirs sombres*
> *Plus comme un grand coup sur les yeux*
> *Visages de papier brûlé*
> *Dans la mémoire rien que cendres*
> *La rose froide de l'oubli*
> *Pourtant Desnos Pourtant Péri*
> *Crémieux Fondane Pierre Unik*
> *Sylvain Itkine Jean Jausion...*

Aragon has done the same thing, when writing of Maï Politzer who died in Auschwitz ; a play on words becomes a line that is more remembered than perhaps any other in the poem (*Le Musée Grévin,* p. 73) :

> *On dit que Danielle et que Maï*
> *Ah déferont-ils maille à maille*
>
> . . . .
>
> *Maï et Danielle y puis-je croire*
>
> . . . .
>
> *Je vous salue Marie de France aux cent visages...*

Weimar has now become more famous for the site of Buchenwald than for other more poetic, historical causes. Babi-Yar has become infamous thanks to the Yevtushenko poem. The name invariably evokes the holocaust. This has been the way — or one of the ways — that literature has been able to immortalize the holocaust, in a way that history never could. This is perhaps the culmination of myth.

It is important to point out that there exists what we might call 'false myth', that is, an attempt at sentimentalizing, romanticizing, at creating heroes by distortions of fact, or by other means. In this manner, true myth cannot be created and these efforts are always unsuccessful : they are false. Myth can never be a sentimental version of historical fact. On the contrary, it is a deep, a profound, rather than romanticized perspective. We will show here one example which dominates the hagiographic literature of Auschwitz.

The character (in the Pirandello sense of the term) that we will consider is Danielle Casanova, posthumously decorated with the *Légion d'honneur*. All the Communist municipalities in the Parisian suburbs have a street named 'rue Danielle-Casanova'. A part of the Parisian street 'rue des Petits-Champs' is named 'rue Danielle-Casanova'. Her pictures hang in all the 'Foyers de la Jeunesse Communiste' and there are pictures and even one sculpture of her on display all over France though few of them resemble her. In 1949, the Communist Party commissioned Simone Téry to write a book about the life of Danielle *(Du Soleil Plein le Cœur)*. The idea was to create a heroine that would serve the party purposes. Danielle fitted the bill : she was well known as a party member before the war and she was active in the Resistance although not more so than many of her fellow-deportees, and she died in Auschwitz. Téry's book recounts the life of a saint named Danielle. It omits the unsavory details, the details that would show that Danielle was human, and that she was far from saintly. It creates a character that never lived, a character who is not human and who would not be a heroine even if she had lived as the story tells us that she did. It forgets that Danielle had several faults, that her carelessness was the cause of her own arrest. She went to bring coal to Georges and Maï Politzer and met the police. She had no way of knowing they were followed, but she had no right to break one of the group rules : never visit a co-worker at home, never meet with one unless authorized to do so. Another version of this story is even more serious as it shows that Danielle caused the arrest of Maï and Georges Politzer. Téry also recounts the story of Danielle's death among her comrades in Auschwitz, in the midst of the worst conditions that the camp could offer, but this is not how she died. She died in an infirmary reserved for Kapos, with 'all the comforts of home' — hardly a condition that she shared with her co-deportees. But all this would not matter ; Danielle could have been a heroine if only Téry had remembered that heroines have faults too. While it is true that Danielle offered strength to her comrades, that she had a certain very admiring entourage that was blind to her faults, and that this might be enough to make her a heroine, it is not true that she was a faultless and saintly human being.

We know from the account of one of her comrades from Auschwitz (see *Le Convoi du 24 janvier*) that Danielle was the only beautiful corpse ever seen in Birkenau because she led a privileged life there. As a dentist she enjoyed special treatment and since, in actual fact, she put her chances for survival above all else, she sacrificed anything and everything rather than endanger her chances of return. Yet she failed. Those who loved her deeply, those who wanted her to return to tell her story, and their own, those who were sure that she would live and that they would die, those who wanted her to return to look after their sons and daughters, were heartbroken when she died on May 9, 1943, in Birkenau. This love that others had for her could have immortalized Danielle, but the deliberate distortions on the part of her biographer only create false myth and they do not add to the personality cult of Danielle, nor do they make her a saint in the eyes of those who know the truth.

For Grotowski, there is the primordial myth, in addition to the general myth outlined previously. There is the exaggeration, the *in extremis* of any physical condition. It is the confrontation of man and his body and the testing of man's body to withstand certain conditions that heretofore were unexplored, inexistent. As we have seen constantly, man was tested, in the camps, to a degree which humanity had never known before. It seems almost unnecessary to speak of a particular work about concentration camps to illustrate this concept. The whole *'univers concentrationnaire'* is an illustration of it. Grotowski is giving us a label for a *'condition humaine'* in a context other than the one for which he uses the term, but which applies exactly to concentration camps. The extremity of the conditions of camp are the first level of myth : the physical, the primary, the biological.

Because the authors writing about concentration camps are con·fronted with a reality that is unbelievable, they have to find a way to communicate to their readers this meeting of myth and reality. The technique of realism is inadequate. We have found that a strict adherence to detail is not effective because the details furnished to the reader do not fit into a pre-existing frame of reference in his mind. Something else, something more is necessary to evoke the camp, to create myth. We find that this has been done most effectively by certain authors : on the physical level by Delbo, Antelme, among others, and on levels of mythology in its purest forms, Wiesel, Semprun and Delbo. Upon asking ourselves what it is that makes these works distinctive, we come to realize that it is the fact that these books enter the realm of myth on varied levels, and that it is for that precise reason that they are true works of art, of literature.

We have already discussed, in great detail, Charlotte Delbo's *Aucun de nous ne reviendra.* Our analysis, though, shows, in addition to certain aesthetic techniques of the author, the absorption of the totality of the phenomenon and how this is transmitted to the reader. We did not, though, define what makes the work a literary masterpiece. The answer seems to be in the fact that it is the creation of myth, on several levels. It is the most intense, the most powerful, usage of myth that we have encountered. Its preoccupation with death, with thirst, with the snow and the cold, are biological preoccupations. The fact that they are shown, without overwhelming and precise details, to be such an exaggeration of normal physical conditions makes this book a contribution to myth as well as to literature. The same is true of *Une connaissance inutile.* One chapter illustrates the idea most clearly. In 'Boire', the author states that for her, at that time in the camp, nothing else existed other than water ; before she gets it, it is the desire for it that suppresses any other feelings. Once she is in possession of the water, and is able to gorge herself with it, neither people nor other objects exist for her. This same singularity of phenomena is found in the chapter entitled 'Le ruisseau' where it is again the preoccupation with water, but this time for ablutions. And the author clearly states that nothing but the spring of water and the parts of the body she is to wash exist for her at the moment she washes. Robert Antelme (*L'Espèce humaine*) has created an entire work evolving around one feature of myth : hunger. The thought of approaching food, the food itself, the lack of food, recipes, endless discussions of food, these dominate his *témoignage.* It is the basis for myth : a total preoccupation with the physical condition of hunger. Food replaces the woman ; hunger replaces sexual desire, satisfaction replaces the love for the woman : for Antelme, in *L'Espèce humaine*, there is nothing but food, just as for Grotowski's *Constant Prince* nothing but his own martyrdom exists. Antelme's book and Delbo's works are perhaps the two best examples of myth, but in actuality, the entire holocaust is an adventure into the realm of myth.

Time permits a certain transcendence of reality. Because of a lapse in time, both the author's mind and his literary creation objectify the experience he has undergone, in this case, the camp, and permit him to present it to us as if he were two : first, the man who has undergone the experience, and second, the one who has witnessed it (vicariously seen it undergone by another self). This is the highest level of what we choose to call myth — the creation that is produced by this *dédoublement de soi* which is based in reality and adds another dimension to it. This is present in only a few of the works about concentration camps, and we conclude that it is only in the superior authors that we can find this literary manifestation. There are hints of it in several of the *témoignages.* Gaussen, in *Le Kapo*, writes : 'L'irréalité de cette potence insignifiante que rapetissait encore la neige...' (p. 105). The '*potence*' was actually omnipotent, but now, to Gaussen, next to the snow, it has become insignificant, perhaps because of the lapse in time. It has become part of myth.

Weinberg, in *Le Printemps des cendres*, has passages that approach the level of myth. The emphasis is on the lapse in time and the creation of myth permitted by this time lapse, no matter how small. The camp and what he has undergone have not changed, but time has permitted him to transmute them :

J'eus honte de ressentir de la pitié devant ces gens qui me racontaient leurs souffrances... ce sentiment me montrait que je regardais ces gens 'd'en face', que j'étais l'autre, que je n'étais plus eux, et qu'ils n'étaient plus moi. Déjà, le temps avait changé. La souffrance s'éloignait. La vie reprenait, avec tous les sentiments 'nobles' et, parmi eux la pitié. (p. 47.)

We feel that for Weinberg, this creation of myth is not a positive phenomenon ; it is rather one that he prefers not to acknowledge. It is the creation of a *dédoublement de soi* but this term does not necessarily imply a positive concept.

Jorge Semprun, in *Le Grand voyage,* written many years after the experience, has forgotten the trip and takes it again in order to create myth. It is perhaps the seventeen years since the experience that have permitted Semprun to forget and to create :

Pendant seize ans j'ai essayé d'oublier ce voyage et j'ai oublié ce voyage. Nul ne pense plus, autour de moi, que j'ai fait ce voyage. Mais en réalité, j'ai oublié ce voyage tout en sachant pertinemment qu'un jour j'aurais à refaire ce voyage. (p. 26.)

Semprun describes to us the first time he sees the camp as myth when, after the liberation, he is still there and acts as guide for the young girls who want to visit it :

La grande place d'appel était déserte, sous le soleil du printemps, et je me suis arrêté, le cœur battant. Je ne l'avais jamais vue vide, il faut dire, je ne l'avais jamais vue réellement. Ce qu'on appelle voir, je ne l'avais pas encore vue vraiment... Je voyais ce paysage, qui avait été le décor de ma vie, deux ans durant, et je le voyais pour la première fois. Je le voyais de l'extérieur, comme si ce paysage qui avait été ma vie jusqu'à avant-hier, se trouvait de l'autre côté du miroir... (p. 71.)

There are times when the camp becomes '*un... pays étranger*' (p. 114) for Semprun. It is the double of Semprun that sees the camp as a foreign country. The other Semprun is so intertwined with those he left behind and their deaths that became part of his life in camp that he is inseparable from them :

Je pense qu'il faut avoir vécu leur mort comme nous l'avons fait, nous qui avons survécu, pour poser sur eux ce regard pur et fraternel. (p. 76.)

The camp as pure myth becomes unreal before the greater reality of the present moment. At the moment of the liberation, he realizes that he has survived for this single moment but at the same time he knows that he has '... râté cet instant unique' (because he realizes that he is not yet ready and that the time is not right for the creation of myth). The lapse of several years, particularly in the mind of the author, is therefore necessary :

J'ai essayé de réaliser que c'est un instant unique, que nous avons tenacement survécu pour cet instant unique, où nous pourrions regarder le camp, de l'extérieur. Mais je n'y arrive pas. Je n'arrive pas à saisir ce qu'il y a d'unique, cet instant unique. Je me dis : mon vieux, regarde, c'est un instant unique, il y a des tas de copains qui sont morts, ils rêvaient à cet instant unique où nous pourrions regarder le camp, comme ceci, de l'extérieur, où nous ne serions plus dedans mais dehors... mais ça ne m'emballe pas. (p. 116.)

At the moment of the liberation, even the life outside becomes myth. It is real, it is life, but because of what the author has just left, because of his experiences over the past two years, another dimension of experience which he adds to the outside makes it myth to him ; it is the concept of freedom that we discussed much earlier, in reference to Semprun, that comes to the fore here :

Et puis, voilà, ce n'était pas la vie au dehors, ce n'était qu'une autre façon d'être dedans, d'être à l'intérieur de ce même monde de l'oppression systématique. (p. 122.)

Not only does Semprun create the mythology of time and place, both inside and outside the camp, but he also creates a myth of characters — for example, the Ilse Koch-Sigrid myth, as we choose to call it. Sigrid, 'la jeune Allemande aux yeux verts' (p. 147), forms the basis for Semprun's definition and explanation of what we call myth :

Quand cette soirée sera finie et que je me souviendrai de cette soirée où tout à coup, le rappel aigu de ce passé si bien oublié, si parfaitement enfoui dans ma mémoire, m'a réveillé du rêve qu'était ma vie, quand j'essayerai de raconter cette histoire confuse, traversée d'événements, peut-être futiles, mais remplis pour moi de signification, je vais réaliser que... Sigrid... dans mon récit devient le pivot de cette soirée, de cette nuit ensuite. (p. 147.)

Sigrid becomes the pivotal point not only of that night but also of the past and the attempt to forget the past, in other words, the creation of myth. He thinks perhaps that her face is there to make him forget, to make civilization forget Ilse Koch, because there is a resemblance and a difference between the two of them. Ilse Koch has become a myth, not only for Semprun, but for all readers about the deportation. There is an attempt to make a replacement : the myth of Sigrid, symbolizing the German non-Nazis, whom Semprun finds difficult to differentiate from the Nazis, and the Ilse Kochs. The myth remains intertwined.

While creating myth, Semprun explains how he does so :

Il faut avoir été dedans, pour comprendre ce besoin physique de regarder du dehors. Elle ne peut pas comprendre.
'Elle' = anyone who has not been 'dedans'. (p. 153.)

The things that happened while he was 'dedans' will never lose their reality for him, he tells us. All the same, he is creating myth. Semprun himself explains the same framework for creating myth that

Grotowski defines : the physical level, the importance of time, and extending this, the metaphysical level created by *dédoublement.*

It is the second part of *Le Grand voyage* that shows us the finest example of the creation of myth. Gérard has just undergone the transition from subject to object of the *récit* and he is entering the camp and he remembers what has happened to him not long before, but the memory has been transformed by the ride in the cattle-car, by the events that have happened since :

Cette avenue, ces colonnes de pierre, ces aigles hautains sont faits pour durer. Ce camp vers lequel on marche n'est pas une entreprise provisoire. Il y a des siècles, il a marché vers un camp, déjà, dans la forêt de Compiègne. (p. 221.)

At the close of the book, Gérard, by becoming an object of the Nazi domination, receives the myth invented by these Germans and is forced to accept it, while simultaneously remaining in reality and weaving his own myth around it :

... ce paysage démesuré où ne manque que la musique, noble et grave, de quelque opéra fabuleux. Gérard essaie de conserver la mémoire de tout ceci, tout en pensant d'une manière vague qu'il est dans le domaine des choses possibles que la mort prochaine de tous les spectateurs vienne effacer à tout jamais la mémoire de ce spectacle, ce qui serait dommage, il ne sait pourquoi... (pp. 223-224.)

Robert Antelme has certain passages in *L'Espèce humaine* which reveal the camp as myth. The myth of décor is among them :

On va arriver. Maintenant le décor de Buchenwald se recompose en entier dans le souvenir : l'immense creux de la carrière et cette gravitation d'êtres minuscules avec la pierre sur l'épaule, devant la plaine d'Iéna ; la parade du départ pour le travail, le matin, avant le jour, sur la place d'appel... la hantise des quinze jours de corvée de merde passés dans la merde... (p. 33.)

Antelme tells us a few pages later that this décor no longer exists. The décor has become myth :

Ces parades, ces décors, n'existeront plus maintenant. Mais nous sommes formés. Chacun de nous, où qu'il soit, transforme désormais l'ordinaire. Sans créma-

toire, sans musique, sans phares, nous y suffirons... (p. 35.) Ils doivent tenir
compte de nous tant que nous vivons, et il dépend encore de nous, de notre
acharnement à être, qu'au moment où ils viendront nous faire mourir ils aient la
certitude d'avoir été entièrement volés. Ils ne peuvent pas non plus enrayer
l'histoire qui doit faire plus fécondes ces cendres sèches que le gras squelette
du lagerführer. (p. 49.)

Each deportee, then, by the very fact that he returns, by the fact
that he survives his executioner, is, in a way, creating myth.

Elie Wiesel has built a whole novel around the concept of myth.
In *La Ville de la chance,* Wiesel takes one incident : the man who
looks out of his window while the Wiesel family is being deported
and does nothing to give Elie Wiesel's sister Tsipora, crying that
she is thirsty, any water. This incident haunts him, as does the town
from which he was deported, Sighet. In *La Ville de la chance,* this
town becomes Szerencseváros, meaning 'city of luck'. The protagonist wants to return to this town, to recapture it, to find it again,
after a lapse of many years, some of which he spent in camp. But
the town has become myth. The town which, at first, is just the town
from which he was deported, the beginning of the trip, has become
other than what he envisages. There are two reasons for this : time
has elapsed and he has become a different person because of what
he has undergone ; he sees things through different eyes. And then,
the town itself has undergone a metamorphosis : all its Jews, or
almost, have gone. A new kind of life has settled over it. Sighet, in
becoming Szerencseváros, has become myth. Wiesel, or the protagonist, returns there after many years and a long struggle to find
that it is a different town. It is no longer the place where he grew
up, the place where he studied Talmud and Jewish customs and
thought. Wiesel creates myth here because he is seeking another
dimension of reality ; he is seeking to find, in reality, the myth he
unconsciously creates by an emotional and intellectual process.
Szerencseváros becomes a mythical place, both for the reader and the
author. But, in reality, it is Sighet that he sees and cannot find. He

cannot find it because he has transmuted reality into myth. All of the construction, or reconstruction, through flashbacks, that we see in the book, takes place during an interrogation ; the police are trying to find out why he illegally entered the country. The flashbacks, the fact that the story is told through them, and the distance that they create, are an element of myth. The novel is pure myth : not to say, of course, that it is pure fiction. We know, from reading all the other of Wiesel's works, that this book is completely based on reality. It never loses, even for an instant, its verisimilitude. It is myth because it is a return, it is a seeing from the outside, just as Gérard will see the camp from the outside, because it is an artistic creation for the reader, in which the city surpasses the physical boundaries of Sighet.

Throughout this treatise, time has been the key element. All the authors who write about deportation were undoubtedly affected by the passing of time since the events took place until they were able to write about them. Many refuse to acknowledge this and it is probably in this acknowledgement that the greatness of the author lies. The greatest authors, the artistically creative ones, are not only aware of the importance of the passage of time but are able to utilize it to its greatest advantage and thus create what we choose to call the concentration camp as myth, all the while producing a work that in no way distorts the facts. The other lesser writers, the less talented ones, choose to forget that time has passed and choose to write as if the events were taking place at that moment. In some cases, this produces a good *témoignage* : it never produces great works of art, for myth and true artistic creation are, in this sense, synonymous, and form the immortality of the camp.

Mauthausen, je l'ai réduit à sa forme primitive, à ses clôtures originelles, des hommes moustachus et méfiants tournant autour des carrioles et des diligences. Moi, j'ai payé mon dû, les papiers sont en règle, je peux passer, la barrière se lève. J'apaise cette terre, ce vieux mot boueux, je l'exorcise, je le fais prononcer par un enfant, je le décrasse, je le frotte contre la vie, à nouveau les saisons le font verdir ou sécher.

C'est en répétant ce mot que je nie sa fatalité : la durée du supplice. Je le mélange aux autres mots, à la fumée d'une haleine, je l'évoque dans son origine, je le renvoie aux hommes. A eux d'en faire bon usage !
Mauthausen n'a pas sauté.
(Jean CAYROL, *Je l'entends encore*, p. 223.)

Conclusion

Nazi concentration camps gave rise to hundreds of books in France and elsewhere. There are few other events, if any, in the history of modern man that have inspired so many works. We have attempted here to examine the content of these works, to show their general trends and themes. We have wished to show that almost all of these works stress the same themes, bring out the same salient features of camp life. The majority of the works that we have discussed, which means the works in existence, from France, are in the category of *témoignages*.

The content of these works about camp rarely varies. Thus, no true conclusions can be arrived at. We prefer to make certain statements, which are the result of our reading, as to the aesthetic quality of the works under consideration, in lieu of conclusion. The *témoignages*, which are generally mediocre, in respect to literary qualities, what one person has called 'Tartempion à Ravensbrück', are descriptions of what has taken place but do not demonstrate any literary talent on the part of the author. Having been in camp does not suffice to create a work of art. However, among these *témoignages*, there are some which, although they are not more than *témoignages*, are very fine in their genre and stand out because they have certain literary, and at times, poetic qualities. Interestingly enough, they are generally the work of writers (that is to say, those who have published other things with some success, those who have created before and since). Among these : *La Nuit* (Elie Wiesel), *L'Homme et la bête* (Louis Martin-Chauffier), *L'Espèce humaine* (Robert Antelme), *L'Univers concentrationnaire* (David Rousset), * *Mauthausen* (Paul Til-

---

* It is interesting to note that when David Rousset attempts to change genres

lard), *Les Morts inutiles* (Francis Wetterwald) and certain of the works of Jean Cayrol. In a slightly different vein, Robert Merle's *La Mort est mon métier,* and Christian Pineau's *Krematorium.*

There are, however, very few authors who have surpassed the *témoignages* and have been able to create a true literary masterpiece around the theme of camp. Semprun in *Le Grand voyage* has done so and he is now considered a renowned writer. In *Une connaissance inutile, Aucun de nous ne reviendra,* and *Mesure de nos jours,* we feel that Charlotte Delbo has created perhaps the purest and most sensitive *chants tragiques* about concentration camps, to say nothing of *Qui rapportera ces paroles.* They are contributions not only to literature but to the immortality of the camps. She too is an accomplished author on subjects other than the camps. In *La Ville de la chance* which is somewhat removed from the camp experience but stems from it, Elie Wiesel has created a work which we consider to be among his finest and which is a literary creation of the highest caliber. Of course, André Schwarz-Bart, the only one of this group who was not deported, has used the theme of deportation in part of *Le Dernier des justes* which is a literary masterpiece.

We wish to dwell for a moment on the problem of those writers who use the theme of deportation and its aftermaths in their works, but who were not themselves deported. We mention here Aragon, Fleg, Eluard, Gary, Langfus, Ikor, Vercors, Del Castillo, * Wallet, Simenon, Triolet, Steiner, Bernadac and Reiner as examples of those who have done so. If we have not mentioned at any previous time, in the body of this treatise, Steiner's *Treblinka* and Reiner's *Et la terre sera pure,* it is because we refuse, in this book, to utilize

---

and to create a novel, *Les Jours de notre mort,* he does not succeed, and the result is frankly boring to the reader.

* We have consistently, in this treatise, referred to Del Castillo as a non-deportee because this is our conviction. There is some question about the matter and since Del Castillo himself has not chosen to rectify it, we stand on our position.

material which is in any way dishonest or which does not acknowledge its sources. It has been proven (there was a judicial proceeding in this matter) that Sylvain Reiner, in *Et la terre sera pure,* plagiarized passages directly from Miklos Nyisli's *Médecin à Auschwitz* (French adaptation by Tibère Kremer) without citing his sources. * The discovery was made by the historian Vidal-Naquet in *Le Monde.* In the case of Steiner, a book entitled *Treblinka,* by Vassili Grossman, was published several years before Steiner's own *Treblinka.* He omits reference to Grossman's book. We refuse to discuss either of these works any further because they are part of a trend which we abhor.

Immediately following the 1945 liberation, *témoignages* appeared and have continued to do so in great number. Twenty years later, Semprun and Delbo published their highly literary works. Very recently, twenty-five years after the liberation, certain 'writers' (a term we use for lack of any other) take advantage of an era in which violence, rape, blood, murder and horror are very much appreciated. They use Auschwitz as a basis for their sensationalism. It is these last ones that we find deplorable. Of course, Auschwitz and all the camps are never ending gold mines of violence. But this is *sang à la une* in its most grotesque form ; it is writing a book to create sensationalism, and using the basest means to impress and attract the reader. This is putting Auschwitz on the same level as *faits divers* — abject sensationalism — and we find this to be a horrifying example of commercialism on a literary level : dishonesty and distortion. We, therefore, refuse to propagate it. For this reason, we have not discussed the books that we find do fit in this grouping : Bernadac's, Steiner's and Reiner's (see Bibliography for documentation).

Few very well-known writers are in our group of several hundred who have written about the camps. We conclude that they feel as Clara Malraux does :

---

* S. Reiner has recently re-edited his book to rectify this.

La déportation m'a toujours semblé une expérience si totale, si incomparable à aucune autre, que, ne l'ayant pas connue, je ne me suis pas cru autorisée à en parler dans mes livres.
(Letter written to us, dated March 4, 1970.)

The exceptions are, among others, those listed above. Fortunately, certain authors do dare to violate this self-imposed taboo and we feel greatly indebted to them. If fifty years from now, there will be no living survivors of the deportation and our great writers refuse to touch upon the subject, it will not live in the minds of future generations. We feel, however, that the non-deportee rather than trying to create a *témoignage* on the subject, or even a novel taking place in camp, has been infinitely more successful and authentic when he has tried to do other things. Both Aragon, Fleg and, of course, Eluard have written little, it is true, but sufficient because effective poems on the subject. Anna Langfus, Simenon, Ikor, Elsa Triolet and Vercors have used the problems of readaptation or of the camp itself as themes to weave into their literary creations : the results are highly successful. Since poetry is the art of universalizing individual feelings, poems surpass *témoignages* by their very nature. They have thus become a literary theme. True, the works in which deportation is spoken of are not entirely devoted to that subject alone, but this is not important to us. What is important is that the theme of Nazi concentration camps enter literature, be thought of, reflected upon, written about and that it remain simultaneously in the realm of the sacred and in the realm of the literary, that certain literary forms do adopt it, without deforming it and incorporate it within themselves. Perhaps the most successful example of this attempt is Vercors' *Les Armes de la nuit*.

Certain writers, such as Del Castillo, have used the theme of the deportation to illustrate other social principles. The fact that Del Castillo concludes his book by showing that Tanguy remains as unadapted after camp as in the camp is Del Castillo's personal judgment which explains his concept of the world but which cannot stand as an interpretation of the camp. It enlightens us, therefore, about the author himself and not about the camp, since we do not have the feeling that it is the camp that rendered Tanguy inadaptable. We cannot accept what he has done because we feel it is a deformation of fact. The perspective in which they show the camp is distorted ; while we do not disagree with social criticism as they formulate it, we vehemently disagree with their way of presentation. The worst ills of society do not come close to the best of camp conditions. This is not our idle conclusion since the proof of it is in the fact that no deportee, in writing or speaking, that we have come across, has ever presented such a point of view.

Although we do not agree at all with the ideas of Del Castillo (discussed previously), and we do not find that Regina Wallet's work is truly a contribution to literature, we are indebted to those authors for trying to penetrate this realm of the macabre. Historians, of course whom we eliminate from the body of this book, have contributed to its formation and have furnished the background necessary for its creation. They are not deportees. Perhaps the most competent, Olga Wormser-Migot, was not deported and has published several works on the deportation which show to what extent a non-deportee can become involved with the subject and contribute to its immortality. Our only rebuke is directed against the form which the non-deportee uses to express himself on the question. We feel that the subject is not at all taboo, but because some do not have first-hand experience, they must restrict themselves to forms that do not diminish the authenticity and verisimilitude of what they write.

The traditional interpretation of the phenomenon of concentration camps, as explained by Communist Party doctrine, is that the camp is the inevitable end-product of the Capitalist society, and that it is the reduction of Capitalism to a caricature which exaggerates but does not basically distort. We do not agree with this interpretation. We agree with David Rousset when he says, in *L'Univers concentrationnaire* (p. 186), 'L'existence des camps est un avertissement'

13

but we cannot agree with the part of certain works that expresses the Party line. It is, however, entirely possible for the author to concur with the Party line and at the same time present an authentic image of camp life. We feel that Lafitte, Daix, Semprun and others may concur with the traditional party interpretation of the Nazi camps, but this in no way distorts the documentation presented in the works nor does it alter their literary quality or lack of it. Using the concentration camps as a political weapon is certainly as valid an idea as any, however the writer must be certain, we feel, not to distort facts in the process.

We do not have the pretention, in this treatise, of establishing the *palmarès* of the works that posterity will conserve but, by studying the various categories of works about concentration camps, we have hoped to show the criteria in the name of which they can be judged and at times, audaciously perhaps, attempted to guess which will remain as works of art in the eyes of future generations.

Appendix

I. CERTAIN LINGUISTIC PHENOMENA

Concentration camps were a strange phenomenon. They were a primitive phenomenon. They were a phenomenon new to their inmates and their staffs. They were a sacred phenomenon. This appendix is an attempt at elucidation of one part of the strange phenomenon : its linguistic manifestations. We shall attempt here to explain the meaning of various words. They were all words that were used in concentration camps, either by the SS or by the deportees. We have divided them into two groups accordingly. These words give a clue to the preoccupations of the inmates, their thoughts, their ways of manifesting their emotions, their relationships with their torturers. These words are important not only as vocabulary but when explicated will permit us to understand many of the books written about the camps. They are also a clue to the psychology of the Gestapo, the SS and the deportees. We learn, from these words alone, the mockery with which the torturers treated the inmates, the disdain which they showed them, the humility which they forced them to show. It is interesting to note that ordinary words appear out of place in the concentration camp context. For example, when André Bléton in *Le Temps du purgatoire* (p. 63) uses the word *'dîner'* to indicate that he would like to eat, it appears almost *précieux*. Françoise, in *Qui rapportera ces paroles* (p. 14), catches herself using the expression *'prendre froid'* and says *'cocasse'* : the most common idiom becomes foreign.

Since concentration camps were a phenomenon new to the history of man, since they contained many objects and places and involved many concepts not only foreign but previously non-existent, it was necessary to build a new vocabulary to deal with the phenomenon.

This was done in several ways : the master-slave relationship existing between men in the Roman Empire was revived and the more educated Nazis drew inspiration from this. More frequently, the SS and the Nazis built words from smaller words, as is common custom in the German language. But what was different there was that the words will give us one meaning and this is a new meaning : they never meant this before. The words will be both distortions and neologisms. Why were these neologisms necessary ? Calming the inmates, disillusioning them, were two techniques most basic to the Nazi psychology because the Nazis themselves could not face the horror of what they were doing. We know this to be case in certain instances. We also realize that the horror they felt was secondary to both the pleasure received from the abhorrent acts and the supposed necessity of their enactment. The words coined by the deportees were in some cases also neologisms, coming from a fear of death and a fear of spreading fear itself. They are also the result of the fact that the deportees came from different milieux, had different educational levels, spoke different languages and above all, that all of them did not understand German and that the SS and other *Proeminents* did not speak any other language. Therefore, the words were often corruptions of German words mouthed by the SS. For the Appendix, we have chosen, of the vocabulary used by the deportees, only those words which the French inmates would use and those likely to be found in books in French literature about the camps.

A. Deportees' Vocabulary

Achtzehn

Literally, eighteen in German. However, a corruption of *Achtung* made by the French deportees to mean 'someone is coming, be on the look-out'. (Bléton, p. 91.)

A la Tour

Literally, in French, to the tower. A corruption of the German *am Tore,* meaning 'to the door or at the gate'. To the prisoner it meant 'being called to the *Politische Abteilung*'. (Wormser-Migot.)

Aller se faire savon

Literally 'to have oneself made into soap'. This was used by the deportees as a synonym for 'to die' because the deportees knew the Nazis made soap from human bodies. (Borwicz, p. 108.)

Aller se faire matelas

Literally 'to have oneself made into a mattress'. Same meaning and explanation as for *aller se faire savon*. (Borwicz, p. 108.)

Anweisehrin

This appears with many spelling variations. It is a noun used by the deportees to designate one who guarded over them — another deportee. Corruption of the German verb *anweisen,* 'to supervise' and of *sehen,* 'to see'.

Armbinde

This literally means an armband. By extension, it came to mean a person — deportee — having a function within the camp, e.g. *Blockälteste.* Used by those deportees who spoke German to indicate : 'Es geht eine Armbinde'. (Documentation furnished by Dr. Mieczyslaw Maneli, of Polish origin, who spoke Polish and German. Incarcerated in May, 1943, first in Maidanek, then Auschwitz, and Monowitz. Escaped in transport in 1945.)

Auge

The German substantive *Auge* is the word for 'eye'. The word for 'look' in verb form is *sehen. Auge* was used among deportees as a substitute command for *sieh.* (Rousset, *Les Jours de notre mort,* p. 770.)

Bauernhäuser

Literally 'farmhouses'. In Auschwitz especially among the older deportees, the name given to the gas chambers. The name comes from the fact that in the beginning at the camp before the modern gas chambers were installed there were two miniature ones in the peasants' huts. (Borwicz, p. 108.)

Bétribe

Corrupt spelling, coined in Ravensbrück to designate the German word *Betrieb,* meaning 'a factory'. In Ravensbrück, the place where the deportees worked at sewing and other such tasks. (Documentation furnished by Charlotte Delbo, French, non-Jewish, political prisoner. Spoke some German. Auschwitz, Raisko, Ravensbrück, repatriated via Sweden in June 1945.)

Bibleforscher

Constructed from two separate German words : *Bibel* and *forschen,* meaning 'to seek'. This was the title of Jehovah's witnesses who were incarcerated in certain minor camps and generally not put into death camps ; they worked as babysitters, housemaids, etc., for the SS — were considered dangerous by the Nazis when free because of their beliefs and non-conformity. They were left to roam freely in the camp because they were obedient and thus trusted by the SS. (Source : see *Bétribe.*)

Café au lait

This is a corruption made by the French deportees of the words *Kaffee holen,* which literally means 'to get coffee'. The literal translation of the French words is 'coffee with milk'. This has nothing to do with the meaning of the expression in camp. It is the reproduction by a Frenchman not speaking German of a German command meaning to fetch the green tea and bring it to the barracks for the deportees. Term comes from Auschwitz-Birkenau ; may have been used elsewhere. (Documentation furnished by Lulu Thévenin, of French origin, speaking only French. Itinerary : Auschwitz, Raisko, Ravensbrück,

	Beendorf, repatriated via Sweden in June 1945.)

Canada

Term used in Auschwitz-Birkenau by deportees of all nationalities. The word had no other meaning for those not in camp except the geographical designation. However, in Auschwitz, it was the place where all clothes, baggage, and other personal effects were left by those entering the camp either to be gassed or become inmates. The deportees who worked here were closely watched to prevent stealing. It therefore sometimes signified a state of affluence because some stealing did take place. The word has now come to mean, in modern Polish, a state of wealth. (Source : see *Bétribe.*)

Chaise-colonne

As it is, this word has no meaning in French. Separately, the first part means 'chair' and the second means 'column'. In Ravensbrück, however, a corruption of the German *Scheisskolonne,* literally, 'shit-column'. The word does not exist as such in German but its two component words exist separately. This Kommando was in charge of emptying excrement, *Kolonne* being synonymous with Kommando in this case. This work was a punishment for a misdemeanor in camp. (Source : see *Café au lait.*)

Chusselle

This is the corruption of the German word *Schüssel* meaning 'a bowl'. The corruption was made by the French inmates. It specifically referred to a bowl in which soup was served, made of reddish-brown enamel, containing one liter. (Documentation furnished by Madeleine Doiret, itinerary same as that of Charlotte Delbo, speaks only French.)

Cigogne

In French, this literally means 'the stork'. However, in camp, it was the corruption of the German *Zigeuner,* meaning 'gypsy'. The normal French word for 'gypsy' is either *gitane, tsigane* or *tzigane.* (Source : see *Café au lait.*)

Claquette

Literally, in French, 'rattle of a musical instrument or rattling noise'. In Auschwitz, the shoes worn by the men, in Ravensbrück, by everyone. They are shoes with a cloth top and a wooden sole which makes a clopping or rattling sound when one walks, from whence their name. (Source : see *Chusselle.*)

Coiffe-tout

Corruption made by the French deportees of the German *Kopftuch,* 'kerchief' which all female deportees wore on their heads ; literally translated from the French it would be 'cap-all'. (Source : see *Chusselle.*)

C'te vache

Literally in French, this means 'this cow'. Corruption made by the French of the Polish order given by the Blockhova, *Stavache,* meaning 'stand up'. This was the command given to rouse the inmates to roll-call. Also possibly *te vache* or *cette vache.* (Source : see *Café au lait.*)

Draussen

This word exists in modern German and means 'to be outside, out of doors'. It had a special meaning among deportees whose native language was German : it meant 'to be free, out of camp, after the liberation' thus expressing a projection of the inmates into the future. (Source : see *Armbinde.*)

Gummi

Literally, in German, 'rubber'. A nightstick used to discipline the deportees, adopted as a word by all inmates in all camps, all nationalities.

Kapo	Word used in camp referring to a deportee with a function, usually head of a team or a column of deportees. Its origin has several possibilities : from Latin *caput,* meaning 'head' and by extension 'chief', or an abbreviation of *Kaporal,* or from the contraction of *Kamerad Polizei.* (Rousset, p. 771 ; see also *Armbinde* for source.)
Meister	Literally 'a master'. In camp, the civilian foreman.
Micheline	French corruption of the German word *Mischlinge,* meaning 'a half-Jew'. These were generally sent to camps such as Ravensbrück, not *Vernichtungsläger.* (Source : see *Café au lait.*)
Musulman	Literally, 'a Moslem', however, in camp, a deportee dying of typhus. The word probably derives from the thought of thin, starving Arabs. Characterized by brown skin, huge eyes and also by the fact that the *musulman* always wrapped himself in his blanket in the manner of the Arabs. Can be used either as a noun or an adjective, e. g. 'At that time, I was still a *musulman*' — in this case, it would mean 'not yet cured of typhus'. (Documentation furnished by Maria-Elisa Nordman, Auschwitz, Raisko, Ravensbrück, Mauthausen, repatriated June 30, 1945, speaks French and some German.)
Nachlage	This does not exist as a German substantive. It exists as *nachlegen,* meaning 'to add to'. In camp, 'a spoonful of supplementary soup when there was some left in the bottom of the pot'. Also see *Rab.* (Source : see *Chusselle.*)
Narchich	Literally, 'night-layer' and by extension 'night-shift'. Our spelling is the French corruption

of the German *Nachtschicht*. In camp, came to mean 'a Kommando sent out to work at night'. (Source : see *Musulman*.)

Officiérine

Same meaning as *Anweiserin*, except that it wass an SS female guard. Same derivation. (Source : see *Café au lait*.)

Organiser

In German, *organisieren*, meaning 'to organize'. But, in all camps, meaning 'to steal' : e. g. 'I organized an onion'. (Source : see *Bétribe*.)

Pipel

Also spelled *Piepel*. Origin ambiguous. A boy selected by the Block Chiefs for their sexual practices. Used in Auschwitz, possibily elsewhere, to designate the boy that would engage in these activities with the men. (Katzetnik 135 633, *Atrocity*. New York, 1963, p. 7.)

Pitchipoi

Used in Drancy to indicate Auschwitz. A neologism, probably coined by the children as their corruption of 'Pithiviers', another camp in France from which people were deported. Connotation in Drancy : 'a place that inspired fear'. (Documentation furnished by Mina Arker, Drancy 1942-1945, speaking French only.)

Proeminent

From the Latin *prominens, prominentis*. Designated a camp VIP. Had always a pejorative meaning when used by camp left-wingers. Could refer to a deportee in charge or an SS. In this book, however, it has a pejorative meaning and is used to indicate any functionary considered part of 'them'. (Source : see *Armbinde*.)

Rał

Shortening for *rabiot,* used by the French army to designate 'a food supplement'. Same meaning in camp. (Source : see *Musulman*.)

Révir

Corruption of the German *Krankenrevier* made

by the French. Literally, 'sick-bay'. Used to designate the camp infirmary which was sometimes one of the worst places in the camp.

Shmusstik

This is a corruption of the German *Schmutzstück*, literally meaning 'dirty piece'. The word does not exist in normal German. It could refer to a young boy engaging in homosexual relations with an SS man. Otherwise, it was a term used by the SS to designate 'a deportee'. Variation *Shmustik*. (Source : see *Café au lait*.)

Sortir par la cheminée

Literally, 'to leave by the chimney'. Used by the prisoners to designate 'dying and being cremated'. (Borwicz, p. 105.)

Standstehen

This word does not exist in normal German. Literally, 'to stay standing'. In Auschwitz, collective punishment that consisted of standing still for many hours in ranks. (Source : see *Café au lait*.)

Trage

Also spelled *trague*. German for 'handbarrow' that was adopted by all deportees to mean the same. (Source : see *Café au lait*.)

Transport

Used in all languages to mean a group of deportees taken from one camp to another, or taken out of camp to do work. Destination always unknown to the deportees.

Transport noir

Transport from a camp to a death camp, e. g. from Plaszow to Auschwitz. (Source : see *Café au lait*.)

Tsoulage

Corruption of the German *Zulage*, meaning 'a food supplement', in camp usually bread. (Documentation furnished by Christine Borras, whose itinerary follows that of Thévenin, Lulu. Speaks only French.)

Verfugtbar	French corruption possibly of the German *furchtbar,* meaning 'awful' or *verfügbar,* meaning 'available'. Meant the deportees employed at the worst jobs. (Source : see *Tsoulage.*)

B. Nazi and SS Terminology

The comparative ranks of the American army and the SS (Collin and Lapierre, *Is Paris Burning?*, p. 345).

SS Reichsführer	General of the Army
Oberstgruppenführer	General
Gruppenführer	Major General
Brigadeführer	Brigadeer General
Oberführer	- - - - - - - - - - -
Standartenführer	Colonel
Obergruppenführer	Lieutenant General
Obersturmbannführer	Lieutenant Colonel
Sturmbannführer	Major
Hauptsturmführer	Captain
Obersturmführer	First Lieutenant
Untersturmführer	Second Lieutenant
Hauptscharführer	Warrant Officer

Abdirigieren	This word does not exist in spoken German. The word *dirigieren,* which does exist, means 'to give a command'. With the separable prefix *ab,* the word comes to mean 'to countermand'. For the Nazis, a neologism for 'to kill' or possibly 'to direct away', 'to cancel out a life'. (Borwicz, p. 98 ; explanation is ours.)
Abholen	This word exists in spoken German. It means 'to fetch' or 'to collect' referring either to people or objects. The meaning here is 'to lead back to', as to lead back to from whence we have come...' Dust to dust... (Borwicz, p. 98.)

Abschieben	The word exists in modern German and has the meaning 'to push' or 'to shove off'. The meaning here is 'to push off the earth', by extension a neologism for 'to kill'. (Borwicz, p. 98.)
Abtransportieren	This word exists in German and has the meaning of 'to relocate', 'send away' or 'transfer'. Neologism for 'putting to death', in the sense of relocating, as from ghetto to gas chamber. (Borwicz, p. 98.)
Abziehen	This word exists in German and means 'to borrow' or 'take away from'. In an idiomatic use, can mean 'to skin', as to skin an animal. Neologism for 'to kill', possibly as an extension of 'to skin alive' or 'to take life away from'. (Borwicz, p. 98.)
Auffliegen	Normally means 'to fly up'. Neologism for 'to kill', as an extension of 'to fly to heaven'. (Borwicz, p. 98.) The number of neologisms that we have found for 'to kill' is suprising and shows an interesting trend. It is even more curious to us that the Nazis would conceive of a heaven or that they presume that those they kill would go there — one does not usually presume that the scum of the earth will go to heaven.
Aufgehen	Usually 'to open' or, idiomatically, 'to rise', as a cake does. When used in camp, meant 'to open ranks'. (Rousset, p. 770.)
Aufheben	'To lift up', as in 'to lift up something in one's hand', or 'to keep', or 'to deprive'. Another neologism — 'to deprive of life' or 'to kill'. (Borwicz, p. 98.)
Auflösen	In regular German this word means 'to dissolve'. By extension, it could mean 'to dis-

solve a human life', and in this way become another neologism for 'to kill'. (Borwicz, p. 98.)

Behandler

The usual German word for a medical doctor is *Arzt,* but this term implies some respect. The verb used to describe what a doctor does to his patients, 'to treat', is *behandeln. Behandler* was a noun coined from a verb by the SS to designate 'an incarcerated Jewish doctor', working as a doctor in the camp. (Source : see *Armbinde.*)

Blockälteste

Composed by the Nazis in camp from two German words, *Block,* meaning 'a barrack' *Alteste,* meaning 'senior' or 'elder'. Thus, the deportee designated as head of the *Block.*

Blockhova

A combination made from the German *Block* and the Polish ending *hova* designating a woman. Same as *Blockälteste.*

Dreiecke

Literally, 'triangle'. Different triangles were used to designate the deportees and the same color generally meant the same thing in all camps :
Blue : Spanish — only in Mauthausen.
Pink : homosexuals.
Red : political prisoners.
Violet : Jehovah's Witnesses.
Green : robbers, common criminals.
Black : droit communs, asociaux. Also, a German woman who cuckholded her husband with a prisoner of war or a Jew, etc.

Duschen

Literally, 'showers'. Euphemism for gas chambers.

Effektenkammer

Word not existing in normal German but compounded from two normal words : *Kammer,* meaning 'room' and *Effekten,* meaning 'effects'

as in the effects of the dead. Where the effects of the inmates were stored until they left and where uniforms were kept. (Source : see *Café au lait*.)
Also, *Effekts*.

Entlassen   Literally, 'to release' or 'set free', but a neologism for 'putting to death'. (Borwicz, p. 98.)

Entnehmen   German word meaning 'to take out', 'to get from' ; meaning in camp same as *abziehen*. (Borwicz, p. 98.)

Entziehen   Same as *Entnehmen*.

Erledigen   In German, 'to finish', as to finish work. For the Nazis, 'to finish off', as to 'finish him off', 'to kill'. Another neologism. (Borwicz, p. 98.)

Fertig werden   Literally, 'to come to the end'. Explanation same as above.

Figur   Literally, 'a statue', 'figure' or 'shape'. Used by the camp hierarchy to designate a man in a very pejorative sense : e. g. 'let the *Figur* bring the rocks'. (Source : see *Armbinde*.)

Fundsachen   Literally, 'found things'. The confiscated goods of the inmates or gassed deportees. (Rousset, p. 770.)

Gestapo   Shortening of *Geheime Staatspolizei*. The security organization of the Nazi Party that inflicted its reign of terror. (Wiesenthal, p. 105.)

Goldjuden   Literally, 'the Jews of Gold'. Those Jews who sorted out gold, money, jewels, etc., brought to camp by those to be gassed. (Source : see *Tsoulage*.)

Häftlingszahnstation   Word found in official German documents and used in camp to mean the place where gold was removed from the teeth of gassed deportees. When broken down : 'prisoner dental station'. Word used to camouflage the purpose of the 'station'. (Borwicz, p. 98.)

Himmelfahrtblock

Literally, 'ascension barrack', by extension, 'the road to heaven'. The barrack where those who were about to die were kept. (Borwicz, p. 98.)

Himmelkommando

Compound meaning 'heaven' and 'squad'. Refers to those who worked in the crematorium. Same as *Sonderkommando*.

Kalifaktor

Word probably coined from the German *Kali*, meaning 'potash', which is the reusable residue of a burnt body, and *Faktor*, German for 'factor'. In camp : 'one who cleaned', 'one who helped', a manservant of an SS man : one of the best jobs. (Source : see *Armbinde*.)

Kaninchen

Literally, 'rabbits'. Shortening in camp for *Versuchskaninchen*, meaning 'guinea-pigs'. In camp, the human beings upon whom medical experiments were performed. (Source : see *Bétribe*.)

Krankenbau

For meaning, see *Révir*. The normal word for hospital in German is *Krankenhaus*. However, since the deportees were not human, they could not have a house. Their hospital was literally called 'building of the sick'. (Source : see *Armbinde*.)

Kugelaktion

Literally, 'bullet-action'. In Mauthausen, the assassination of prisoners of war, sometimes with a bullet in the back of the head as they walked down a long corridor, the SS behind them. (Borwicz, p. 102.)

Lagerschutz

Literally, 'camp protection'. Police used to protect the SS in the camp and see that they were respected. (Borwicz, p. 102.)

Meeresschaumaktion	Literally, 'the action of the waves of the sea'. Used by the SS of Buchenwald to designate 'prisoners in transport from Compiègne'. (Borwicz, p. 101.)
Mensch	German word for 'human being'. However, in camp, this word had a derogatory undertone, implying sub-humanity. Parallel to *Figur*. Very often a dog was called a '*Mensch*' and a man was called a '*Hund*'.
NN	Abbreviation for *Nacht und Nebel,* 'a deportee kept in isolation'. Literally, 'night and fog'. In camp, deportees not permitted letters or packages in or out. (Source : see *Bétribe*.)
Operation Rheinhardt	Thus designated in hommage to Heydrich Rheinhardt who began this operation, continued by the Czechoslovakians. The recuperation of the fortunes, personal effects and jewels, gold, of the deportees, in all camps, but especially of the Jews, later sent to the Reich banks.
Politische Abteilung	Literally, 'the Political Division' where deportees might be interrogated — and tortured. The *état civil*. (Delbo, *Le Convoi du 24 janvier,* p. 21.)
Schutzstaffel	Protection group : the SS.
Sicherheitsdienst	Literally, 'security service'. For the Nazis, the SD, 'elite of the SS'. (Wiesenthal, p. 339.)
Sonderkommando	Literally, 'special squad'. Came to mean same as *Himmelkommando*. (Abbreviation : *Sonder*.)
Straffblock	Literally, 'punishment barrack', where the deportees were sent to be punished.
Straffkolonne	Also called *Straffkommando,* a discipline squad where deportees were sent to work at the worst jobs as punishment for misdemeanors. (Delbo, *Le Convoi du 24 janvier,* p. 217.)

Stubendienst	Literally, 'room employment'. By extension, the one who did the barrack housework.
Stubhova	Same as *Stubälteste,* derives as does *Blockhova.*
Stück	Literally, 'a thing'. Used to designate a man by the SS in a derogatory way. (Source : see *Café au lait.*)
Tischälteste	Literally, 'table-senior'. There were no tables in most camps, so this designated 'the person who distributed bread'. (Source : see *Armbinde.*)
Totenjuden	The Jews who handled the bodies and the gas chambers. Literally, 'the Jews of the dead'. (Source : see *Armbinde.*)
Zu fünf	'To five', the command to line up in ranks of five.

2. LIST OF PRINCIPAL CAMPS*

AUSCHWITZ-BIRKENAU	(Kattowice)
BELZEC	(Lvov)
BERGEN-BELSEN	(Hanover)
BUCHENWALD	(Weimar)
DACHAU	(Munich)
DORA	(Leipzig)
ESTERWEGEN	(Oldenburg)
FLOSSENBURG	(Pilsen)
GROSS-ROSEN	(Breslaw)
MAIDANEK-LUBLIN	(Lublin)
MAUTHAUSEN	(Linz)
NATZWEILER-STRUTHOF	(Strasburg)
NEUBREMM	(Carlsruhe)
NEUENGAMME	(Hamburg)
OSNABRUCK	(Münster)
PLASZOW	(Cracow)
RAVENSBRUCK	(Berlin)
RIGA	(Lettonia)
SACHSENHAUSEN-ORANIENBURG	(Berlin)
SOBIBOR	(Brest-Litovsk)
STUTTHOF	(Danzig)
THERESIENSTADT	(Prague)
TREBLINKA	(Warsaw)

* Olga Wormser-Migot, *Quand les Alliés ouvrirent les portes* (Paris, 1965), from map on pages 15-16. City in parenthesis is the city nearest to which the camp site was located.

14 *

3. Principal 'Kommandos'* and the Camps they depended upon

Kommando	Camp
Barth	Ravensbrück
Buna	Auschwitz
Ebensee	Mauthausen
Ellrich	Dora
Gandersheim	Buchenwald
Gleiwitz	Auschwitz
Gusen	Mauthausen
Hartheim	Mauthausen
Holleischen	Ravensbrück
Hradisko	Flossenburg
Jawischowitz	Auschwitz
Laura	Dora
Mackenrode	Buchenwald
Melk	Mauthausen
Monowitz	Auschwitz
Neubrandenburg	Ravensbrück
Nordhausen	Dora
Porta Westphalica	Neuengamme
Raisko	Auschwitz
Ratibor	Auschwitz
Siemens	Ravensbrück
Tarnowitz	Auschwitz
Torgau	Ravensbrück
Vaihingen	Buchenwald
Wattenstedt	Neuengamme
Zwodau	Ravensbrück

* Term used to designate a camp affiliate. Also, a group of deportees designated for a particular job (e.g. Painting Kommando). Further used to mean 'a transport' (i.e. 'to go out in a Kommando'). List compiled in consultation with O. Wormser-Migot.

Bibliography

LIST OF WORKS CONSULTED

This book is based on works of French literature only. It does not include works of any other nationality. However, it will be noted that in this bibliography, there are occasionally English and other language titles. These are generally either secondary sources or background material used to document the historical portion of this book. There is virtually no secondary source material on this subject : while there are newspaper and magazine articles of criticism on the books, usually appearing shortly after their publication, we have generally not included them because we find that they had little if any influence on the work presented here. It is very interesting to note that many of these works were published without editor, that is to say, at the author's expense. This indicates to us a strong desire to tell, to make known, a desire that surpassed any financial considerations, which we find both unusual and commendable. These works are very difficult to locate : some are found in the Jewish Memorial in Paris, at the Bibliothèque Nationale, and others, only *chez l'auteur.* We have attempted to make this bibliography as complete as possible, not so much in the listing of historical documentation, as rather in the *témoignages,* etc., that compose the basis for the body of the study. As an addendum we have indicated those works (this list is only partial) in which deportation, or deportees, is mentioned, but where this is not the principal subject of the work. These are generally the works of non-deportees. The bibliography was compiled principally at Yivo Institute in New York, the Bibliothèque du Centre de documentation juive contemporaine in Paris (called the Jewish Memorial elsewhere here) and utilized other bibliographies compiled previously — for example, those of Olga Wormser-Migot and Chantal d'Audiffret, among others. There are few bibliographies of French literature on the camps and we can only hope that our list is complete.

Aimé Denise (1945), *Relais des errants,* Paris, Desclée de Brouwer.

Alcan Louise (1945), *Sans armes et sans bagages,* Limoges, Imprimerie d'Art.

Alexandre Henri (1959), *Ceux qu'emporte le train,* Paris, Scorpion.

Almeras Charles (1958), *Le Christ... au bagne,* Paris, Paulines.

Alter Robert (1969), *After the Tradition,* New York, Dutton. (Secondary source on Elie Wiesel)

Amery Odette and Champier Martin G. (1945), *Nuit et brouillard,* Paris, Berger-Levrault.

Ammar Charles (1948), *KW 4,* Lyon, Editions du Coq.

Antelme Robert (1947), *L'Espèce humaine,* Paris, Gallimard.

Anthologie des poèmes de Buchenwald (1946), Paris, Laffont.

Aragon Louis (1946), *Le musée Grévin,* Paris, Editeurs Français Réunis.

Arega Léon (1964), *Aucune trace,* Paris, Gallimard.
— (1964), *Comme si c'était fini,* Paris, Gallimard.

Armand and Givre, Abbés (1948), *Un témoin du Christ parmi les déportés,* Paris, Témoignage Chrétien.

Aroneanu Eugène (1945), *Camps de concentration,* Paris, Office français d'édition (Collection : Témoignages).

Arvet Henri and Boissard F. (1948), *Des geôles de la Gestapo de Dijon à l'enfer de Buchenwald et Dora,* Dijon, Darantière.

Audiffret Chantal d' (1959), *Essai de bibliographie sur l'histoire de la déportation française dans les camps de concentration nazis* (Diplôme de documentaliste, Conservatoire des Arts et Métiers, Institut national des techniques documentaires).

Bannerot Hélène (1962), *La Conjoncture,* Paris, Casterman.

Baranski Jan (1956), *Mon pays perdu, 1939-1951,* Paris, Les Iles d'or.

Barber J. (1946), *Les Spectres de la faim,* Paris, Janot.

Barondeau R. P. (1948), *Une Ordination sacerdotale au KZ de Dachau,* Strasbourg, Le Roux.

Bauer Anne-Marie (1957), *La Vigie aveugle,* Paris, Mercure de France.
— (1959), *La route qui poudroie,* Paris, Corti.

Bent Philippe (1958), *L'Attente de la mort dans les camps du Neckar,* Toulouse, Imprimerie Régionale.

Berger Pierre (1960), *Robert Desnos,* Paris, Seghers (Collection : Poètes d'aujourd'hui).

Bernadac Christian (1967), *Les Médecins maudits,* Paris, France-Empire.
— (1968), *Les Médecins de l'impossible,* Paris, France-Empire.

Bernard Jean-Jacques (1944), *Le Camp de la mort lente,* Paris, Albin-Michel.

Bernard Martha H. (1958), *Deux ans dans les camps de concentration nazis,* Paris, Le Déporté.

Bernet Claude (1946), *Rescapé 57961,* Paris, Godet.

Berrard Germain (1947), *La Route du bagne,* Nîmes, Imprimerie Richelieu.

Beschet (1946), *Mission en Thuringe,* Paris, Editions Ouvrières.

Bessy Maurice (1960), *Car c'est Dieu qu'on enterre,* Paris, Albin-Michel.

Billig Joseph (1967), *L'Hitlérisme et le système concentrationnaire,* Paris, Presses Universitaires de France.

Biosca Marius (1947), *De la Résistance à Dachau,* Nîmes, Imprimerie Richelieu.

Birin Frère (n.d.), *Seize mois de bagnes,* Epernay, Dauville.

Birkenau, bagne de femmes (1945), Paris, Nathan (Collection : Révélations, Petite Encyclopédie de la Résistance).

Birnbaum Suzanne (1945), *Une Française juive est revenue,* Paris, Edition du Livre Français.

Blanc Aimé (1947), *Français ne l'oubliez pas,* Paris, Plon.

Blécourt André (1945), *De la Résistance au bagne,* Paris, Nathan.

Bléton André (1953), *Le Temps du Purgatoire,* Paris, Tequi.

Bonifas Aimé (1968), *Détenu 20801,* Paris, Delachaux et Nestlé.

Bonte Florimond (1964), *6 Millions de crimes,* Paris, Editions Sociales.

Borwicz Michel (1954), *Ecrits des condamnés à mort,* Paris, Presses Universitaires de France.

Bosquet Adrien (1945), *Hors des barbelés,* Paris. Spes.

Boutbien Léon (n.d.), *Le Gourou,* chez l'auteur.

Bouteille Marie-Jeanne (1946), *Infernal rébus,* Moulins, Crépin Leblond.
— (1948), *Carrefour en Bohème,* Vichy, Imprimerie Wallon.

Bradley Jean (1948), *Jours francs,* Paris, Julliard.

Briquet Georges (1945), *Rescapé de l'enfer nazi,* Paris, La France au Cantal.

Bulawko Henry (1954), *Les Jeux de la mort et de l'espoir,* Paris, A.A.D.J.F.

Cayrol Jean (1946), *Poèmes de la nuit et du brouillard,* Paris, Seghers.
— (1947), *Je vivrai l'amour des autres,* Paris, Seuil.
— (1949), *Les Poètes emprisonnés,* Paris, Seghers.
— (1950), *Lazare parmi nous,* Paris, Seuil.
— (1968), *Je l'entends encore,* Paris, Seuil.

Chambon Albert (1961), *81490*, Paris, Flammarion.

Chansonniers à Buchenwald (1949), Paris, Templier.

Chaplet Pierre (1947), *Häftling 43485*, Paris, Charlot.

Chateau Gilberte (1949), *L'Enfer de Ravensbrück*, Paris, Rouff.

Chauvenec André (n.d.), *Une expérience de l'esclavage*, Paris, Office Général du Livre.

Chetaneau Abbé Roger (1947), *Le Christ chez les rayés par le n° 31397*, Fontenay, Lussand.

Cigalette (1946), *Poèmes de la captivité*, Paris, Egix.

Closset René (1964), *L'Aumônier de l'enfer*, Mulhouse, Salvation.

Cohen Albert (1954), *Le Livre de ma mère*, Paris, Gallimard. *

Cohen Guy (1954), *Retour d'Auschwitz*, Paris, Leroi.

Collette Paul (1946), *J'ai tiré sur Laval*, Caen, Ozanne.

Coquet James de (1945), *Nous sommes les occupants*, Paris, Fayard.

Couroble Alice (1946), *Amie des Juifs*, Paris, Bloud et Gay.

Crémieux Julie Dunand (1945), *La Vie à Drancy*, Paris, Gedalge.

Daix Pierre (n.d.), *La Dernière forteresse*, Paris, Editeurs Français Réunis.

Darriet Claude (1946), *Intermède*, Paris, Susse.

David Abbé (1950), *Du bagne français au bagne nazi*, Saint-Lô, Leclerc.

Daville J. and Wichene S. (1945), *Drancy la Juive*, Paris, Berger Frères.

Debouzi Roger (1949), *A marée basse*, Paris, Achesse.

Debrise Gilbert (1945), *Cimetières sans tombeaux*, Paris, Bibliothèque française.

Delarue Jacques (1962), *L'Histoire de la Gestapo*, Paris, Fayard.

Delbo Charlotte (1965), *Aucun de nous ne reviendra*, Paris, Gonthier ; and (1970), Paris, Editions de Minuit.

— (1965), *Le Convoi du 24 janvier*, Paris, Editions de Minuit.

— (1970), *Une connaissance inutile*, Paris, Editions de Minuit.

— (1971), *Mesure de nos jours*, Paris, Editions de Minuit.

— *Ceux qui avaient choisi*, chez l'auteur.

— *Une scène jouée dans la mémoire*, chez l'auteur.

— *Un métro nommé Lénine*, chez l'auteur.

— *Qui rapportera ces paroles*, chez l'auteur.

* Prix Goncourt.

Del Castillo Michel (1957), *Tanguy,* Paris, Julliard.

Delfieu Maurice (1947), *Récits d'un revenant,* Paris, Indicateur Universel des P.T.T.

Demaine Michèle (1946), *La Banque de Dante,* Paris, Rivade.

Déportation (La) (1967), Ouvrage collectif, F.N.D.I.R.P.

Desanti Dominique (1960), *Les Grands sentiments,* Paris, Grasset.

Desnos Robert : see Pierre Berger.

Desnos Youki (1957), *Les Confidences de Youki,* Paris, Fayard.

Diamant-Berger (1947), *La Prison tragique,* Monte-Carlo, Solar.

Dory Henny (1960), *La Nuit de la Passion,* Paris, Julliard.

Drori Paul (1948), *Matricule 5586,* Paris, Polyglottes.

Dufournier Denise (1945), *La Maison des mortes,* Paris, Hachette.

Du Fresne Madeleine (1947), *De l'enfer des hommes à la cité de Dieu,* Paris, Spes.

Dumur Renée (1948), *Le Train de la mort,* Paris.

Ecrivains en prison (1945), Paris, Seghers.

Elina Odette (1948), *Sans fleurs ni couronnes,* Bourges, Boulet.

Eluard Paul (1952), *Poèmes pour tous,* Paris, Editeurs Français réunis.

Enfants de Buchenwald (Les) (1946), Geneva, Union O.S.E.

Eskenazi Raoul (1962), *Elie le Malvenu,* Paris, Julliard.

Eydoux Emmanuel (1960), *Ghetto à Varsovie,* Marseille, chez l'auteur.
— (1967), *Le Dernier pourimspiel des orphelins du docteur Janusz Korkczak.* Marseille, chez l'auteur.

Felloni Madeleine (n.d.), *Voyage en enfer,* Châlons-sur-Marne, Imprimerie Union Républicaine de la Marne.

Fleg Edmond 1954), *Ecoute Israël,* Paris, Flammarion.

Fliecx Michel (n.d.), *Pour délit d'espérance,* Evreux, Imprimerie Merissy.

Fronzac Charles (1947), *Le Fil d'Ariane,* Paris, Aux Armes de France.

Fournier Emile (1945), *En prison,* Badonviller, Poupier-Wernert.

Fournier Pierre (1953), *Le Temps des morts,* Paris, Gallimard.

Françaises à Ravensbrück (Les) (1965), Paris, Gallimard. (Collected eye-witness reports, edited by the Amicale de Ravensbrück and Association des Déportés et Internés de la Résistance.)

Francis Louis (1947), *Jusqu'à Bergen,* Paris, Vigneau.

Franqueville Robert (1946), *Rien à signaler,* Paris, Attinger.

Fraysse René (1946), *De Francfort à Dachau,* Annonay, Editions du Sol.

Frejafon D. (1947), *Bergen-Belsen,* Paris, Valois.

Friang Brigitte (1970), *Regarde-toi qui meurs,* Paris, Laffont.

Frossard L. (1945), *La Maison des otages,* Paris, Editions du Livre Français.

Garin J.-P. (1946), *La Vie dure,* Lyon, Audin.

Garnier Roger (1948), *Ils ont ainsi vécu,* Besançon, Imprimerie Jacques et Demonhard.

Gascar Pierre (1953), *Le Temps des morts,* Paris, Gallimard. *

Gatti Armand (n.d.), *L'Enfant rat,* Paris, Seuil.

— (n.d.), *La Deuxième existence du camp de Tatenberg,* Paris, Seuil.

Gatti Armand and Michaud Jean (1962), *L'Enclos,* Paris, Fayard.

Gaussen Dominique (1966), *Le Kapo,* Paris, France-Empire.

Gavet Jacqueline (1945), *Pierre Argout,* Auxerre, Imprimerie de l'Yonne Républicaine.

Gely Roger (1947), *Neuengamme,* Clermont-Ferrand, Nouvelle Imprimerie Moderne.

Geoffroy Jean (1948), *Au Temps des crématoires,* Cavaillon, Imprimerie Michal.

Granier Jacques (1948), *Schirmeck,* Strasbourg, Dernières Nouvelles.

Grenard Michel (1953), *La Nuit, les armes et l'amour,* Paris, Seghers.

Grenier Fernand (1959), *C'était ainsi,* Paris, Editions Sociales.

Grossmann Vassili (1945), *L'Enfer de Treblinka,* Paris, Arthaud.

Grotowski Jerzy (n.d.), *Exemple d'un traitement de texte : Acropolis.* Wroclaw.

Guillon Denis (1946), *Matricule 51186,* Paris, Imprimerie Mary.

Halkin Léon (1947), *A l'ombre de la mort,* Paris, Casterman.

Heim Roger (1947), *La Sombre route,* Paris, Corti.

Henocque Abbé (1947), *Les Antres de la bête,* Paris, Durassie.

Hertz Robert (1946), *La Mort,* Paris, Editions de Minuit.

Hervé Annie (1946), *Rencontres internationales,* Paris, Chroniques de Minuit.

Hessel Stéphane (1946), 'Entre leurs mains', *Temps Modernes,* I, 6 (mars) : 1009-1083.

* Prix Goncourt.

Honel Maurice (1947), *Prophétie des accouchements,* Paris, F.N.D.I.R.P.

Hornung Albert (1945), *Le Struthof,* Paris, La Nouvelle Revue Critique.

Huk Cécile (1958), *Et le ciel restera bleu,* Paris, Scorpion.

Janvier Emile (1952), *Retour,* Alençon, Imprimerie Alençonnaise.

Jauzine (1946), *Quatre ans dans les bagnes hitlériens,* n.p.

Jean Paul (1947), *Matricule 39727, chaînes et lumières,* Béthune, Logier.

Jorand Abbé (n.d.), *Les Camps de la mort,* Nancy, Wagner.

Joyon Charles (1957), *Qu'as-tu fait de ta jeunesse?* Paris, Lacoste.

Julitte Pierre (1965), *L'Arbre de Goethe,* Paris, Presses de la Cité.

Kahn Lothar (1968), *Mirrors of the Jewish Mind,* Cranbury, Yoseloff.

Kauffman Charles (1946), *L'Entreprise de la mort lente,* Nancy, Imprimerie Nancéenne.

Kessel Joseph (1963), *Tous n'étaient pas des anges,* Paris, Plon.

Kessel Sim (1970), *Pendu à Auschwitz,* Paris, Solar.

Kogon Eugène (n.d.), *The Theory and Practice of Hell,* New York, Farrar and Straus. (Translation of *Der Staat SS.*)

Kozlik François (1945), *Le Struthof,* Strasbourg, Sedal.

Lacour-Gayet Michel (1947), *Un déporté comme un autre,* Paris, S.P.I.D.

Lafitte Jean (1947), *Ceux qui vivent,* Paris, Hier et Aujourd'hui.

— (1965), *Le lac aux rêves,* Paris, Hier et Aujourd'hui.

Lafond-Masudet Etienne (1946), *Buchenwald, Dora, etc.,* Louviers, Drai.

Lahaye Simone (1954), *Les Rachetées,* Paris, Durassie.

— (1954), *Un homme libre parmi les morts,* Paris, Durassie.

Laks Simon and Coudy René (1948), *Musique d'un autre monde,* Paris, Mercure de France.

Lang André (1960), *Bagage à la Consigne,* Paris, Gallimard.

Lapierre Dominique and Collins Larry (1965), *Is Paris Burning?,* New York, Simon and Schuster.

Laromiguière Jean de (1946), *La Dame à l'ombrelle,* Paris, Lacoste.

Lebas Maurice (1948), *Pierre de Porcaro,* Paris, Lethie.

Leboucher Marcel (1950), *Souvenirs de bagne d'un grand-père — de Caen à Oranienburg,* Caen, Ozanne.

Le Gallois J. (1948), *Combat pour nos cadavres,* Paris, Fortuny.

Le Guillerme Marc (1946), *Hors la vie,* Paris, Fasquelle.

Leloir Père (1945), *Je reviens de l'enfer,* Paris, Rendez-Vous.

Lemeur Léon (1948), *L'Abbé Joseph Tanguy,* Anjou, Imprimerie de l'Anjou.

Leproux Marc (1947), *Nous les terroristes,* Monte-Carlo.

Levasseur Raymond (1948), *Les Loups de Germanie,* Pacy-sur-Eure, Imprimerie de la Vallée d'Eure.

Leverrier G. (1945), *Une Française dans la tourmente,* Paris, Emile-Paul.

Lhotte Céline (1947), *Et pendant six ans,* Paris, Bloud et Gay.

Livre du pain et de la peur (Le) (1946), Paris, Solar.

Lohéac Paul (1949), *Un médecin français en déportation,* Paris, Bonne Presse.

Loustaunau-Lacau Georges (1945), *Chiens maudits,* Paris, Durassie.

— (1948), *Mémoires d'un Français rebelle,* Paris, Laffont.

Lusseyran Jacques (n.d.), *Et la Lumière fut,* Paris, La Table Ronde.

— (n.d.), *Silence des Hommes,* Paris, La Table Ronde.

Magnan Pierre (1945), *L'Aube insolite,* Paris, Julliard.

Mallat Robert (1965), *Poèmes de la mort juive,* Honfleur, Pierre-Jean Oswald.

Mallet Mireille (1949), *Sous le signe du triangle,* Dijon, Jotard.

Malraux André (1965), *Anti-mémoires,* Paris, Gallimard.

Manchester William (1964), *The Arms of Krupp,* Boston, Little Brown.

Marette Fanny (1954), *J'étais le n° 47177,* Paris, Laffont.

Marnot René (1945), *18 Mois au bagne de Buchenwald,* Tours, La Nouvelle République.

Martin-Chauffier Louis (1947), *L'Homme et la bête,* Paris, Gallimard.

Masset Robert (1949), *A l'ombre de la croix gammée,* Argenton-sur-Creuse, Langlois.

Masurel Etienne (n.d.), *Buchenwald,* Louviers, Drai.

Matricule 55310. Birkenau (1945), Anonymous, Paris, Nathan.

Maurel Micheline (1957), *Un camp très ordinaire,* Paris, Editions de Minuit.

— (1958), *La Vie normale,* Paris, Editions de Minuit.

— (1965), *La Passion selon Ravensbrück,* Paris, Editions de Minuit.

Maurice Violette (1946), *N N.* Saint Etienne, S.P.E.R.

Maury Louis (1947), *Quand la haine élève un temple,* Evreux, Imprimerie de l'Eure.

Mazeaud H.L.J.P. (1946), *Visages dans la tourmente,* Paris, Albin-Michel.

Mennesson Hortense (1949), *Ma vie au bagne,* Laon, Bruneteau.

Meri Michel (n.d.), *Histoires d'un autre monde,* Toulouse, Victoire.

Merisse (n.d.), *Poèmes et chants du camp de Dora,* Cosne, Poussière.

Merle Robert (1952), *La Mort est mon métier,* Paris, Gallimard.

Michaut François and Edouard (1945), *Esclavage pour une résurrection,* Bagneux, Le Cep.

Michelet Edmond (1955), *La Rue de la Liberté,* Paris, Seuil,

Miller Serge (1947), *Le Laminoir,* Paris, Calmann-Lévy.

Monteyron Camille (n.d.), *Une victime de Flossenburg — le colonel François de Sauvebœuf,* Niort, Imprimerie Saint-Denis.

Morelli M.-G. (1947), *Terre de détresse,* Paris, Bloud et Gay.

Morse Arthur (1968), *While Six Million Died,* New York, Random House.

Mutter André (1944), *Face à la Gestapo,* Paris, Librairie Champion.

Mutz Pierre (1946), *6773,* chez l'auteur.

Naas Marcel (1943), *Mémoires de quatre ans et demi KL,* Mulhouse, Imprimerie Union.

Nassiet Robert (1949), *A l'ombre de la croix gammée,* Indre, Langlois.

Nonn Hughes (1943), *La Victoire des vivants,* Paris, Denoël.

Nordmann Roger (1946), *Le Bain,* Paris, La Porte Etroite.

Nouveau Louis (1961), *Un autre monde,* Paris, Calmann-Lévy.

Onfray Joseph (1946), *L'Ame résiste,* Alençon, Imprimerie Alençonnaise.

Orset Marcel (1948), *Misère et mort, nos deux compagnes,* Châlons-sur-Saône, Imprimerie Perroux.

Ourisson Dunia (1946), *Le Secret du bureau politique d'Auschwitz,* Paris, F.N.D.I.R.P.

Pagniez Yvonne (1947), *Scènes de la vie du bagne,* Paris, Flammarion.
— (1949), *Evasion 44,* Paris, Flammarion.
— (1950), *Ils ressuscitèrent d'entre les morts,* Paris, Flammarion.

Parguel Paul (1946), *De mon presbytère aux bagnes nazis,* Paris, Spes.

Pelissier Jean (1945), *Camps de la mort,* Paris, Mellottée.

Philippe Père (1949), *Un martyr des camps, le Père Jacques 1900-1945,* Paris, Tallandier.

Piguet Gabriel (1947), *Prison et déportation,* Paris, Spes.

Pineau Christian (1969), *Krematorium,* Paris, Presses Pocket.

Ploton Abbé (1946), *De Montluc à Dora,* Paris, Dumas.

Poirmeur André (n.d.), *Compiègne 1939-45,* chez l'auteur.

Poliakov Léon (1951), *Bréviaire de la haine,* Paris, Calmann-Lévy.

— (1964), *Auschwitz,* Paris, Julliard.

Pontoiseau André (1947), *Dora la Mort,* Tours, Imprimerie Arrault.

Portefaix Raymond (n.d.), *L'Enfer que Dante n'avait pas prévu,* Aurinac, Imprimerie Moderne.

Pottier René (1946), *Au seuil de l'enfer,* Paris, Nouvelles Editions Latines.

Pouzet Richard (1946), *Dora, propos d'un bagnard à ses enfants,* Paris, Castet.

Puissant Jean (1945), *La Colline sans oiseaux,* Paris, Rond Point.

Ragot André (1948), *Nuit et brouillard,* St.-Julien-de-Soult, Cooped.

Ravensbruck (1946), Paris, Seuil (G. Tillion, A. Fernier, V. Maurice, etc.).

Razola Manuel and Constante Mancino (1969), *Triangle bleu,* Paris, Gallimard.

Reine Charles (1945), *Sous le signe de l'étoile,* New York, Brentano.

Reiner Sylvain (1969), *Et la terre sera pure,* Paris, Fayard.

Rémy (1950), *Mais le temple fut bâti,* Monte-Carlo, Sabor.

Renault Maisie (1948), *La Grande misère,* Paris, Chavane.

Rendu François (1947), *Souvenirs de déportation,* Lyon, Imprimerie du Sud-Est.

Respaut André (1946), *Buchenwald,* Narbonne, Imprimeurs Réunis.

Retten Luce (1951), *Juive ou Française,* Belfort, Imprimerie Gerber.

Reynaud E.-M. (1945), *Potence et pots de fleurs,* Rouen, Defontaine.

Ribard André (1950), *Introduction à la vie publique,* Paris, Robin.

Richet Charles, *et al.* (1945), *Trois bagnes,* Paris, G. Ferenczi.

Rodriguez F.-E. and Hervet Robert (1958), *L'Escalier de fer,* Paris, France-Empire.

Rogerie André (1946), *Vivre c'est vaincre,* Paris, Imprimerie Curial-Archereau.

Roos Georges (1945), *Buchenwald,* Paris, Médicis.

Rosane (1946), *Terre de cendres,* Paris, Les Œuvres Françaises.

Rosenstein (1946), *Dieu a sauvé,* Paris, Imprimerie S.N.I.E.

Rossignot A. (1958), *Matricule 10122,* Cannes, Aegitna.

Rousset David (1946), *L'Univers concentrationnaire,* Paris, Le Pavois.

— (1947), *Les Jours de notre mort,* Paris, Le Pavois.

— (1948), *Le Pître ne rit pas,* Paris, Le Pavois.

Rousset Jean (n.d.), *Chez les barbares,* Lyon, chez l'auteur.

Roux Catherine (1948), *Triangle rouge,* Paris, France-Empire.

Roy Claude (1946), *Saison violente,* Paris, Julliard.

Sabine Madeleine (1961), *Changer le sable en or,* Paris, Fayard.

Saint-Clair Simone (1945), *Ravensbrück, l'enfer des femmes,* Paris, Tallandier.

Salan Georges (1946), *Prisons de France et bagnes allemands,* Nîmes, Imprimerie de l'Ouvrière.

Sang des poètes (1958), Bucarest, Editions de l'Etat.

Saveria Jacqueline (1954), *Ni sains ni saufs,* Paris, Laffont.

Schreiber Marianne (1947), *La Passion de Myriam Block,* Paris, Fasquelle.

Schwarz-Bart André (1959), *Le Dernier des Justes,* Paris, Seuil.

Semprun Jorge (1963), *Le Grand voyage,* Paris, Gallimard.

Simon Sacha (n.d.), *La Mort dans l'âme,* Nancy, Wagner.

Simone et ses compagnons (1946),Anonymous, Paris, Défense de l'Homme.

Songy Jacques (n.d.), *Fortes impressions de Dachau,* Châlons-sur-Marne, Union Républicaine de la Marne.

Spitz Aimé (n.d.), *Struthof, bagne nazi en Alsace,* Selestal, Alsatia.

Steinberg Lucien (1970), *La Révolte des Justes,* Paris, Fayard.

Steiner Jean-François (1966), *Treblinka,* Paris, Fayard.

Suire Pierre (1947), *Il fut un temps,* Niort, Soulisse-Martin.

Surchamp Henry (1964), *6 000 000 de morts,* Paris, Desclée de Brouwer.

Tauzin (1945), *Quatre ans dans les bagnes hitlériens,* Corbeil, Crété.

Témoignages strasbourgeois (1954), *De l'université aux camps de concentration.* Ouvrage collectif, Strasbourg, éd. Les Belles Lettres.

Témoins qui se firent égorger (Les) (1946), Anonymous, Paris, Défense de la France.

Téry Simone (1949), *Du soleil plein le cœur,* Paris, Hier et Aujourd'hui.

Tillard Paul (1945), *Mauthausen,* Paris, Editions Sociales.

— (1953), *Les Triomphants,* Paris, Editeurs français réunis.

— (1965), *Le Pain des temps maudits,* Paris, Julliard.

Tisseau Pierre (1948), *Nous les bandits,* Poitiers, chez l'auteur.

Un des trente-six (L') (1946), Anonymus, Paris, Kyoum.

Unger Julien (1946), *Le Sang et l'or,* Paris, Gallimard.

Vaillant-Couturier Marie-Claude (1946), *Mes 27 mois entre Auschwitz et Ravensbrück*, Paris, Editions du Mail.

Vercors (1951), *Les Armes de la nuit* and *La Puissance du jour*, Paris, Albin-Michel.

— (1960), 'Clémentine', in *Sur ce rivage*, Paris, Albin-Michel.

Verdet André (1948), *La Nuit n'est pas la nuit*, Paris, Pré aux Clercs.

— (1949), *Les Jours, les nuits et puis, l'aurore*, Paris, F.N.D.I.R.P.

Verine (1947), *Chercheurs de Dieu*, Paris, Spes.

Viallet Francis (1945), *La Cuisine du diable*, Paris, Hier et Aujourd'hui.

Wallet Regina (1962), *Celles qui ne voulaient pas mourir*, Paris, La Tour.

Wanda Andrée (Carliez Lambert de Loulay) (1945), *Déporté 50 440*, Paris, Bonne Presse.

Weinberg Joseph (1966), *Le Printemps des cendres*, Paris.

Wellers Georges (1946), *De Drancy à Auschwitz*, Paris, Editions du Centre.

Wetterwald Francis (1946), *Les Morts inutiles*, Paris, Editions de Minuit.

Wiesel Elie (1958), *La Nuit*, Editions de Minuit. *

— (1960), *L'Aube*, Paris, Seuil.

— (1961), *Le Jour*, Paris, Seuil.

— (1962), *La Ville de la chance*, Paris, Seuil.

— (1966), *Les Juifs du silence*, Paris, Seuil.

— (1966), *Le Chant des morts*, Paris, Seuil.

— (1970), *Entre les deux soleils*, Paris, Seuil.

Wiesenthal Simon (1967), *The Murderers Among Us*, New York, McGraw-Hill.

Wilborts Suzanne (1946), *Pour la France*, Paris, Lavauzelle.

Winovska Maria (1950), *Le Feu de Notre-Dame*, Paris, Bonne Presse.

Wormser-Migot Olga (1959), 'Le système concentrationnaire nazi', *L'Information historique*, Paris, n° 2, pp. 85-89.

---

* We realize that this work is a translation and the original appeared in Yiddish, but we have included it in this book even though we have restricted the book to works written only in French originally, that is to say, no translations, because the author translated it himself, because the rest of his work is in French and because we feel that given our understanding of the author's purposes, it belongs as an integral part of this book.

— (1964), 'La déportation', *Cahiers pédagogiques,* n° 17.

— (1965), *Quand les Alliés ouvrirent les portes,* Paris, Laffont.

— (1968), *Le Système concentrationnaire nazi,* Paris, Presses Universitaires de France.

— (1969), 'Le système concentrationnaire nazi', *Historia,* Paris, n° 64, pp. 1773-1778 and n° 78, pp. 2179-2184.

Wormser-Migot Olga and Michel Henri (1955), *Tragédie de la déportation,* Paris, Hachette.

ADDENDUM I

Beauvoir Simone de (1964), *Le Deuxième sexe,* Paris, Gallimard.

Billetdoux François (n. d.), *Pitchipoi,* chez l'auteur.

Doubrovsky Serge (1969), *La Dispersion,* Paris, Mercure de France.

Gary Romain (1969), *La Danse de Genghis Cohn,* Paris, Livre de Poche.

Langfus Anna (1963), *Le Sel et le soufre,* Paris, Gallimard.

— (1965), *Les Bagages de sable,* Paris, Gallimard.

Rohmer Charles (1951), *L'Autre,* Paris, Gallimard.

Semprun Jorge (1969), *La Deuxième mort de Ramon Mercader,* Paris, Gallimard.

Spiraux Alain (1957), *La Dénonciation,* Paris, Sedimo.

Triolet Elsa (1944), *Les Amants d'Avignon,* Geneva, Trois Collines.

— (1963), *L'Ame,* Paris, Gallimard.

ADDENDUM II

Claudel Paul (n.d.), 'Ballade', in *Les Plus belles poésies françaises,* Paris, Delachaux et Nestlé.

Ganzfried Rabbi (1961), *Shulhan Aruh* [Code of Jewish Law], New York, Hebrew Publ. Co.

Index of Authors

ACHEVÉ D'IMPRIMER SUR LES PRESSES DE
L'IMPRIMERIE AUBIN 86 LIGUGÉ / VIENNE
LE 10 MAI 1973

Dépôt légal, 2ᵉ trimestre 1973. — Imprimeur, 7017.
Imprimé en France